JEWISH WOMEN WRITERS
IN BRITAIN

JEWISH WOMEN WRITERS IN BRITAIN

EDITED BY NADIA VALMAN

Wayne State University Press

Detroit

© 2014 by Wayne State University Press, Detroit, Michigan 48201.
Manufactured in the United States of America.

18 17 16 15 14   5 4 3 2 1

ISBN 978-0-8143-3238-2 (paperback)
ISBN 978-0-8143-3914-5 (e-book)

Library of Congress Control Number: 2014936566

Designed and typeset by Bryce Schimanski
Composed in Chapparal Pro and Aracne

In memory of my grandmothers
Etty Weiss née Schechter z"l (1900–1997)
Lily (Leah) Valman née Swiegals z"l (1908–2009)

CONTENTS

ACKNOWLEDGMENTS

This project was initiated during a fellowship at the Center for Advanced Judaic Studies, University of Pennsylvania, Philadelphia, in 2004–5; my thanks to the director, Professor David B. Ruderman, fellows, and staff at the center.

I gratefully acknowledge permission to quote from the following: "Lisson Grove," "To Cross," "Out," "Renaissance Feb. 7," and "Amy Levy" by Elaine Feinstein from *Selected Poems* (Carcanet 1994) and *Daylight* (Carcanet 1997); "Definition," "My Position in the History of the Twentieth Century," "Cages," "Hymn," "Ego-Death," "Solo Scrabble," "My Grandparents," "Paradise," "Green," "Animal Trainer," "The English Country Cottage," "House Guests," and "At Home at Last" by Ruth Fainlight from *Another Full Moon* (Hutchinson, 1976), *Selected Poems* (Sinclair-Stevenson, 1995), *Cages* (Macmillan, 1966), *To See the Matter Clearly* (Macmillan, 1968), *The Region's Violence* (Hutchinson, 1973), *Sibyls and Others* (Hutchinson, 1980), *Burning Wire* (Bloodaxe, 2002), © Ruth Fainlight; "Assimilation," "Inheritance," "Across the City," "Stereoptica," "Rooms," "Crows Over the Wheatfields," "The Gold Cutter's Daughter," and "Eurydice" by Sue Hubbard from *Everything Begins with the Skin* (Enitharmon Press, 1994) and *Ghost Station* (Salt, 2004).

An earlier version of chapter 8 appeared as Louise Sylvester, "Troping the Other: Anita Brookner's Jews" in *English* 50 (2001), 47–58, and is reproduced with the permission of Oxford University Press. Chapter 9 appears in a different version in Phyllis Lassner, *Anglo-Jewish Women Writing the Holocaust: Displaced Witnesses* (2008, Palgrave), and is reproduced with the permission of Palgrave Macmillan.

Thanks to Sarah Lightman, an extraordinary documentarist of her experience as a British Jewish woman, for the beautiful painting on the book's cover. Thanks to Orlando Valman for photographs of Sue Hubbard's

"Eurydice." Throughout this project it has been a pleasure to work with Wayne State University Press, and my thanks are especially due to Mindy Brown for meticulous copyediting, to Kristina Stonehill for support with rights, and finally to Kathy Wildfong for her enthusiastic editorial support for this book from its very beginnings.

INTRODUCTION

Feeling at Home: Jewish Women
Writers in Britain, 1830–2010

NADIA VALMAN

In a spare, haunting poem written in 1996, the Anglo-Jewish poet Elaine Feinstein claimed a literary forebear, the young Victorian writer Amy Levy.[1] Appearing to her in a dream set in Cambridge, where both women studied, the ghostly Levy describes her experience of double estrangement—on the one hand as a Jew at the ancient university, on the other as a writer from the philistine environment of bourgeois Anglo-Jewry, where "I am alien because I sing." In the final line of the poem, Levy unexpectedly turns to the modern-day poet with a direct challenge: "A hundred years on, is it still the same?"—the last word a partial echo of "strange" at the end of the previous line. Aurally propelling the reader forward through the twentieth century to the present, Levy's question is ambiguous. It seems partly to express the hope of a woman at the threshold of modernity, conscious of the emergent social and political changes that are set to sweep away the causes of her "unhappiness"; partly a rhetorical question, reflecting with irony on the subsequent failure of such hopes. At the same time, though, it is these very estrangements that provide a productive resource for Levy's work as a writer and, Feinstein suggests, that of her contemporary counterparts. Most interestingly of all, therefore, Feinstein's Levy seems conscious of the lineage she is inaugurating: "I am," she declares, "the first of my kind."

As this collection of essays illustrates, Levy was not quite the first of her kind, but she is an apt muse for the generations of British Jewish women writers who have returned again and again to the experience of alienation, of living between worlds, as a source of critique and creativity. "To be a Jew, a

1

Briton and a woman," writes the contemporary novelist Tamar Yellin, "means to live in a vortex of contradictory forces: loss, longing, pride, guilt. Exile and alienation. Only by writing is it possible to harness these forces and make my contradictions whole."[2] Initiated in the 1830s as Jews started for the first time to claim a place in the political life of the nation, British Jewish women's literature began with didactic intentions, and a strong strain of political engagement marked subsequent writing as well. In the last century of geographic, demographic, and social change for Jews in Britain, their position was never straightforward. This is evident in Jewish writing of the early to mid-twentieth century, which frequently dramatized the pressure to assimilate, or conform to dominant social and cultural norms, that peaked in the wake of the mass immigration of Eastern European Jews and again in the 1930s with the arrival of refugees from Nazi Europe. Jewish literature also registers the changing class position of Jews in Britain, from the deep fractures between immigrant and native Jews in the late nineteenth century to the rapid embourgeoisement of the postwar years. Across the nineteenth and twentieth centuries, the meanings of Jewish identity have been reconfigured as social and cultural shifts in British life have altered the terms of national belonging. Once perceived simply as a dissenting religious community, later as an alien race, Jews in Britain—secular, religious, or ethnic—now form part of a postimperial cosmopolitan nation in which cultural heritage, religious affiliation, and local identity intersect in dizzyingly plural ways.[3]

In the last twenty years, the history of British Jewry has been rescued from obscurity by the path-breaking work of a new generation of scholars.[4] Their studies have documented the religious and ethnic subcultures of Britain's Jews and argued strongly for an understanding of how public debates involving Jews repeatedly intersected with key questions of national identity, memory, and belonging. For the most part, however, historians of British Jewry have paid little attention to gender.[5] As an oral history research group noted in 1989, "Jewish women's experiences and perceptions have either been obscured or absorbed into descriptions of men's lives."[6] British Jewish literature, in the same way, has typically centered on the drama of the Jewish hero. For Arnold Wesker in *Chicken Soup with Barley* (1956), Alexander Baron in *The Low Life* (1963), or Bernice Rubens in *The Elected Member* (1969), for example, the symbolic story of the Jewish minority experience in Britain is that of a young man burdened with existential questions and torn apart by the competing demands of family expectations and personal aspirations. While some women writers, including Rubens, Elaine Feinstein, and Betty Miller, reproduced this trope in their novels, others expanded the Jewish cultural narrative in new directions with fiction and poetry exploring the female body, maternity, sexual politics, and the transmission of memory.

Jewish Women Writers in Britain aims to examine the distinctive perspectives that women have brought not only to interpreting their experience as Jews but also to imaginatively transforming it for a wide general readership.[7] Subjectivities produced by dislocation, for example, are the incentive for a great deal of literary inventiveness. Experiments in narrative autobiography by the refugee writer Karen Gershon and in dramaturgy by the playwright Diane Samuels pursue multiple ways of representing the radical disjunction between young and adult self. Both the Victorian Amy Levy and the contemporary Ruth Fainlight explore precarious states of social and sexual inbetweenness in their poetry. In Sue Hubbard's innovative forms of public poetry, reflections on place and belonging spring directly from Hubbard's uneasy sense of displacement in her Home Counties upbringing. For Ova, half-Jewish poetic persona of the modernist Mina Loy, meanwhile, the experience of alterity is formative in shaping an assertive opposition to all ideologies of exclusion, including antisemitism and imperialism.

Such partial Jewish identities provide complex perspectives on questions of affiliation and belonging. Almost all the writers discussed in this book have an oblique, complicated, or mobile relationship to Jewishness, and it figures in their work in highly varied and often unexpected ways. Grace Aguilar came from a pious family but as a female was religiously undereducated and more familiar with contemporary Christian values than Jewish texts; Amy Levy had a secular upbringing and an intellectual interest in "the Jewish question." For Anita Brookner, Judaism is universalized and understood as a "moral code"; for Mina Loy it is a psychic or philosophical inheritance. The refugee writers discussed in chapter 5 were defined as racially Jewish by the Nazi regime but considered themselves Germans. Others, like Linda Grant and Jenny Diski, evince a strong sense of Jewish ethnic belonging without a religious dimension. For Ruth Fainlight, meanwhile, militant secularism goes hand in hand with a strong identification with a Jewish history of persecution.

A further complicating factor is the extent to which Jewish identity has been inflected by the class structure of British society. For nineteenth-century writers like Aguilar and Lily Montagu, the sharp social divisions between lower- and upper-class Jews disturbed and confused their sense of a common religious culture. Twentieth-century writers have sought, on the other hand, to explore the differences and specificities of working-class and middle-class

Jewish identity. For Grant and Diski, however, class was a system into which they, raised in immigrant families, did not clearly fit. Furthermore, some of the writers in this book seek to question the notion of stable or tangible personal identity, Jewish or otherwise. In Anita Brookner's novels, assimilation—the movement between Jewish and English identity—is represented not as an outcome but as an ongoing and incomplete process, in which identities are always in flux. In the theater of Diane Samuels, the body of the Jewish woman is remarkable for being unmarked—for its potential to "pass" and disappear from visibility. Shaped on the one hand by the changing status and experience of Jews in Britain, and on the other by variations of class, family background, birthplace, political commitment, and religious affiliation, these writers attach radically different meanings to Jewishness.

The other key contribution women writers make to the representation of British Jewish experience is their thoroughgoing interrogation of Jewish domestic life. The mythology of the Jewish family goes back to the mid-nineteenth century, when Grace Aguilar used it as part of her argument that Jews were worthy of full political equality in England, proclaiming: "The virtues of the Jews are essentially of the domestic and social kind. The English are noted for the comfort and happiness of their firesides, and in this loveliest school of virtue, the Hebrews not only equal, but in some instances surpass, their neighbours."[8] This perception persisted even at times when public responses to Jews were at their most hostile or baffled: journalists observing Eastern European immigrants in early twentieth-century London, for example, often commented on the "happy and contented home life" that Jews managed to sustain despite conditions of overcrowding and poverty.[9] In writing by Jewish women throughout this period, however, we see very different perspectives on the popular idea of the warm, cohesive Jewish family. Many of the writers examined in this volume suggest that, far from offering a refuge from the external world, the domestic realm is where external social and political hostilities are projected inward and brutally played out on an intimate level. In the work of Eva Figes and Anita Brookner, harrowing experiences are submerged or displaced but surface irresistibly in domestic life. More directly articulated rage is evident in the writing of Diane Samuels and Jenny Diski, where the dislocated or disrupted Jewish family is a site of rejection and betrayal rather than protection. In contrast to the familiar narrative formula of the Jewish hero in conflict with an emasculating mother figure, these texts foreground more ambivalent, more bewildering relationships between mothers and daughters. For many, it is essential to understand the dynamics of dysfunctional families not via the customary narratives of stereotype but as a crucible of historical trauma.

It is not only in terms of subject matter that the work of these writers is interesting. They engage, also, with a series of aesthetic questions uniquely arising from their positions as women and as Jews. Victorian Jewish poets, for example, were writing in a period when poetic authority was characteristically invoked through intertextual relationships to existing literary traditions, and grounded on a close relationship between poetry and religion. If unable to share the Christian assumptions of Victorian poetics, some, like Amy Levy, were nonetheless able to lay claim to specifically Hebrew poetic forms, such as the lyric tradition of deferred resolution or the lament of exile; or, like Nina Salaman, to forge a link through translation to a heritage of classical Jewish poetry. Alternatively, like Grace Aguilar and Alice Lucas, they adapted Christian models of didactic or devotional writing for use in Jewish contexts. A different kind of adaptation of familiar literary form can be seen in the rewriting of the *Bildungsroman,* the novel of personal development, by refugee writers. And while Anita Brookner's measured sentences invite comparisons with Jane Austen, her narratives of perilously repressed emotion implicitly critique the control they enact at the level of style.

An unavoidable challenge for the writers under discussion here is the prevalence of stereotypes of Jews in nineteenth- and twentieth-century literary culture. Some, like Miller or Loy, reproduce traits attributed to Jews in this period and associate Jewishness with a neurotic hypersensitivity, or (conversely) an uninhibited physicality. Critics have been particularly perplexed by Jewish writers who deploy the language of race. Amy Levy and Mina Loy both knowingly use terminology, recognizable from the lexicon of antisemitism and eugenics, that associates Jews with physical and psychic pathologies—a move interpreted alternately as ironic or self-hating.[10] Yet this persistent difficulty in pinning down their tone points to a more productive way of reading their work: as a deliberate attempt to destabilize clear signifiers of identity. Thus the mix of incommensurate linguistic registers in Loy's poetry forms a polyglot, "mongrelized" discourse in which all category systems lose authority. Elsewhere Loy, as well as other writers explored here, invokes semitic stereotypes to mess more creatively with them. She recasts the "wandering Jew" of Christian legend and recent European history as a "wondering Jew," the intellectually restless subject of modernity—at home in language rather than any place.

Regarded in the context of their reflections on the condition of Jews and women, then, the experimental aspects of these writers' work come more fully into focus. Levy's subtle modulations of poetic form, for example, can be seen as a challenge to the universal assumptions of genre conventions. The ungainly lines of Loy's poetry, similarly, signal a reverence for the imperfect, unruly, vulgar body that expresses her opposition to English xenophobia. Betty Miller's psychological portrait of a Jew divided between ethnic belonging and assimilation leads to an ongoing exploration in her fiction of the self as fundamentally divided between instinct and conformity. Writers attempting to represent direct or inherited memories of the Holocaust, meanwhile, push their creative practice in a number of disparate directions, from the oblique suggestiveness and abstraction of Eva Figes's fiction, to Anita Brookner's use of understatement and narrative omission, to Diane Samuels's on-stage deployment of the shadow, connoting simultaneous absence and presence. In Sue Hubbard's site-specific poetry, in contrast, the familiar trope of the Jew as exile, and the binary of belonging/non-belonging central to the concerns of many Jewish writers, are themselves challenged as Hubbard considers instead the ways the self is constituted as a product and process of the spatial relations it inhabits.

While the work of many of the writers discussed in this volume is shaped by their ambiguous place within British culture, for others it is Jewish institutions and customs that have alienated women. As far back as the nineteenth century, British Jewish women's writing established a tradition of critique. Emily Marion Harris, Amy Levy, and Lily Montagu in the late Victorian period used the form of the novel to uncover the interior life of the contemporary Jewish woman, suggesting an imminent crisis in Anglo-Jewry if the vocational and spiritual potential of women continued to be suppressed. The prophetic feminist voice is present in the poetry of Mina Loy, too, when she points out the survival among secular Jews and Christians of religious beliefs about the impurity of the female body—which she proceeds to flout.

For other writers in this volume, however, critique was more often directed at a complacent and unthinking majority culture. Sue Hubbard's poetry, inscribed on the windows and walls of Birmingham's Jewellery Quarter, is a ghostly reminder of the forgotten role of the Jewish minority in the city's industrial past. In reanimating the hidden lives of a Jewish woman deported from Guernsey, or of a Jewish child refugee superseded by her gentile adult self, Julia Pascal and Diane Samuels use the occluded figure of the Jewish woman in history to reconsider Britain's self-narrative as a safe haven for the persecuted. These literary acts of memorialization go back even further, to the early Victorian Celia Moss, writing of Jewish women massacred in medieval York. While Moss's male contemporaries publicly embraced British identity and repeatedly insisted on their patriotism, Moss boldly reminds her readers of Britain's history of intolerance. In the interwar period Mina Loy and Betty Miller similarly offer a view of England from the margins; in their writing Jews are associated with the pleasures of the body, throwing into stark relief the repression and froideur of the English. Although the history of British Jewish literature is often told as a trajectory "from apology to revolt," it is clear from the writers in this volume that to follow a line of Jewish women's writing from the nineteenth century to the present day is to follow a company of rebels all the way.[11]

Jewish religious ritual plays an intermittent role in the writing examined here, from the devotional texts composed by Victorian poets to the festive eating in Miller's fiction to the many writers struggling against human fallibility and the inadequacies of language to observe the religious injunction to remember. The trope of Exodus, the wandering in the desert, the figure of Moses as leader: scriptural references, often radically rewritten, continue to inform the work of Loy, Figes, and Feinstein. But what should also be noted is the potential for transgression inevitably provided by a religious framework. In the specific context of the loss of Jewish lives in the Holocaust, Ruth Fainlight's rejection of all categories of identity is both a logical and a sacrilegious response; even more peculiarly fraught are her images of transcendence through bodily pain. The memoirs of Eva Figes, Jenny Diski, and Linda Grant, meanwhile, are also deliberately taboo-breaking: candid accounts of childhood neglect and adult hostility that knowingly contravene the commandment to honor one's parents.

Yet in what is surely the most transgressive novel by a British Jewish woman writer in recent years, Naomi Alderman turns to a subject that has been all but absent since Grace Aguilar and Lily Montagu first wrote about God and gender in the Victorian period. Alderman's novel *Disobedience* (2006) is set in the insular milieu of contemporary north London ultra-Orthodoxy—synonymous, in the mind of Ronit, the alienated heroine, with retrograde sexism and social conformity.[12] But the novel juxtaposes the conservative social world of Orthodoxy with its sinuous textual culture: witty, erudite Talmudic addresses to the reader exploring concepts in Jewish thought, such as the commandment to be happy, the meaning of the Sabbath, and, above all, the importance of free will—the capacity to disobey. It is this principle that brings together the novel's two protagonists, once schoolgirl lovers—Ronit, the prodigal who has fled to America to live a free and secular life, and Esti, who has outwardly conformed and remained silent about her sexuality. Both protagonists finally forge a difficult bond between incompatible aspects of themselves, recognizing not only the legitimacy of their desires but also their attachment to home. The novel proposes that Orthodox Judaism (in which ethical conflict is central) in its British incarnation (which honors habits of discretion and respect for privacy) is a surprisingly favorable environment for queer Jews.

Disobedience points toward new directions for British Jewish women's writing at the beginning of the twenty-first century. While earlier generations were haunted by a traumatic European heritage or wary of a history of British antisemitism, poets and novelists now imagine relationships to Jewishness that are no longer exclusively dominated by the past. The ongoing story of Jewish writers' vigorous engagement with a religious establishment and social conventions that constrain women's public freedoms nonetheless continues. And while the theme of conflicted Jewish identity still forms the core compelling subject of their writing, it no longer leads inevitably to bleak paralysis but opens up, instead, to a future of new retellings.

Notes

1. Elaine Feinstein, "Amy Levy," *Collected Poems and Translations* (Manchester: Carcanet, 2002), 156.
2. Tamar Yellin, "The Newspaper Man," in *Mordecai's First Brush with Love: New Stories by Jewish Women in Britain,* ed. Laura Phillips and Marion Baraitser (London: Loki Books, 2004), 57–70 (57).
3. On the history of British Jewish writing from the late nineteenth century to the present day, see Bryan Cheyette, "Introduction," *Contemporary Jewish Writing in Britain and Ireland: An Anthology* (London: Peter Halban, 1998), xiii–lxxi.
4. Todd M. Endelman, *The Jews of Britain, 1656 to 2000* (Berkeley: University of California Press, 2002); idem, *Radical Assimilation in English Jewish History, 1656–1945* (Bloomington: Indiana University Press, 1990); David Feldman, *Englishmen and Jews: Social Relations and Political Culture, 1840–1914* (New Haven, CT: Yale University Press, 1994); Eugene C. Black, *The Social Politics of Anglo-Jewry* (Oxford: Basil Blackwell, 1988); David Cesarani, *The Making of Modern Anglo-Jewry,* 1880–1920 (Oxford: Basil Blackwell, 1990); Tony Kushner, ed., *The Jewish Heritage in British History: Englishness and Jewishness* (London: Frank Cass, 1992); Tony Kushner, *Anglo-Jewry since 1066: Place, Locality and Memory* (Manchester: Manchester University Press, 2008). On contemporary British Jewry, see Howard Cooper and Paul Morrison, *A Sense of Belonging: Dilemmas of British Jewish Identity* (London: Weidenfeld and Nicholson, 1991).
5. Exceptions include Tony Kushner, "Sex and Semitism: Jewish Women in Britain in War and Peace," in *Minorities in Wartime: National and Racial Groupings in Europe, America and Australia During the Two World Wars,* ed. Panikos Panayi (London: Berg, 1993); Rickie Burman, "The Jewish Woman as Breadwinner: The Changing Value of Women's

Work in a Manchester Immigrant Community," *Oral History* 10.2 (Autumn 1982), 27–39; Rickie Burman, "'She Looketh Well to the Ways of Her Household': The Changing Role of Jewish Women in Religious Life, c.1880–1930," in *Religion in the Lives of English Women,* ed. Gail Malmgreen (London: Croom Helm, 1986); Susan L. Tananbaum, "Philanthropy and Identity: Gender and Ethnicity in London," *Journal of Social History* 30.4 (June 1997), 937–61; Linda Gordon Kuzmack, *Woman's Cause: The Jewish Woman's Movement in England and the United States, 1881–1933* (Columbus: Ohio State University Press, 1990).

6. Jewish Women in London Group, *Generations of Memories: Voices of Jewish Women* (London: Women's Press, 1989), 8.

7. For further essays on Jewish women's writing in Britain, see Claire Tylee, *"In the Open": Jewish Women Writers and British Culture* (Newark: University of Delaware Press, 2006), and Ulrike Behlau and Bernhard Reitz, eds., *Jewish Women's Writing of the 1990s and Beyond in Great Britain and the United States* (Trier: Wissenschaftlicher Verlag Trier, 2004). See also Ruth Gilbert, *Writing Jewish: Contemporary British-Jewish Literature* (Basingstoke: Palgrave Macmillan, 2013), 122–43. The earliest attempt to identify a discernible body of work by British Jewish women writers was Olga Kenyon, "Wandor, Rubens, Feinstein: Jewish Women Writing in Britain," in *Writing Women: Contemporary Women Novelists* (London: Pluto, 1991), 32–50.

8. [Grace Aguilar], "History of the Jews in England," in *Chambers' Miscellany of Useful and Entertaining Tracts,* 18 (Edinburgh: William and Robert Chambers, 1847), 1–37 (18).

9. Nadia Valman, "'The Most Unforgettable Character I've Met': Literary Representations of the Jewish Mother," in *For Generations: Jewish Motherhood,* ed. Mandy Ross and Ronne Randall (Nottingham: Five Leaves, 2005), 58–66 (60–61).

10. See Maeera Shreiber and Keith Tuma, eds., *Mina Loy: Woman and Poet* (Orono, ME: National Poetry Foundation); Naomi Hetherington and Nadia Valman, "Introduction," in *Amy Levy: Critical Essays* (Athens: Ohio University Press, 2010), 1–24.

11. Bryan Cheyette, "From Apology to Revolt: Benjamin Farjeon, Amy Levy and the Post-Emancipation Anglo-Jewish Novel, 1880–1900," *Transactions of the Jewish Historical Society of England* 24 (1982–86), 253–65; Ruth Gilbert, "Contemporary British-Jewish Writing: From Apology to Attitude," *Literature Compass* 5/2 (2008), 394–406.

12. Naomi Alderman, *Disobedience* (London: Viking, 2006).

1

FROM DOMESTIC PARAGON
TO REBELLIOUS DAUGHTER

Victorian Jewish Women Novelists

NADIA VALMAN

Women were central to the emergence and development of the Jewish novel in nineteenth-century England. Anglo-Jewish literature came into being in the early Victorian period in the form of popular didactic fiction, a form to which women writers had privileged access. Their novels were conceived to help press the Jewish claim for equal citizenship and to counter the pressure from Protestant missionaries to convert to Christianity. The Jewish woman, moreover, was repeatedly the subject of their writing. Aimed at both Jewish and non-Jewish readers, early Victorian Anglo-Jewish fiction sought to position the Jewess as an ideal type of steadfast piety—a paragon of bourgeois values, steering the Jewish family through adversity toward moral uprightness and national loyalty.

Jewish women writers in Victorian England continued to write popular fiction, and their novels were produced against a background of increasing political and social integration and dramatic demographic changes. Again and again they returned to the figure of the Jewess as the conduit of religious or ethical principles even as these principles were challenged and reconfigured. In this chapter, I trace this thread through the work of three writers whose work exemplifies Anglo-Jewry's shifting concerns, from the domestic writing of Grace Aguilar (1816–1847), who, in responding to the political and religious demands of mid-nineteenth-century England, established the model of the idealized Jewess, through to the *fin-de-siècle* writers Emily Marion Harris (?–1900) and Lily Montagu (1873–1963), whose novels are shaped by class conflict, religious skepticism, and the Woman Question.

Since the 1980s, scholars have begun to recover the work of nineteenth-century Anglo-Jewish writers with great enthusiasm. Aguilar, for example, has been read as a pioneer of social and religious reform in Anglo-Jewry, whose fiction boldly challenged both the male Anglo-Jewish establishment and Christian conversionists, and drew on discernibly Jewish literary forms.[1] The late Victorian poet, novelist, and essayist Amy Levy, meanwhile, has risen to critical prominence for her sharp social satire—seen variously as a "revolt" against the tradition of Anglo-Jewish apologia, a liberal feminist polemic, a critique of contemporary antisemitism, or a complex articulation of the ambivalent identity of late nineteenth-century Jews.[2] Although each of the writers I discuss in this chapter offered distinctive perspectives on the contemporary experience and future potential of Jewish women, I aim here not simply to heroize them. Rather, I seek to uncover the tensions surrounding class, religion, and gender that, throughout the nineteenth century, provided these writers with rich resources for fiction.

Grace Aguilar and the Mother in Israel

Grace Aguilar, the first widely read Jewish writer in Britain, came from a middle-class family active in London's Spanish and Portuguese Jewish congregation. She also encountered Christian influences in her youth, and her writing was highly popular with Evangelical readers. Her most successful books, published after her early death in 1847, were her domestic novels *Home Influence: A Tale for Mothers and Daughters* (1847) and *The Mother's Recompense* (1851), articulations of the early-Victorian bourgeois ideology of gender which conferred exceptional moral power on the figure of the virtuous mother. The few works she published during her lifetime, however, display her as a robust advocate for the Jews. In her most accomplished writing, she brought together political argument and popular fictional genres to represent Judaism in terms comprehensible to the English woman reader.

Aguilar's writing was produced and published during the early decades of the campaign for Jewish emancipation, and she aimed to play her part by illustrating the merits of the Jews in both past and present. Her earliest published fiction, *Records of Israel* (1844), historical romances showcasing the deep patriotism and heroic suffering of the Iberian Jews under the Inquisition, is "offered to the public generally, in the hope that some vulgar errors concerning Jewish feelings, faith and character may, in some measure, be corrected."[3] Like her popular novel about the persecution of Spanish crypto-Jews, *The Vale of Cedars; or, The Martyr* (1850), it draws on the strong anti-Catholic feeling of the 1840s and seeks to identify the beleaguered heroine with the Protestant reader. Both texts adapt the generic and ideological conventions of popular middle-class fiction to promote the cause of Jewish equality.

Aguilar's second concern in her writing was to combat the threat of Evangelical missionaries to the Jews, an early nineteenth-century phenomenon that attended the Protestant millennialist belief in the urgent need for Jewish conversion. One weapon in their armory was the novel. Published prolifically in the period, conversion tales typically featured an unhappy Jewess who rejects the law of her father, learns the spiritual joy of true religion from a Christian woman friend, and is relentlessly persecuted while she clings to it.[4] For Jewish readers, Aguilar wrote *The Jewish Faith: Its Spiritual Consolation, Moral Guidance, and Immortal Hope* (1846), which took the form of letters addressed to a Jewish girl facing the temptation of conversion, encouraging her to remain loyal to her faith. In *The Vale of Cedars* she produced a counter-conversion narrative; here the climax of the plot is the Jewish heroine's sacrifice of her female friend's love and her choice of death over Christianity. Aguilar also addressed the Evangelical critique of Judaism directly, insisting that Jews should disregard the authoritarian legal apparatus of their religion and focus on a direct, emotional, unmediated relationship with God.[5]

Among her numerous volumes of bourgeois domestic fiction and Jewish historical romances, aimed at female readers of all religious persuasions, Aguilar's novella of contemporary working-class Anglo-Jewish life, *The Perez Family* (1843), is an apparent anomaly. Commissioned as part of the *Cheap Jewish Library* of improving fiction for Jews of the humbler classes, funded and edited anonymously by the philanthropist Charlotte Montefiore, Aguilar's text was evidently intended as a Jewish version of Hannah More's popular anti-radical *Cheap Repository Tracts* of the late eighteenth century. Although its subject was the lives of impoverished Jews in Liverpool and London, however, the moral framework of *The Perez Family* emphasizes the middle-class virtues of cleanliness, thrift, honesty, and family-feeling that distinctively mark Aguilar's other fiction.

The trials of the poorer class of Jews, moreover—battling poverty and its attendant temptations to sin and despair—offered an especially instructive setting for illustrating the learning and practice of the paramount virtue of humility. Aguilar's story follows the lives of a family of Liverpool Jews who face a series of adversities: their house burns down, the youngest child is blinded, the father dies, the eldest son marries the Christian daughter of his fellow worker, the second son, fiercely loyal to Judaism, brands his brother an apostate, and the niece tries to support her unscrupulous, bankrupt father. As Michael Galchinsky has noted, each subplot becomes an exemplary tale in which Aguilar's characters struggle with the key dilemmas of contemporary Anglo-Jewry: how to balance fidelity to Judaism with the need to prosper in the gentile world, how to respond to religious dissent within Jewry, whether to fulfill the divine commandment to honor a parent who has been publicly disgraced.[6] At each stage, however, tragedy is met with patience and piety by the female members of the family, while the fathers and sons either contribute to the misery or rage impotently against it.

Indeed, the vices commonly attributed to Jews by their detractors in this period, pharisaical dogmatism and material ambition, are embodied by the two sons, Simeon, who *"loved his faith* better than he *loved his God,"* and Reuben, who "was in truth only *nominally* a Jew."[7] In contrast, the narrator says, "[o]f the female members of Perez'[s] family we have little to remark," since they cause little trouble (109). In fact it is the women characters, particularly the mother, Rachel, and her niece and deputy, Sarah, who stand at the moral center of the family, shaping and modeling the spiritual development of the men and younger children. This is evident in the story's most remarkable scene, the Perez family Sabbath Eve, where the ritual, conventionally conducted by the paterfamilias, is led instead by the widowed mother. Rachel not only performs the traditional practice of lighting candles but also directs the reading and family discussion of a verse from the Bible on the importance of faith. While she is "no great scholar," Rachel "had a *trusting spirit and a most humble and childlike mind,"* and is for these reasons a superior interpreter of God's words, according to the narrator—who also pointedly adds: "to every mother in Israel these powers are given" (115; emphasis in original). For Galchinsky, this eccentric version of Jewish Sabbath practice is evidence of Aguilar's own crypto-Jewish heritage, in which the prohibition of public expressions of Judaism had been countered by the continued transmission of traditions in the home.[8] However, Aguilar's emphasis on Rachel's direct access to God's will, through her own reading of scripture in a spirit of "childlike" passivity, links her more with the contemporary theology of Protestant Christianity. In *The Perez Family* Aguilar aligns Jews with the Evangelical model of female spiritual inspiration.

The mother figure is also central to Aguilar's theology. She exemplifies Aguilar's conception of divine authority, which is merciful rather than punitive. Each time the errant Reuben returns from consorting with "strangers" to the family home, Rachel reminds him: "It is never, never too late for a mother's blessing—a mother's love," and continues to offer forgiveness even after his marriage to a Christian woman (120). Rachel's neighbors, meanwhile, advise that such transgression deserves excommunication, but lest the reader should find herself sharing such a view, the narrator makes one of her rare interventions: "We are quite aware that, by far the greater number of our readers, widow Perez will be either violently condemned or contemptuously scorned as a weak, mean-spirited, foolish woman. We can only say that if so, we are sorry so few have the power of understanding her, and that the loving piety, the spiritual religion of her character should find so faint an echo in the Jewish heart" (127). Here Aguilar calls for Jews to turn from attempts to police the beliefs of their co-religionists to the forgiving love—the truer form of piety, in her view—that governs Rachel's relationship with her children. When Sarah responds to the crimes of her father with a similarly maternal compassion, she too becomes a conduit of salvation, continuing to exemplify "the love which was unending, pitying, strengthening, as the gracious Lord from whom it comes" (137). These terms recast Judaism itself as a religion of mercy, with God as a long-suffering mother figure.

If Judaism is feminized in Aguilar's writing, religion is also seen as fulfilling an especially deep need in women. In *The Perez Family* women are repeatedly required to submit to the decisions and actions of men, however much suffering they cause. Thus when Reuben announces that he is marrying a Christian woman, both his mother and Sarah, who is in love with him, conceal their painful feelings and continue to offer him support. After this rejection, Sarah suffers a short-lived crisis of faith but ultimately finds consolation in her close, emotive relationship with God: "Where could she have turned for comfort, had she been taught to regard Him as too far removed from earth and earthly things to love and be approached?" (129). The divinity of Aguilar's (and Rachel's) spiritual imagination provides "comfort" for the sufferings even of—especially of—women, reconciling them to a necessary passivity.

Such resignation, however, is represented as active, indeed heroic. By persisting in their love for those who wrong them, the heroines act as catalysts for the novel's transformations. When Sarah, for example, is summoned to leave her happy home to support her wayward father, Levison, in London, she suppresses her horror at the scene of urban squalor she encounters. She meets the hostility and cynicism of Levison's grumpy neighbor, Esther, with disarming kindness. Although Esther is religiously observant, she is missing out on the benefits of the Bible: "I read it every Saturday, the parts they tell us to read; and I do not find much comfort in them, for they seem to tell me God is too far off to care for such as us" (134). But Sarah's insistence that scripture is for everyone provokes "an ardent desire in the old woman's mind to become thoroughly acquainted with God's holy volume; and many an evening did they sit together, and Esther listened to the sweet pleading voice of her young companion, till she felt with her whole heart that God must be with Sarah" (138). Esther's worldly relations are also revitalized. She reflects: "I must have been cross and harsh myself, which made folks abuse me as they did; since you have been here, I feel an altered creature, and now meet with kindness instead of wrong" (138). Sarah's father, however, is an altogether tougher case and responds to her entreaties with derision. Eventually, though, "the influence of his gentle pious child" works its wonders on him too (149). Wrongly imprisoned in Newgate but unable to clear his name because of his bad reputation, he finds himself drawn to repentance: "It seemed to Levison that if such a being could love and pity him, and cling to him thus even in a prison cell, he could not be cut off from all of heavenly hope—the all pitying love and consoling promises of God appeared to him through her as if by a voice from heaven" (160). In modeling forgiveness for her father, Sarah has awakened in him the possibility of belief in God's mercy.

The novel's repeating pattern of reversion to religion and family—Esther's, Levison's, and finally Reuben's—is made possible, made inevitable, by the human practitioners of the principle of forgiveness. These narratives draw clearly on the genre of conversion narrative, but rather than resolving the characters' spiritual discontents with a turn to Christianity, Aguilar has them return, with renewed faith and intimacy with God, to Judaism.

While several of these ideas are evident in Aguilar's other domestic fiction, the working-class setting of *The Perez Family* makes it a considerably more complex text. If the novel, like Aguilar's other work, explicitly aims to intervene in the public perception of Jews, following established patterns of Anglo-Jewish apologia through the deployment of counter-stereotype, the Perez family offers new representational opportunities. The Evangelical critique of Judaism as lacking in faith and a personal relationship to the deity is, for example, repeatedly contested in the descriptions of Rachel's and Sarah's piety. Even the novel's physical setting is carefully invested with symbolic

meaning: the opening introduces the Perezes' meager dwelling, where "[t]
he garden was carefully and prettily laid out, and planted with the sweetest
flowers; the small parlour and kitchen of the cottage opened into it, and so,
greatly to the disappointment and vexation of the gossips of the alley, nothing could be gleaned of the sayings and doings of its inmates. Within the
cottage the same refinement was visible; the furniture, though old and poor,
was always clean and neatly arranged" (87). Whereas influential contemporary social commentators like William Cobbett and Thomas Carlyle cast
the Jews as alienated from agriculture and inextricably bound to commerce
and the urban, Aguilar's Jews have an intuitive relationship to the land.[9] The
insularity of which Jews were frequently accused is also recast as a proto-
bourgeois impulse toward privacy. The Perez family members are not only
unlike early nineteenth-century stereotypes of Jews; they are also distinct
from their working-class neighbors, practicing middle-class virtues of cleanliness and domestic pride rather than neglecting the home for the communal
pleasures of the street. In the course of the narrative, such values are seen to
alter gentile perceptions of Jews; when Sarah goes into service, for example,
her humility and kindness enable her fellow servants to overcome their prejudices against Jews (148).

Repositioning Jews in the gentile imagination, however, is only one
aspect of Aguilar's didacticism in *The Perez Family*. Equally, and more directly,
she is concerned to instruct Jews themselves—in particular regarding Jewish
intolerance toward non-Jews. If Sarah's virtue leads to the gentile servants'
enlightenment, in a parallel subplot her dogmatic cousin Simeon learns to
conquer his own narrow-mindedness because of the kindness of a Christian
stranger who cared for him during an illness and challenged his belief that
piety must be narrow: "*that heart alone in sincerity loves God, who can see, in
every pious man, a brother, despite of difference of creed*" (171; italics in original).
This view echoes that of the narrator, who has earlier declared: "An earnest
and heartfelt love of God can never permit an emotion so violent as hatred to
any of God's creatures. It is no test of our sincerity to condemn or disbelieve
in that of others" (107).

Such tolerance of religious difference is apparently exemplified by Reuben when he marries Jeanie, the daughter of his gentile employer. Jeanie's
father, Reuben explains to his family, "has made no condition in giving me his
daughter, except that she may follow her own faith, which I were indeed prejudiced and foolish to deny. He believes as I do; to believe in God is enough—all
religions are the same before Him" (122). But in fact, while Jeanie and Reuben

"believed there was a God, at least they said they did," both are only nominal adherents to their respective religions, and as yet their faith remains untested (129). Problems arise when Jeanie becomes more seriously Christian, and, on her deathbed, begs Reuben to have their daughter baptized. Hoping to comply, Reuben studies Christianity conscientiously with Mr. Vaughan, a minister "whose very kindness and true piety in spirit made his arguments more difficult to resist, than had they been harshly and determinately enforced," but is unable to convert and brings his own soul and that of his daughter back to Judaism (153). Aguilar here uses the example of the dilemmas of raising a child born of parents of different faiths to illustrate the impracticality of assuming that "to believe in God is enough." While Reuben intends not to be "prejudiced," tolerance cannot be grounded on secularity or rational choice. In fact, it is only the clarification of Reuben's convictions as a Jew that leads to genuine religious understanding, as he and Mr. Vaughan become "true friends" who have "strengthened themselves in their own peculiar doctrines, without in the least shaking each other's" (172). As Aguilar's narrator puts it earlier in the novel, "prejudice is almost the only feeling which reason cannot conquer—religion may" (107).

Aguilar's representation of Judaism and Jews in *The Perez Family* is also inflected by the text's explicit address to a working-class readership. Sarah's travails in finding employment due to the public perception of the Jewish worker, therefore, function as an admonition to the working-class Jewish reader. Potential employers repeatedly inform Sarah that the Jews' "pride and ignorance were beyond all bounds, and as for a proper deference towards their superiors, a willingness to be taught or guided, it was not in their nature" (140). That these views are not simply gentile bigotry is underlined by Esther, who also laments the tendency of Jewish workers to regard themselves as social equals among other Jews. Jews like herself, she declares, need "to be taught our proper duties . . . it is all very true about being lazy and sometimes insolent" (141). For Aguilar, this permissiveness is a result of the impiety of the Jewish lower orders, as exemplified by Esther. The proper interpretation and practice of their religion, however, would produce Jews like Sarah, whose public behavior is shaped by spiritual meekness: "Her duty to her God had, she hoped, taught her proper deference towards her superiors on earth" (140). The example of Sarah and her cousins demonstrates to the world that Jews are in fact hardworking and self-sufficient, but perhaps most crucially of all, at the same time happily passive, and contented with their position within the social hierarchy. The material prosperity that returns to the Perez family at the end of the story is, therefore, a result of the men's renunciation of personal ambition in favor of working together in a small-scale family business—in emulation of the humility shown habitually by the women. The lessons in obedience learned by the novel's characters thus have a political as well as a religious resonance; Judaism appears here as a crucial guarantor of class stability. If the text seeks to inculcate bourgeois values in the lower orders, it also seeks to keep them in their place.

The complex political dimensions of Aguilar's novel are even more apparent in the novel's final miraculous plot turns, which, despite the repeated emphasis on submission to God's will, are in fact enacted by human agency. Miss Leon, a philanthropist impressed by Sarah's good conduct, takes it upon herself to train the blind Perez daughter, Ruth, in order to render her self-supporting. Later, she notices a change in Ruth's eyes, and takes her to an oculist, who is able to restore her sight. Meanwhile, Miss Leon has also been the means of vindicating Levison, having discovered the crucial witness who can attest to his innocence. Although the rhetoric of *The Perez Family*, like many of Aguilar's other books, insists that the working-class widow Rachel is God's deputy in the home, the plot actually requires the intervention of a compassionate middle-class figure of authority—the female philanthropist—to reverse misfortunes in the lives of the poor. This somewhat clunky plot construction symbolically interpolates the figure of the benevolent bourgeois reader into the text, flatteringly reminding her of her power, responsibility, and righteousness. It also makes manifest the multiple and competing class interests at work in Aguilar's didactic fiction, which ostensibly addresses the working-class reader while including in the picture the elite patronesses who distributed the tracts, as well as the shadowy presence of the gentile reader.

The novella's reception among those to whom it was issued is unknown; on its reprinting for a middle-class readership a few years later, however, it was most warmly received.[10] If the message and medium of *The Perez Family* are too narrowly instructional for a modern reader, and its representation of Jews too apologetic, nonetheless its use of the rhetoric of feminized religion to mediate differences of social class makes this text enduringly interesting. These same themes, moreover, continued to echo in Anglo-Jewish fiction as the century progressed.

Emily Marion Harris and the Jewish New Woman

During the half-century that followed, the economic, social, and legal status of Jews in Britain changed rapidly. If Aguilar's impoverished Perez family was typical of the majority of Anglo-Jewry in the mid-nineteenth century, by the 1870s Jews were overwhelmingly middle class. The bourgeois values that Aguilar projected onto her idealized working-class family were now in reality embodied and practiced by the large majority of British Jews.[11] There were renewed causes for anxiety, though, in the public debate about the Jews' capacity for patriotism and, toward the end of the century, in the open hostility stirred by the arrival of large numbers of immigrants from Eastern Europe.[12] In this context, Bryan Cheyette has argued, Anglo-Jewish literature of the 1870s continued its earlier tradition of reactive defensiveness: a second wave of apologetic writing sought to shape the image of Anglo-Jewry within public discourse. By the 1880s, however, many Jewish novelists adopted a position of "revolt" against Anglo-Jewry's conservative self-image.[13]

Absent from Cheyette's discussion, however, is the gender dimension of this literary history. In this section I discuss the work of Emily Marion Harris, one of several Jewish novelists of "revolt" who foregrounded women's experience within Anglo-Jewry. Harris, the (mostly anonymous) author of a number of middlebrow courtship novels for a female readership between the 1870s and 1890s, published two novels about Anglo-Jewry, *Estelle* (1878) and *Benedictus* (1887), in which the protagonists are bourgeois Jewish women.[14] Harris also pursued a vocation in welfare work. For many years she led the West Central Friday Night Club, the first leisure club for Jewish working girls, established in 1885 by the philanthropist Lady Louise Rothschild to provide girls with social, educational, and recreational opportunities.[15] Harris herself thus directly participated in the same effort to shape the behavior and values of the Jewish working class as the *Cheap Jewish Library* of the 1840s, but she was working in the fraught new context of the mass Jewish immigration of the late nineteenth century. While in some ways her fiction continues the apologetic tradition established by Aguilar, Harris also exposes the social fissures that *The Perez Family* labors to disguise. Oscillating between apology and revolt, her middle-class Jewish heroines experience the political pressure to be a "good citizen" primarily as the social and familial demands on them to be pious and patient women.

The strain of these demands on the middle-class Jewish woman is evident in Harris's earlier novel, *Estelle,* the story of a young aspiring artist whose hopes to develop her talent are quashed by the austere strictures of her Orthodox father. Although in public Estelle is an energetic defender of Judaism as "a code full of humanity, of gentleness, and an exquisite tenderness" rather than "greed or avarice," in private she is in "unuttered rebellion" against her father's insistence that "[h]ome was, or should be, sufficient to girls."[16]

She also tentatively cultivates a romantic friendship with a gentile neighbor. When her father dies suddenly, however, Estelle renounces both professional and romantic aspirations in order to work as a teacher to support her younger siblings.[17] This sacrificial destiny, however, has been anticipated earlier in the novel, in its first description of her: "Sombre, appealing, almost tragic in its calm and force, that face of Estelle Hofer's, leaning against the oak-panelled, many-paned window, comes to her as an inheritance from her race. Majesty and melancholy, dignity and the habitual humility sprung from centuries of oppression, assert each their separate power in her straight features, and, combining, cause hers to be a most distinctive and interesting type."[18]

The story of Estelle's thwarted ambition is already imprinted, proleptically, on her features. The "humility" with which she embraces self-denial is not, as in Aguilar's heroines, resolute submission to God's will but an inherited "habit," produced not by virtue but by "oppression." In the absence of an explicitly didactic narrator in this text, much more weight is given to the individual protagonist and her interior life, emphasizing the competing claims that shape her subjectivity. The novel's unresolved tensions suggest that the early Victorian feminine ideal of humble resignation continued to serve an apologetic agenda for Jewish writers in the 1870s but that this paradigm was now under heavy pressure. Although the notion of self-denial remains highly idealized in *Estelle,* it is at the same time cast more ambivalently as "shrinking reserve, pathetically characteristic of the esteem—or want of esteem—in which the Jews held the women of their nation."[19]

In the novel's sequel, *Benedictus,* published nine years later, these tensions erupt. The central figures in Harris's depiction of Jewish London in the 1880s are not the simple pious Jews of earlier Anglo-Jewish literature but the cosmopolitan, assimilated, and worldly Freund family, especially their opinionated daughter, Thyra, a former pupil of Estelle's. Thyra resists her parents' efforts to pressure her into marriage and devotes herself and her substantial fortune to social work in the East End. Even Estelle has managed to shake off her hereditary passivity to advance a career as an artist. In this new context, the principle of female domesticity has become virtually unworkable. The family unity that Estelle strove so hard to maintain as a young woman, meanwhile, is at the point of collapse in *Benedictus,* with each of her siblings ultimately going their separate ways, both within and beyond the Jewish community. Broader social divisions among Jews, moreover, even if mediated, as in Aguilar's fiction, by the figure of the female philanthropist, are sharper and more unbridgeable.

While Aguilar sought to represent the Jewish working class as a nascent bourgeoisie, Harris's fiction is not too squeamish to detail the overwhelming "squalor and poverty" that limits their self-betterment.[20] The opening of *Benedictus* is set in the East End of London among the decaying ruins of once-prosperous houses, now a neighborhood that is "one to be shunned."[21] Like the East End itself, the Jews who live there have fallen from former glory. Harris regards them not, like Aguilar, as humble, industrious workers aspiring to virtuous citizenship but as picturesque relics of a lost world, whose identity is rooted in the biblical past: "Behind narrow counters, or bending above heavy garments are assembled many a specimen of a kingdom whose descendants bear the trace of its royalty, and greatness yet, in the flash of the dark eye, in the gestures of the grand figure, strikingly apparent at times" (I: 4). Practicing ancient religious rituals amid dirt and dilapidation, the East End Jews in Harris's fiction are "Oriental," exotic, and mournful (I: 21). Unlike Aguilar, for whom Judaism functioned as an analog of conservative Anglicanism, inculcating obedience and respectability in the lower orders, Harris represents immigrant Jews as tragic exiles. They resist adaptation, Thyra says: "[T]heir ways and habits are ancestral; unchanged they continue from one generation to another" (II: 70). Also in contrast to Aguilar, the narrator suggests sympathy with the burden of this racial memory, affectionately noting, for example, the Jewish working girl who "abhors domestic service, as a bondage allied to the former experience of her ancestry in Egypt" (II: 91). This romanticized representation of immigrants as ruined aristocrats, however, repeats Aguilar's efforts to cast the much-maligned Jewish working class in a positive light.

A more nuanced account of class relations in Anglo-Jewry unfolds in the novel's depiction of the encounter between philanthropists and their clientele. Describing a cultural evening organized by Thyra and Estelle to distract Jewish working women and girls "from the temptations of pleasures not so temperately wholesome," Harris uses a form of free indirect narrative to produce a multivocal account of the different relationships of power and self-interest that structure the encounter (II: 84). The narrator begins this chapter with a detached, ironic tone evocative of committees and condescension: "Multiplied, truly, are the public meetings of this century, for the entertainment of the poor" (II: 78). Abruptly shifting perspective, the narrative attends to the detail of the audience's often astute response: their bafflement at the domestic economy lecture, their enthusiasm for the refreshments, their hilarity at an improving tale of "good work effected among savage tribes," and their adulation of Thyra as a glamorous celebrity (II: 96). It includes also the uneasiness felt by Thyra's rich father, who "would like even to speak to them, but . . . furtively fingers his watch, and can find no fitting sentence with which to offer his sympathy or pity," and the needy, middle-aged spinster Miss Nugent, who wants to do good but is cowed by the vociferous young women and physically repulsed by a "dirty shawl and its dirty wearer's proximity" (II: 91; 94). The narration is not omniscient and does not therefore imply a single viewpoint. Instead, a mobile narrating consciousness expresses the unvoiced thoughts of the various participants, suggesting the middle-class discomfort with the noise, smell, and profligacy that underlies their efforts to influence the lives of the poor, as well as the pleasure, mockery, and self-possession of the girls themselves.

Acknowledging their limitations, however, the novel at the same time applauds the work of the West End women who "strove to beautify and to widen the aims of the poor work-girls' lives" through music and poetry performance (II: 83). This objective contrasts with that of the Romanian Jewish philanthropist Adrian Benedictus, a cynical newcomer on the London scene who has expended his fortune in a failed effort to alleviate the suffering of Jews living under political oppression in Romania. Unlike Thyra, Benedictus aimed at a thorough reformation of the Jews but discovered in the process that "[t]he world he was so anxious to regenerate cared not for his model lodging houses and new plans" and resisted his program of emigration (I: 129). While Benedictus himself concluded that "his countrymen were not alone the victims of men's persecution, but under the yoke of an infatuated formalism, such as curbed them in almost as much force as this visible cruelty of their rulers," the reader might well infer that it was his authoritarianism, rather than their overzealous orthodoxy, that inhibited their incentive for change (I: 92). In contrast, the less ambitious and more interpersonal approach of Thyra and her companions makes small but certain inroads into the deprived lives of the London Jewish poor. Nonetheless, Benedictus's despondency about the greater impact of philanthropy subtly pervades the novel, producing an atmosphere of vague pessimism. The East End itself seems to defy hope for progress: the snow, for example, "is defiled as it descends. The smoky air checks its delicate work of decoration, spoils its chilly bracelets round the lamp posts, blots the beauty of its icy fringes under the eaves" (II: 8).

Stylistically, then, *Benedictus* suggests the breaking down of authority and certainty. This is also apparent in the novel's religious landscape. Thyra's East End project is designed to offer an alternative to Christian social gatherings, and her enterprise is marred by "no bigotry or formalism. Everyone tacitly accepted things as they were, and if the meeting, mainly formed of one particular creed, received occasionally those of another, it was taken as a matter of course by its presidents" (II: 84–85). Yet this is not so much a progressive principle of ecumenism as a general indifference to religious questions on the part of both organizer and audience. Thyra's Quaker friends help run the cultural evening, for example, but the edifying tale of Christian faith under duress that one of them reads out loud is met with amused tolerance rather than either affront or inspiration. For both East and West Enders, religion is an attenuated rather than a formative aspect of their identity.

As *Benedictus* returns at its close to focus once again on the story of Estelle, moreover, it creates similar confusion and ambivalence about the meaning of Judaism to its heroine. Estelle, now an established artist, unexpectedly reencounters her first (and only) love, the gentile Cecil Haye. Cecil is now a widower, and Estelle is no longer subject to the will of her Orthodox father, and he proposes marriage to her a second time. Although she longs to agree, Estelle refuses once again, later experiencing a physical breakdown under the strain. The novel ends with Estelle's death as a result of her disregarding her doctor's order not to exacerbate the heart condition from which she is suffering. This could be read as her fulfillment of "the grand ideal of being true to her inclination for sacrifice" by preserving her loyalty to Jewish law, renouncing romantic happiness, and succumbing to the resulting emotional suffering (II: 235). In an alternative reading, however, we can see Harris linking Estelle's death to her determination not to curtail her professional ambition. "Be content with moderate success, and do not tear physical and mental strength to tatters," advises her doctor. "Look down on the daisy, figuratively; paint that . . . lead an uneventful domestic life"—he recommends, in other words, a reversion to the repressed Estelle of her youth (II: 218–19). However, refusing to confine herself to daisies, Estelle chooses a life that is active, though inevitably foreshortened. The nobility of Estelle's final sacrifice, then, is not clearly attached to her religious fidelity; it is just as much motivated by her devotion to her vocation.

In this respect, Harris's novel demonstrates affinities with the themes that were to coalesce in the 1890s in the more well-known fiction associated with the New Woman. The struggle of female characters for economic independence and vocational self-fulfillment structured the narratives of Olive Schreiner's *The Story of an African Farm* (1883) and Ella Hepworth Dixon's *The Story of a Modern Woman* (1894), yet these novels frequently end with frustration or failure.[22] Alison Ives, the upper-class philanthropist in Dixon's novel, for example, defies her parents' plans for a society marriage and instead goes slumming in the East End of London, where she catches a fatal infection. In concluding Estelle's story with solitude and self-sacrifice, therefore, Harris was revisiting tropes no longer especially linked to Jewishness but rather to the questions that dominated feminist fiction more generally at the *fin de siècle*.

Lily Montagu and the Renewal of Faith

If the novels of Emily Marion Harris register in both thematic and formal terms the uncertainties around Anglo-Jewish identity in the late nineteenth century, the work of Lily Montagu imagined new answers. Montagu had a prominent public role as an innovator in both religion and social work. She was one of the founders, in 1909, of the Liberal Jewish Synagogue, which brought the Reform theology successful in Germany and America to a generation of English Jews who wanted to reconcile loyalty to ancestral tradition with more recent thinking on the historical origins of the Bible and the scientific account of creation. She went on to become the first Jewish woman preacher in Europe and a suffragist. Starting in clubs for working-class Jewish girls in the 1890s, moreover, Montagu built a career as a social worker and organizer in the national youth club movement. Yet while these aspects of her work have been recognized by historians, Montagu's writing has been all but neglected.[23] In looking closely at her fiction and autobiographical texts, I want to explore how she not only brought together her experience of religious crisis, female subjectivity, and social inequality, but also brought it to bear on the same set of concerns that had preoccupied the Jewish women writers who preceded her. Although Ellen Umansky claims that Montagu showed no interest in Anglo-Jewish literature, it is clear, I would argue, that her stories of the spiritual development of a young woman in fact consciously rewrote the novels that had helped define previous generations of Anglo-Jewish women.[24]

In foregrounding the perspective of a lower-class Jewish woman in her fiction, Montagu may well have been influenced by one of the period's most well-known novels of Anglo-Jewish life, *Reuben Sachs: A Sketch* (1888), by the liberal feminist writer Amy Levy. Having published an anonymous polemic in the *Jewish Chronicle* against Anglo-Jewry's suppression of female emotional and intellectual potential, Levy caused a stir with *Reuben Sachs*'s outspoken critique of the materialistic ethos of West End Jewry. At the center of the novel is the tragedy of Judith Quixano, a young woman from a shabby genteel Jewish family who, "despite her beauty, her intelligence, her power of feeling, saw herself merely as one of a vast crowd of girls awaiting their promotion by marriage."[25] Unthinkingly obedient to social and religious convention, Judith feels a vague alienation in synagogue on the Day of Atonement, where the congregation is "bored" and the repeated prayers have no resonance with her "personal needs . . . human longings."[26] Judith thus has no resources with which to face the catastrophe of her life—her sudden abandonment by her lover Reuben, who is driven, like the rest of his society, by social aspiration and material ambition. It is only by chance that she finds consolation reading Swinburne's poetry, where she discovers her longings—"feelings which had not their basis in material relationships"—at last legitimized.[27] In structuring her narrative around Judith's discontent, her suffering and her spiritual awakening, Levy shows the influence of the novel of conversion, which had been so formative in representations of the Jewish woman throughout the century.[28] For Levy, the self-consciousness that Judith attains at the end of the novel is grasped through the secular revelation of poetry. For Montagu, on the other hand, the only power that could ground self-realization was a revitalized religious faith.

Montagu's own *Bildungsroman* resembled that of a character from Emily Marion Harris's fiction. She came from a wealthy Anglo-Jewish family and began her encounter with the immigrant milieu teaching literature and history to East End girls. In fact the connection was even closer: Montagu's introduction to what was to become a lifelong career in social work came through Harris herself, whom she met in 1892 at the age of nineteen at Harris's Sabbath club for Jewish working girls in Bloomsbury.[29] Montagu's identification with the interests of the Jewish working class, however, had other sources too. Her father was the maverick financier and Liberal MP for Whitechapel, Samuel Montagu. Unlike Tory members of the Anglo-Jewish elite, Samuel Montagu was a supporter of trade unions and the financial backer of the Federation of small Orthodox immigrant synagogues in the East End.[30] Montagu was a self-made millionaire; his children were brought up in a relatively austere atmosphere and, Lily later recalled, actively encouraged "to assist others less fortunately placed than ourselves."[31]

In her autobiography, *The Faith of a Jewish Woman* (1943), however, Montagu represented the story of her youth as a conversion narrative. Focusing on the development of her spiritual life, she sketched an Orthodox childhood in the 1880s during which "my religion was definitely shaped by my father," and characterized by the "small regulations which, in the name of Judaism, restricted my liberty" (2). Her experience of prayer was passive, like the endless "recital" of grace after meals (7). In particular, she describes her feelings of alienation during the synagogue service on the Day of Atonement, where she obediently sits in the women's gallery, remote from the leaders of the service. Like Judith Quixano, Montagu observes a congregation whose religion entails no reverence or emotion; "they really seemed unaffected by the contents of the prayers" (10). To her further bewilderment, after the end of a long day intended for contemplation and repentance, the worshippers eagerly rush home to resume everyday life: "The *solemn day* seemed to have made so little difference" (10; italics in original). In contrast, the young Montagu reveals her private feelings of unfulfilled longing and unarticulated doubt.

Montagu's account of a religious practice dominated by ceremonialism that is in conflict with her own intuitive spirituality follows the familiar pattern of the conversion novel. Before long, the heroine's vague feelings of discontent begin to coalesce into rebellion. Her friendship with the theologian Claude Montefiore leads her to the principles of Liberal Judaism, which he had articulated as "a living, growing, spiritual conception, not a hard and fast collection of laws. It helped man to live and to think, to hope and to pray, not merely to obey and to sacrifice" (27).[32] She describes these ideas as a "new revelation," a "teaching [that] seemed to set me free from my spiritual fetters" (25, 24). Subsequently, Montagu's conversion to Liberal Judaism, like all conversions, is authenticated by its high emotional cost. She "suffered greatly" because of her father's deep opposition to the creation of a schismatic religious movement, but her loyalty to her newly found faith is stronger (33). Although he wants her to renounce it, she is able to resist by drawing on a religious authority that she regards as greater even than his: "I felt that by doing so I should betray the God-given truth which had been shown me" (36).

For Montagu, the drama of conversion expresses more than her personal spiritual autobiography; it tells of a wider crisis within Anglo-Jewry. "The history of a community," she declared in an essay published in 1899 in the liberal intellectual journal the *Jewish Quarterly Review*, "like the history of an individual, is marked by the recurrence of periods of self-consciousness and self-analysis. . . . For many years self-consciousness has been growing among English Jews, and they have expressed, in whispers to one another, dissatisfaction with their spiritual state." She contended that "the highest Jewish influences are . . . dormant, and have ceased to inspire our lives."[33] In her first novel, *Naomi's Exodus* (1901), Montagu boldly used the figure of a young Jewish shopgirl to explore the nature and extent of the crisis. As she had concluded through her work in girls' clubs, unreformed Judaism was especially unsatisfying for immigrant girls and women, who on the one hand "were not expected to join

in public worship" but on the other bore the brunt of the economic strain of festival observance.[34] While it evidently drew on her club work as well as her own
experience of Orthodox Judaism, *Naomi's Exodus* is also a confident parody of
and challenge to the tradition of the Jewish conversion novel.

As in *Reuben Sachs,* the novel's heroine, Naomi Saul, is a young woman
who has never thoughtfully considered the religion in which she has been
raised. The prologue describes a Friday night at the home of her Orthodox
aunt and guardian, in which "[Naomi] did not understand the words that
were being sung. She was hardly conscious that they had a sacred meaning,
but she was as zealous and sincere as her aunt in wishing that every portion
of the service should be exactly fulfilled."[35] A similarly unreflective conven-
tionality governs Naomi's relationship with her fiancé, Jacob: "Like most of
her friends, she was deeply imbued with the belief that marriage was a necessity and spinsterhood a degradation. Therefore she had accepted the engagement merely as a necessary episode in the natural course of events; love as a
romantic idea never occurred to them" (xiii). Montagu's opening scene thus
introduces her heroine as a figure familiar from conversion literature: a Jewess unwittingly deprived of spiritual and emotional fulfillment.

Naomi's exodus from her enslavement also begins conventionally, with
her meeting with an older woman, a Christian, whose unflappable serenity
provokes a crisis in Naomi's sense of wellbeing. She finds herself "strangely
troubled and discontented," alienated from her family and friends, and
"began, almost in spite of herself, to question the significance and importance
of some of the observances which were rigidly followed in her home, and
which had hitherto possessed a strong hold over her everyday life. . . . Never
having realised the presence of God, or even thought much about Him, she
had satisfied herself with a vague feeling that willing obedience meant piety,
and was in fact what God wanted. It made her 'good'" (5–6). Her aesthetic
capacities are also awakened: looking at paintings in the National Gallery with
her new friend, she "felt for the first time humbled in the presence of their
beauty" (9). Trouble begins when Jacob reports to Naomi's aunt that he has
seen her "with a Schickse [non-Jewish] woman, a fine lady in black. . . . She
kissed her most affectionate. I tell you that Schickses have got hold of our
Naomi" (29–30). When confronted by her aunt, Naomi refuses to deny that
she's been converted, and painfully decides that the only avenue open to her
is to leave home. Wandering the London streets and witnessing poverty and
domestic violence, she realizes that her concept of a distant, punitive God
inhibits her capacity for compassion for the suffering of others.

Here, instead of following through on narrative expectation, *Naomi's Exodus* takes an unanticipated direction. In her hour of need, Naomi is taken in by some factory girls who introduce her to a lady philanthropist, Miss Miles, the organizer of a club for working girls. Miss Miles's upper-class Jewish friend Clement Marks comes to the club as part of his well-meaning but insensitively executed investigation of tenement conditions, and a romance unfolds between him and Naomi. Yet although Clement expands her horizons by involving her in his political work, it is not he who is to be her salvation. Recognizing that he is uncomfortable with their social difference, Naomi voluntarily renounces him. This is the novel's turning point, for only now, stricken with grief and loneliness, is Naomi able to give herself over to prayer, and her idolatrous love is transmuted into love for humanity. No longer dependent on Clement's attention, she can define her own mission to "make herself useful" serving others in the London slums (164). The novel represents the advent, through suffering, of an ethical impulse in Naomi's life as the dawning of a genuine religious consciousness.

This point is driven home through the novel's double ending. The first, emotional climax is the momentous scene of Naomi's homecoming. It is with this move that Montagu decisively rejects the narrative of Christian conversion and links her text instead with the celebrated scenes in European Jewish literature—in Leopold Kompert's *The Peddler* (1849) or Israel Zangwill's *Children of the Ghetto* (1892), for example—which end with the return of a prodigal child to his or her ghetto home.[36] Naomi returns apprehensively to her aunt's house, anticipating "how she would long in vain to escape from it" and crave the opportunities for "free development" that she has come to see as the source of happiness (188–89). However, to the reader's surprise, her newly awakened powers of perception immediately find routes to religious feeling everywhere:

> There was the high dresser, with its rows of plates and dishes shining as brightly as they did on that Sabbath eve—now so far distant—when Jacob had come to celebrate the anniversary of their engagement. But the prosaic application of hot water could never have given them the splendour with which to Naomi's tired eyes they seemed endowed on this evening of her home-coming. The familiar Sabbath candles, too, appeared strangely unfamiliar to-night. The glow which they threw on the spotless tablecloth, seemed possessed with a mysterious sanctity which Naomi had never noticed before.

Thus often, when our souls have wandered far away from the old home objects, does the renewed contact cause us to bow our heads in reverent, silent wonder where before we were indifferent or noisily critical. (190–91)

This is not the tribal loyalty that had so often moved other Jewish writers of the homecoming scene, but "the immanent divine presence" whose general absence in Orthodox life Montagu had lamented in her 1899 essay.[37] Naomi moves seamlessly from noticing the "sanctity" in everyday life to embracing a new role as sympathetic supporter of her ailing aunt. In revisiting the same Friday night tableau with which the novel opened, now transfigured by the mature consciousness of the protagonist, Montagu suggests that ritual is not an obstacle to spirituality but, potentially, a pathway to it. But like Montagu herself, according to her autobiography, Naomi comes to a new understanding of Judaism not through theological inquiry but through intuition and experience.

The unfolding of Naomi's new life is indicated in the second ending, an epilogue set fifteen years later in which Naomi, now "serving others" as a successful head nurse at a large London hospital, reencounters Clement Marks. Unhappily married, he pleads with her to restart their friendship, but she refuses. Naomi's reflection as she watches him leave, in the final line of the novel, "He seemed quite an old man," indicates that, in contrast, she remains invigorated, empowered by her sacrifice (207). Montagu's work has been generally regarded in the context of the conservative values that, as part of the club movement, she aimed to instill in her charges—the values of moral discipline, respectability, and refinement through which the elite leaders hoped to tame unruly youthful energies.[38] But insofar as she follows Emily Harris in orchestrating her heroine's economic and emotional independence from men and successful pursuit of vocation, Montagu's writing suggests the modern, feminist potential within the ideology of the civilizing mission.

Naomi's Exodus is also significant in the history of Anglo-Jewish literature because it takes seriously the individuality and interior life of a young working woman; the novel's narration is almost entirely from Naomi's perspective. A brief excursus into the life story of Miss Miles, the middle-class club leader, reveals that she too has overcome romantic loss to find her vocation in social service, but the novel treats this subplot as evidence of the essentially common experience and potential of women regardless of social status. This was particularly the case for Jewish women, in Montagu's view. In her autobiographical writing she frequently referred to her intimate understanding of the frustrations and dilemmas of Jewish working girls whose subjectivities were shaped by cultural assumptions similar to those of her own family. "My father's attitude towards religious observance," she noted, "was shared by the fathers of our Club members," and it was through her conversations with the daughters that "I learned most about this strange, pseudo Orthodoxy which I was myself beginning to question fundamentally."[39] For Montagu, their common experience as Jewish women provided the grounding for the cross-class friendships that she saw as key to her work of raising girls' aspirations. Equally, in her early forays into leading synagogue services, she favored a democratic structure of worship in which "the leader must actually pray with the Congregation as one of the group . . . she must invite her congregation to seek God with her, realizing the dignity and the difficulty of the search, never speaking for them."[40] In Montagu's writing, similarly, narrative hierarchy is flattened: she diminishes the authority of the omniscient narrator, positioning the reader alongside the protagonist in her spiritual journey.

Although, in her various autobiographical writings, Lily Montagu continued to reaffirm these principles all her life, her fiction also registered some degree of doubt. Her later collection of short stories, *What Can a Mother Do?* (1926), focusing on scenes from the lives of Jewish seamstresses and typists, evokes with even sharper poignancy the longings of lively, intelligent young women chafing against long working hours, narrow horizons, and authoritarian parents. One is tempted by an upper-class philanderer, another by a kind gentile colleague, and a third is offered the opportunity to study art, supported by the labor of her best friend. Each, however, renounces the possibility of a new life, returning home to her family responsibilities in dutiful if resentful resignation. In these failed conversion narratives, the homecoming of the rebellious daughter is bitter and futile: her renunciation does not herald spiritual growth.

The title story, for example, holds the idea of female autonomy and the moral force of self-sacrifice in an ambivalent balance. The heroine, Kitty Solomon, escapes her cramped family apartment, her mother's ingrained passivity, and a life focused on physical subsistence to a pleasant suburb, where "[s]he had a room to herself, with a window which opened; she had a little table next to her bed and a bookshelf full of the novels and books of poetry she had learned to love. Her cheeks became fuller and took a healthy colour. She seemed to grow beautiful."[41] But Kitty is unable to enjoy these pleasures wholeheartedly, because "[i]n her heart was the consciousness of her mother's love, and she felt that she must go back to the stream of inevitability, for away from it, she would be lost" (18–19). Kitty's action is compelled by a force beyond her that she is unable to resist and barely comprehends: "She understood dimly that she must follow her mother down the stream to share her agony—that was the inevitable" (19). At the end of the story, the narrator intervenes, heavy-handedly, to put a positive cast on her choice to return: Kitty's hope of alleviating her mother's misery has brought her in touch with the "Spirit of Love." Yet as she voluntarily denies herself the basic pleasures enjoyed by the very readers of her story—books and a room of her own—for the endlessly repeating "stream of inevitability," the effect is chilling rather than uplifting.

Until the 1920s, then, Lily Montagu continued to rewrite the story of the spiritual crisis of the Jewish woman. In some ways her emphasis on the moral value of self-sacrifice is a throwback to the domestic ideology of Grace Aguilar. Yet Montagu's stories are very different from the didactic tales of the early Victorian period, in which generic characters embodied abstract attributes like humility or pride, and played a designated role in the exemplary narrative. Montagu sought instead to present her Jewish heroines' conflicts of allegiance within the specific context of the immigrant second generation, torn between the opportunities for female independence in the modern urban environment and the tradition of collective responsibility, especially to other women. For Montagu these competing imperatives could be resolved through the principles of Liberal Judaism, which offered women a new, imaginative framework to understand service to others—as an expression of spiritual love rather than a religious obligation.

Conclusion

Jewish women writers in Victorian England are of more than parochial interest. Their novels trace how Jews interpreted the shifting contours of womanhood across the century, from domestic piety to professional vocation to social activism. At the same time, they track the changing status of Jews in England, from the campaign for political emancipation to the impact of immigration, secularization, and religious fragmentation.

Moreover, their use of various genres of popular literature belies a complex texture of competing interests that structure their storylines, shape their characters, and are latent in their narration. Above all, in these texts, we can see how novels about class relations expressed Jews' anxieties about their public image. Always haunted (and often fascinated) by the specter of the Jewish poor, Aguilar, Harris, and Montagu sought to reassure both Jewish

and non-Jewish readers of their essential respectability with idealized portraits of the humble working-class mother, the romantic immigrant, or the
spiritual shopgirl. These novels are not only apologetic, however, as the recur-
rent presence of the philanthropist, at once a mediating, enabling, and disci-
plining figure, suggests. They also examined and questioned the nature of the
Anglo-Jewish collectivity. Thus, increasingly across the century, the figure of
the ardent, struggling, impoverished Jewess came to function self-reflexively.
Her unfulfilled longings were an implicit critique of a religious and social system that undervalued her potential.

Perhaps the most striking feature of the work of these writers is their
eschewal of the heterosexual marriage plot. Aguilar's, Harris's and Montagu's
stories of women who lose or renounce lovers but gain autonomy derive originally from the ideology of female moral superiority in the early nineteenth
century, but by the end of the century carry overtones of first-wave feminism.
Rewriting the formulaic Victorian story of the discontented Jewess and her
conversion, therefore, provided these writers with a ready-made vehicle for
exploring female subjectivity.

Notes

1. Michael Galchinsky, *The Origin of the Modern Jewish Woman Writer: Romance and Reform in Victorian England* (Detroit: Wayne State University Press, 1996).
2. Bryan Cheyette, "From Apology to Revolt: Benjamin Farjeon, Amy Levy and the Post-Emancipation Anglo-Jewish Novel, 1880–1900," *Transactions of the Jewish Histori-cal Society of England* 24 (1982–86), 253–65; Meri-Jane Rochelson, "Jews, Gender, and Genre in Late-Victorian England: Amy Levy's *Reuben Sachs*," *Women's Studies* 25 (1996), 311–28; Linda Hunt Beckman, "Leaving 'The Tribal Duckpond': Amy Levy, Jewish Self-Hatred and Jewish Identity," *Victorian Literature and Culture* 27.1 (1999), 185–201; Susan David Bernstein, "'Mongrel Words': Amy Levy's Jewish Vulgarity," in *Amy Levy: Critical Essays*, ed. Naomi Hetherington and Nadia Valman (Athens: Ohio University Press, 2010), 135–56.
3. Grace Aguilar, *Records of Israel* (London: John Mortimer, 1844), x.
4. Nadia Valman, *The Jewess in Nineteenth-Century British Literary Culture* (Cambridge: Cambridge University Press, 2007), 51–84.
5. For an extended discussion of Aguilar, see Valman, *The Jewess*, 85–114; Galchinsky, *Origin of the Modern Jewish Woman Writer*; and Miriam Elizabeth Burstein, "'Not the Superiority of Belief, But Superiority of True Devotion': Grace Aguilar's Histories of the Spirit," in *Silent Voices: Forgotten Novels by Victorian Women Writers*, ed. Brenda Ayres (Westport, CT: Praeger, 2003), 1–27.
6. Galchinsky, *Origin of the Modern Jewish Woman Writer*, 182.
7. Grace Aguilar, "The Perez Family" (1843), reprinted in *Grace Aguilar: Selected Writings*, ed. Michael Galchinsky (Peterborough, ON: Broadview Press, 2003), 87–179 (107, 108; emphasis in original). Further references to this edition will appear in the text.

8. Galchinsky, *Origin of the Modern Jewish Woman Writer*, 183.

9. T. P. Park, "Thomas Carlyle and the Jews," *Journal of European Studies* 20.1 (1990), 1–21.

10. Galchinsky, *Origin of the Modern Jewish Woman Writer*, 185.

11. Todd Endelman, *The Jews of Britain 1656 to 2000* (Berkeley: University of California Press, 2002), 79.

12. Colin Holmes, *Anti-Semitism in British Society, 1876–1939* (London: Edward Arnold, 1979); Bernard Gainer, *The Alien Invasion: The Origins of the Aliens Act of 1905* (London: Heinemann, 1972); John Garrard, *The English and Immigration, 1880–1910* (London: Oxford University Press, 1971).

13. Bryan Cheyette, "From Apology to Revolt," 253–65.

14. Harris's work remains unexplored by scholars except for Valman, *The Jewess*, 160–71.

15. Linda Gordon Kuzmack, *Woman's Cause: The Jewish Woman's Movement in England and the United States, 1881–1933* (Columbus: Ohio State University Press, 1990), 13.

16. [Emily Marion Harris], *Estelle*, 2 vols. (London: George Bell and Sons, 1878), I: 109; I: 271; I: 84.

17. For a fuller account of the novel, see Valman, *The Jewess*, 160–71.

18. [Harris], *Estelle*, I: 4–5.

19. Ibid., II: 113.

20. Ibid., I: 107.

21. [Emily Marion Harris], *Benedictus*, 2 vols. (London: George Bell and Sons, 1878), I: 2. Further references to this edition will appear in the text.

22. Lyn Pykett, "Portraits of the Artist as a Young Woman: Representations of the Female Artist in the New Woman Fiction of the 1890s," in *Victorian Writers and the Woman Question*, ed. Nicola Diane Thompson (Cambridge: Cambridge University Press, 1999), 135–50; Ann Heilmann, *New Woman Fiction: Women Writing First-Wave Feminism* (Basingstoke: Macmillan, 2000), 155–93.

23. On Montagu's role in the development of Liberal Judaism, see Ellen M. Umansky, *Lily Montagu and the Advancement of Liberal Judaism: From Vision to Vocation* (New York: Edwin Mellen Press, 1983). On her social and campaigning work, see Jean Spence, "Lily Montagu: A Short Biography," *Youth and Policy* 60 (1988), 73–83; Jean Spence, "Working for Jewish Girls: Lily Montagu, Girls' Clubs and Industrial Reform, 1890–1914," *Women's History Review* 13.3 (2004), 491–510; and Sidney Bunt, *Jewish Youth Work in Britain: Past, Present, and Future* (London: Bedford Square Press, 1975). On her suffragist activism, see Kuzmack, *Woman's Cause*, 136–39, and Anne Summers, "Gender, Religion and an Immigrant Minority: Jewish Women and the Suffrage Movement in Britain, *c.* 1900–1920," *Women's History Review* 21.3 (2012), 399–418.

24. Umansky, *Lily Montagu*, 61.

25. Amy Levy, "Reuben Sachs: A Sketch" (1888), reprinted in *The Complete Novels and Selected Writings of Amy Levy, 1861–1889*, ed. Melvyn New (Gainesville: University Press of Florida, 1993), 197–293 (209).

26. Ibid., 230.

27. Ibid., 269.

28. Nadia Valman, "Amy Levy and the Literary Representation of the Jewess," in *Amy Levy: Critical Essays*, ed. Hetherington and Valman, 90–109.

29. Lily H. Montagu, *My Club and I: The Story of the West Central Jewish Club* (London: Herbert Joseph, 1941), 22. Montagu may also have had an indirect connection with Grace

Aguilar; one of her early instructors in Judaism was a "Miss Rebecca Aguilar," probably the author's niece. See Lily H. Montagu, *The Faith of a Jewish Woman* (London: George Allen & Unwin, 1943), 6.

30. David Feldman, *Englishmen and Jews: Social Relations and Political Culture, 1840–1914* (New Haven, CT: Yale University Press, 1994), 220.

31. Montagu, *Faith of a Jewish Woman*, 13. Further references to this edition will appear in the text.

32. For a full account of the intellectual and social context of Liberal Judaism, see Daniel R. Langton, *Claude Montefiore: His Life and Thought* (London: Vallentine Mitchell, 2002), and Eugene C. Black, *The Social Politics of Anglo-Jewry, 1880–1920* (Oxford: Basil Blackwell, 1988), 67–70.

33. Lily H. Montagu, "Spiritual Possibilities of Judaism To-Day," *Jewish Quarterly Review* 11.2 (January 1899), 216–31 (216, 223).

34. Montagu, *Faith of a Jewish Woman*, 22, 25.

35. Lily H. Montagu, *Naomi's Exodus* (London: T. Fisher Unwin, 1901), xiv. Further references to this edition are included in the text.

36. See Jonathan M. Hess, Maurice Samuels, and Nadia Valman, eds., *Nineteenth-Century Jewish Literature: A Reader* (Stanford: Stanford University Press, 2013).

37. Montagu, "Spiritual Possibilities," 218.

38. Black, *Social Politics of Anglo-Jewry*, 133–56.

39. Montagu, *My Club and I*, 2; *Faith of a Jewish Woman*, 22.

40. Montagu, *Faith of a Jewish Woman*, 18.

41. Lily H. Montagu, *What Can a Mother Do? and Other Stories* (London: George Routledge and Sons, 1926), 16. Further references to this edition are included in the text.

2

"AND WE ARE NOT WHAT THEY HAVE BEEN"

Anglo-Jewish Women Poets, 1839–1923

CYNTHIA SCHEINBERG

O do not spurn our untaught lay,

Though clad in simple garb it seem;

For Judah's bards are passed away,

And we are not what they have been.

From "The Conclusion," Celia and Marion Moss, 1839

In 1839, something extraordinary happened in British literary history. Two Jewish women published a volume of poems titled *Early Efforts, A Volume of Poems by the Misses Moss of the Hebrew Nation, Aged 18 and 16.*[1] The volume had a series of subscribers—many, but not all of them Jewish—and proved successful enough to go into a second edition that same year. What was extraordinary about *Early Efforts* was not that it was the first book of poems by Anglo-Jewish women; indeed, Emma Lyon published a volume in 1812, and Grace Aguilar published a volume of poems—*The Magic Wreath*—anonymously in 1835.[2] But neither Lyon's volume nor *The Magic Wreath* take up the idea of what an explicitly female English Jewish poetic identity would look and sound like. In *Early Efforts,* by contrast, the Moss sisters made a bid to define an Anglo-Jewish female poetic identity that both claimed alliances with and challenged Victorian definitions of English female poetic identity.

It may not seem that the Moss sisters were claiming anything particularly extraordinary for themselves in the somewhat self-deprecating concluding lines to their volume quoted in the preceding epigraph, yet many of the questions they raise in this deceptively simple stanza remained central for the Anglo-Jewish woman poet in the century that would follow. On the surface the lines compare their own poetry and that of "Judah's bards"—a reference to the poetry of the Hebrew scriptures and psalms and such Hebrew medieval poets as Yehuda Halevi, so revered in Jewish literary tradition. Thus, on one level, "we are not what they have been" can be read as a self-conscious distinction that differentiates the Mosses from the almost exclusive maleness of the Hebrew poets of old. Yet the line can also be read in a number of other registers. Suggesting their difference from that male trajectory of Hebrew literature, these women articulate one of the major questions to confront any Anglo-Jewish woman poet in this period: What relationship could she claim to Jewish and Hebrew poetic traditions in her work?

Indeed, claiming a link to the tradition of "Judah's bards" was a complex act in nineteenth-century Jewish and Christian cultures. Many Christian writers in the century were debating the importance of this Hebrew poetic tradition. In the early part of the century, renewed interest in the literary characteristics of biblical verse was supported by the work of Johann Gottfried Herder in Germany and Bishop Lowth in England; this reverence for psalms and biblical poetry can be seen in a number of Victorian texts throughout the century. In 1878, the eminent literary critic J. B. Selkirk suggested that Hebrew poetry typified the ideal relationship between poetry and religion: "Nor could it be well otherwise with a people [the English] whose moral modes of thinking have been so largely grafted upon the Hebrew Scriptures, those ever-flowing rivers of consolation that have quenched the thirst of so many of earth's pilgrims, and in which the perfect and harmonious fusion of the two instincts, religious and poetical, find so complete an illustration."[3] Selkirk's comments, moreover, are not isolated but representative of a school of Victorian criticism that idealized biblical Hebrew poetry.

On the other side of the dialogue, Matthew Arnold in *Culture and Anarchy* (1869) argued that the true roots of English poetic identity were found not in what he termed the "Hebraism" of British middle-class culture—the dull-witted call to duty and religion—but rather in the "sweetness and light" of "Hellenism." Thus, when Anglo-Jewish women poets claim or ignore their connections to "Judah's bards" in this period, they not only constitute new meanings for their own "Hebraic" identities but necessarily enter into a larger discourse about the respective values of different poetic traditions. In this context, the line "we are not what they have been" can also invoke the difference between modern diasporic Jewish culture and the biblical world depicted in scripture and classical Jewish texts.[4] And, as this chapter explores, Anglo-Jewish women writers also reveal differing relationships to classical Jewish poets, in particular Yehuda Halevi, marking their own differential relationships to Jewish religious and cultural literacy.

Anglo-Jewish women poets who continued in the Moss sisters' tradition—Grace Aguilar (1816–47), Amy Levy (1861–89), Katie Magnus (1844–1924), Alice Lucas (1852–1935), and Nina Salaman (1877–1925)—each took a different approach to the problem of constructing a female Anglo-Jewish literary identity. What this analysis of six Anglo-Jewish women poets suggests is that their poetic identities were always in tension with a number of historical and literary discourses: Hebrew and English literary traditions, England's changing attitudes toward the woman poet and women's education, and emerging class and religious differences within Anglo-Jewish society. Finally, their own understanding of their audiences—Jewish, non-Jewish, assimilated, or religious—affected these women's approach to their writing.

In expressing an anxiety about who "we" resemble and do not resemble, the Mosses suggest other questions about writing and difference. Along with constructing their place in Jewish literary traditions, Anglo-Jewish women poets had to confront the powerful tradition of women's poetry that emerged from the eighteenth century and continued to gain momentum throughout the nineteenth century. Jewish women poets had to confront and coopt a powerful tradition of Christian women's literary identity, and construct a relationship with the cultural icon of "the poetess"—a figure who was implicitly and explicitly associated with Christian womanhood. The Moss sisters and Grace Aguilar had the hugely popular figures of Felicia Hemans (1793–1835) and Letitia Elizabeth Landon ("L.E.L") (1802–1838) directly preceding them, and each successive generation of Anglo-Jewish women poets would have to confront that poetess tradition as it continued to expand and diversify in the work of some of the century's most famous and successful poets: Elizabeth Barrett Browning, Christina Rossetti, Jean Ingelow, and Augusta Webster, to name only a few.[5]

Finally, the idea of "we" and "they" suggests the questions of form that these young Jewish poets encountered. The Moss sisters wrote in distinctly English verse patterns and traditions; the *Early Efforts* volume demonstrates their acute awareness of contemporary literary style and genre, and thus indicates they had to situate themselves in not only a Jewish literary tradition, and a women's literary tradition, but also an English one. Specifically, these poets grapple with the assumption of Romantic lyric identity, issues of universal and minority voice, and changing understandings of the roles poetry plays in British culture as a public and political tool for change, or as a more private and particular form of personal or devotional reflection. And of course, as Jewish women confront the forms and genres of English poetry, their work engages with the Jewish question again, in terms of form. Amy Levy's work articulates most sharply the question of whether English poetic genres themselves make claim to specific Christian orientation, and what generic responses are needed to make English poetry give voice to non-majority speakers. Indeed, each of the women in this essay highlights a particular challenge for Jewish women writers in England: rewriting historical accounts of Jewish oppression, creating Jewish devotional poetry in English, translating Hebrew verse into English, and engaging with a specifically Jewish literary heritage.

Early to Mid-Nineteenth-Century Voices: Writing the Anglo-Jewish Past

Celia Moss (Levetus) was born in 1819 in Portsea; one of twelve children, she and her sister Marion (born 1821) published *Early Efforts* when they were eighteen and sixteen, respectively.[6] *Early Efforts* ranges in poetic style and form, including brief lyrics and extensive historical and dramatic poems, with both authors participating in a wide range of genres. Some poems explore explicitly Jewish themes and genres: "The Passover," "The Feast of the Tabernacle," "Lament for Jerusalem," "The Jewish Captive's Song," "Return from the Captivity," and "The Jewish Girl's Song" call on genres from Hebrew tradition or take up specifically Jewish content; others explore English and non-Jewish themes and topics, as in "The Novice," "The Georgian Girl to Her Lover," "The Battle of Bannockburn," and "Amy Robsart's Complaint to the Earl of Leicester." As such, the diverse topics and styles of poems in the volume demonstrate the breadth of these women's historical and literary knowledge. Michael Galchinsky notes that one source for their poetic literacy came from contemporary British poetry, as "their father read romantic poetry to them while they sewed"[7]; clearly another was their awareness of a tradition of classical Jewish texts, evidence of their Jewish education. Even more than the male Romantics of their father's reading, the Moss sisters were also deeply influenced by the work of women in the Romantic and early Victorian eras, Felicia Hemans and L.E.L.

Drawing on many of the historical poems about female martyrdom by Hemans and Landon, Celia Moss's "The Massacre of the Jews at York" memorializes a tragic event in Anglo-Jewish history from a Jewish perspective, with a focus on the plight of women. Unlike poems of diasporic Jewish history in the later work of Aguilar, "The Massacre of the Jews at York" stands out for its refusal to claim any alliance with Christian England, its coopting of the sentimental trope of gendered martyrdom, and its participation in nineteenth-century medievalism. The poem is also framed by versions of Jewish history drawn from two well-known non-Jewish works. The poem's epigraph is from Byron's "On the Day of the Destruction of Jerusalem by Titus," from his *Hebrew Melodies* (1815): "And scattered and scorn'd as thy people may be, / Our worship, O Father, is only for thee." And the poem closes with a series of footnotes citing Henry Hart Milman's influential *History of the Jews* (1829).[8] In many ways Milman serves as the authoritative source of this historical episode; he describes how, at York, the Jews were besieged by a Christian mob and took refuge in the castle, where they starved until their mass suicide directly prior to the storming of the castle. Linking Byron's appropriation of Hebrew lyric identity to the historical event of Jewish massacre on English soil, Moss challenges the terms of British philosemitism which structure both Byron's and Milman's works.

The poem begins by presenting a seemingly conventional rendering of a major English icon, the medieval castle:

> There is an old and stately hall,
> Hung round with many a spear and shield,
> And sword and buckler on the wall
> Won from the foe in tented field: (1–4)

While appearing to participate in the description of England's past heroic glory, the poem immediately unsettles the idealization of this chivalric, knightly home; the narrator notes "yet there no warrior bands are seen" and describes not the heroic knight or nobleman in this setting but rather "men with care, not age, grown white / Meet in York Castle hall to-night, / And groups of maids and matrons too" (7–9). This opening section concludes by questioning any notion of England as a safe refuge for the Jews:

> What doth the Jew, the wandering race

Of Israel, in such dwelling place?
From persecution's deadly rage
A refuge in those walls they sought,
The zealots of a barb'rous age
Ruin upon their tribes had brought. (13–18)

Moss here poses the radical disjunction of England as a site for Jewish refuge and its absolute unreliability. In quick succession, the poem turns the familiar cultural icons of England's heroic past to images of English Christians as cruel barbarians intent on murdering children, starving Jewish communities, and inflicting atrocities on all Jews with whom they come in contact.

The historical setting of the poem links Moss to her most famous female Christian contemporary poet, Felicia Hemans. David Rothstein has demonstrated how Hemans capitalized on the nineteenth century's "growing cultural appetite for the fantasy of the medieval past that included tales of chivalric heroism, refurbished castles, Gothic furniture and tours of ruined abbeys," and that her poems in this genre helped to "sustain a British national fantasy based on the ideals of traditional social hierarchy, masculine chivalric heroism and domestic harmony."[9] "The Massacre of the Jews at York" surely enters into dialogue with this growing interest in medievalism yet also remains a radical challenge to glorified images of medieval England. Also reminiscent of Hemans is Moss's depiction of women as martyrs faced with moral decisions that make gruesome suicide a viable choice. The question of the moral imperative in the Jews' choice of martyrdom is a major theme in the poem, which tempers its more conventional glorification of martyrdom by depicting particularly graphic deaths of women and children. The omniscient and restrained narrator repeatedly suggests that the mass suicide was in fact the "right" moral choice, as those who resisted martyrdom are, by the end of the poem, "coldly murdered . . . where they stood" or "plunge[d] . . . back into flame till the halls with their shrieking rung" (266–69). Between the introduction and the gruesome ending of the poem, Moss muddies the clarity of the moral choice made by the Jewish men of York.

For, despite the communal acceptance of the decision to commit mass suicide, the women presented in the poem resist their own deaths and the death of a child only to be overpowered by the patriarch, Rabbi Ben Israel, and a young husband of the community, who do indeed kill them. However, one narrative strand serves to defer responsibility from these men even as we are asked to watch them commit murder. After stabbing the "object of [his] fondest cares"—his own daughter Rachael—despite her protestation, the rabbi proceeds to a "babe and his widow'd mother" (98, 213). As he raises his dagger, the mother pleads to let her look on her baby a few more moments; it is the rabbi who points out to the mother that the baby has in fact already died of starvation. This is a crucial moment in the poem, as it essentially decriminalizes the patriarch's act, suggesting that the starvation caused by the Christians is "the sterner hand that hath done the deed." This observation leads the mother to a frenzied shriek that is matched "[b]y one, more wild, more fearful still," namely that of the young bride killed by her new husband (231).

Moss's strategy of focusing specifically on female death and martyrdom as symbolic of the larger communal tragedy connects her work to a tradition of poetry by women like Hemans which highlights female death and infanticide.[10] Yet "Massacre" challenges poems in which female martyrdom can be claimed in a larger heroic cause, and likewise refuses to offer any narrational redemptive closure, save the notion of "glorious death of the brave" in the penultimate section of the poem (243). Thus, whereas other poems in this tradition often allow the women themselves a voice with which to speak about their own heroic redemption, in "Massacre" neither the women nor the narrator say much to redeem their deaths. Instead, death is marked only by their terrified and terrifying shrieks and the image of the murderers rushing away in "awe" and silence from the crime scene of "the silent dead" (276). Moss's minimal narration and thematic focus allow a male speaker (the rabbi) to perform the bulk of the poem's didactic work about the moral imperative to murder women and children to save them from violent Englishmen; by withholding the women's own commentary, "The Massacre of the Jews at York" makes their martyrdom even more disturbing. As perhaps the most political poem in *Early Efforts,* "Massacre" condemns the nineteenth-century fantasy of medievalism through the lens of antisemitism; the poem, like the martyrs within it, seeks to claim a place "in their country's annals"—with a double play on the idea of what country exactly the Jews of York, and by extension the "Misses Moss of the Hebrew Nation," can claim as authentically "theirs" (159).

Grace Aguilar wrote in the same period as the Moss sisters and, like them, explored a number of literary forms. However, her approach to poetry, Jewish history, and English poetic genres is very different from the Mosses', and she suggests a very different set of strategies for a Jewish woman's poetic voice and identity. Aguilar was particularly influenced by the Romantic poetics of Wordsworth and Coleridge, claiming their influence far more overtly than she does that of any female poets of the day. Many of Aguilar's poems also position her in dialogue with the political, activist poems of writers like Elizabeth Barrett Browning, as is evident in her call for political action in "The Hebrew's Appeal: On Occasion of the Late Fearful Ukase Promulgated by the Emperor of Russia" (1844).[11] This poem makes distinct connections to "The Massacre of the Jews at York" in that both seek to describe situations of terrible Jewish suffering at the hands of majority cultures. However, where Moss depicts the atrocities and martyrdom of Jews without overt commentary or self-identification, Aguilar creates a distinct poetic persona who directly calls on English readers not only for sympathy but also for concrete action.

Aguilar begins her poem with a rendering of the inarticulate shriek of Jewish suffering, much like the images of shrieks that punctuate "Massacre."

> Awake! arise! ye friends of Israel's race.
>   The wail of thousands lingers on the air,
> By heavy pinions borne, through realms of space,
>   Till Israel shudd'ring Israel's woe must bear;
> The voice of suffering echoes on the skies,
> And oh not yet one pitying heart replies. (1–6)[12]

If the shrieks in the Moss poem ultimately fade into silence, invoking on the part of an English reader sympathy—if not guilt—for their historical erasure, Aguilar's "wail[ing]" Jewish thousands, on the other hand, "[linger] on the air" and "[echo] on the skies" with the possibility of provoking a response. Indeed, Aguilar calls on England not only as "friends of Israel's race" but also as a nation that has bestowed "Liberty [on] the slave." The poetic voice of the poem is in a constant mode of exhortation, using repeated imperatives, rhetorical questions, and direct pleas. Thus Aguilar takes a more active role than does Moss, becoming a spokesperson for Jewish relief in a specifically Jewish voice, which is at the same time deeply engaged with English poetics.

Stanza 7 begins, "Oh England! thou hast called us to thy breast, / And done to orphans all a mother's part"; here, the "us" refers to Jews and clearly situates the poetic speaker as a Jewish voice and presence. This identity becomes even more pointed in stanza 8, in which the speaker directs a specific plea to English Jews: "And let one prayer from Hebrew hearths ascend / To Israel's God, that he may deign reply, / And yet again his chosen race defend." In other words, "The Hebrew's Appeal" is overtly addressed to both Christians and Jews, both understood to be equally part of "England." While questions of audience are addressed only obliquely in the "Massacre" poem, Aguilar makes the demands of her dual audience explicit.

Where Moss suggests the threat to Jewish identity in British history—
and perhaps mutes her own narrational presence for that reason—Aguilar
instead casts England as heroic for its reputation as a savior of oppressed
peoples and uses a confident narratorial tone: "Will SHE not rise once more,
in mercy clad, / And heal the bleeding heart, and Sorrow's sons make glad?"
The complex gendering of England as the heroic mother healing a "bleeding
heart" and "Sorrow's sons" offers allusions to Christian narratives of the Passion. This reference resembles a characteristic of much of Aguilar's writing, in
which she uses images and ideas that are typically associated with Christianity to describe specifically Jewish referents.[13] In the previous lines, the "bleeding heart" and "Sorrow's sons," then, are not references to Christ but rather to
a persecuted Jewish community. Aguilar's willingness here and elsewhere to
engage with tropes of Christian rhetoric suggests her overt appeal to Christian audiences as well as to assimilated Jews.

Along with the political call to arms in poems like "A Hebrew's Appeal,"
Aguilar also wrote numerous explorations of her approach to Judaism and
her relationship with God, especially in her "Sabbath Thoughts" sequence.
Here Aguilar reveals the personal dimensions of Jewish religious experience,
linking it to universal forms of spirituality. She mediates the difficulties of
speaking as a devout Jew within the terms of English poetics by evincing a
deep commitment to the forms and assumptions of first-generation British
Romanticism.[14] She does so through repeated allusions to Romantic poetry
in her work, but also by claiming a prophetlike voice, a belief in the spiritual power of nature, and a link to personal biography as a source of poetic
authority. While maintaining her Jewish poetic voice through explicit Jewish
content in the majority of her poems, Aguilar was seemingly uninterested in
emulating or referencing Hebrew or Jewish poetic genres; there are no communal laments of exile and few, if any, references to traditional Hebrew poetics. The closest Aguilar came to the classical diasporic lament is her "Song
of the Spanish Jews," a poem ostensibly spoken by medieval Spanish Jews
celebrating their freedoms in Spain; thus on the surface it suggests the success of diasporic existence. Nevertheless, any reader coming to the poem with
knowledge of the imminent Inquisition would recognize the double-edged
irony embedded in the Spanish speakers' praise for Spanish tolerance.[15]

Where later Jewish women poets would claim a more direct link to
"Judah's bards" and the Jewish/Hebrew poetic traditions, Aguilar—perhaps
the most famous Anglo-Jewish writer of her day—seeks alignment instead
with English literary genres. This choice is in part explained by Aguilar's

awareness of her readers, who would have had little grasp of those Jewish literary traditions—and perhaps by the limitations of her own knowledge of classical Jewish sources. Aguilar's lack of interest in establishing a specific relationship to "Judah's bards" is also a direct result of her goals as a writer: understanding all too well the centuries of women's total exclusion from Jewish textual education, she explicitly sought to create a "Jewish literature" in English. Noting that it was important to have a literature that could not only "make the Jew respected, but [also] . . . have JUDAISM rightly reverenced," Aguilar aimed to speak directly to Jews uneducated in their religious traditions, and also to correct false ideas of Judaism and Jews.[16] Aguilar sought to show that Jews could speak much like other English writers, even as she made claims for Judaism's unique spiritual power.

Amy Levy and the Challenge to Christian Poetics

It is hard to imagine a more striking difference from Aguilar's approach to poetry and Anglo-Jewish literary identity than the work of Amy Levy. Writing almost fifty years after Aguilar and the Moss sisters, Levy rejected models of the poetic female "heart" and the poetess tradition, challenged the lyric identity of the Romantic poetic prophet, and articulated a minority voice that is ambiguously Jewish and potentially lesbian. Very little of her poetry utilized explicitly Jewish content. This may be explained by the difference in Levy's experience as a Jew in England compared with those of earlier Jewish writers. For Levy was a true child of Anglo-Jewish emancipation—the series of parliamentary bills and acts from 1832 to 1871 that collectively removed all political and educational restrictions for Jewish citizens. Levy benefited from these reforms, as she was one of the first Jewish women to attend the University of Cambridge, which had previously required the profession of Christianity. Her ensuing career as a novelist, poet, and essayist brought her into contact with both mainstream and avant-garde literary circles that included figures like Oscar Wilde, Havelock Ellis, and Eleanor Marx; nevertheless, she also maintained literary ties with the *Jewish Chronicle* and Jewish literary figures like Lady Katie Magnus.

While the extent of Levy's Jewish education and her relationship to Jewish ritual observance remains unclear, we do know Levy actively sought higher education in a Christian university, and she often criticizes Anglo-Jewish culture for its disregard for women's education.[17] Levy's wide-ranging experience in English educational and literary institutions may also have contributed to her more theoretical exploration of how dominant British culture fails to accommodate forms of difference, a point she repeatedly made through the subject matter and formal experimentation of her poetry and fiction. In addition, recent critics have posited that Levy may have been a lesbian, and many of her poems use a lyric voice that addresses women as objects of desire.[18] Whereas Aguilar made a call for a Jewish literature that could elevate the status of Jews and Judaism in England, Levy demonstrated her willingness to overtly criticize the middle-class Anglo-Jewish society of her day, and to take a profoundly assimilated view of Judaism itself. As a result, Levy's poetic project is less concerned with claiming a Jewish poetic self than with deconstructing the assumptions of Christian poetic identity from an outsider position.[19] What makes Levy a complex figure in this study of Anglo-Jewish women poets is how she articulated a Jewish poetic identity in relation to a mainstream, intellectual, Christian language that she termed the language of "the purest University English."[20]

While Levy does not lay explicit claim to a Jewish poetic identity, in poems like "Captivity" and her translations of Yehuda Halevi some of her work does clearly call on Hebrew literary traditions.[21] Her belief in the value of maintaining some kind of minority identity even while using "University English" is also evident in her poem "Sonnet," published in her 1881 volume *Xantippe and Other Verse.* The collection contains some of Levy's best dramatic monologues, and thus demonstrates her interest in characterization and psychological portraits—often of oppressed or misunderstood historical figures. Yet there are also signs of the developing lyric style and poetic themes that would emerge in her last volume, *A London Plane Tree and Other Verse.* "Sonnet," in its very title, establishes a connection to an English poetic tradition that has roots in both devotional and heterosexual courtly love lyrics, as well as to the Victorian resurgence of interest in the sonnet. The poem explores the sonnet tradition itself, seeking some new relationship between the form and what (and who) it can represent.

> Most wonderful and strange it seems, that I
> Who but a little time ago was tost
> High on the waves of passion and of pain,
> With aching heart and wildly throbbing brain,
> Who peered into the darkness deeming vain
> All things found there if but One thing were lost,
> Thus calm and still and silent here should lie,
> Watching and waiting,—waiting passively.
> The dark has faded, and before mine eyes

Have long, grey flats expanded, dim and bare;
And through the changing guises all things wear
Inevitable Law I recognize:
Yet in my heart a hint of feeling lies
Which half a hope and half is a despair.[22]

This very personal account of some spiritual, psychological, or romantic crisis, one that is left significantly unnamed, focuses not on the speaker's identity per se but rather on the process of crisis and possible recovery the poem recounts. Where Aguilar uses the poem of personal suffering to point repeatedly to the mercy of a Jewish God, Levy's poem demonstrates a far more obscured relationship to any form of spirituality. Thus while Levy's use of capitalization—"One" and "Inevitable Law"—grants the poem the marks of devotional language, this recognition of "Inevitable Law" is theologically indecipherable, possibly even echoing the derogatory Christian notion of Judaism as the religion of law rather than spirit.

If the poem invokes an un-Jewish vision of Judaism, it also challenges conventions of sonnet rhetoric and form. "Sonnet" reworks the underlying premise of sonnet structure, which posits an opening statement or problem in the octet that is "resolved" with a slight imbalance of the sestet, a structure in which the turn, the volta, becomes a central point of transition. In Levy's "Sonnet," however, there is only the "guise" of transformation, for though "[t]he dark has faded" in the pivotal ninth line, it is not replaced by light but rather "long, grey flats expanded, dim and bare"—hardly a clear resolution from darkness. Rather than create a kind of spiritual conversion or transformation of initial premises, Levy's "Sonnet" simply suggests that after crisis comes passivity, with no clarity or direct conclusions. Not only is the refusal to find closure or resolution an act of subversion to the sonnet tradition; such an ending also perhaps connects with the tradition of Hebrew lyric of unresolved longing, like that of the Psalmist lyricist who never can claim a sure conviction of redemption but simply hope.

Perhaps the most challenging part of "Sonnet" is the last four lines. The reference to "changing guises all things wear" suggests a reference to outward forms, poetic or ritualistic, those that the speaker must see "through" to find "Inevitable Law." This unnamed law can refer both to a deeper, transcendent spiritual or psychological truth that is only clothed by the "changing guises" as well as to the "laws" of British literary tradition and genre invoked by the title, "Sonnet." The most important word in the poem is the "Yet" of line 13—"[y]et

in my heart a hint of feeling lies / Which half a hope and half is a despair"—
which positions the "hint of feeling" in the speaker's "heart" as opposed to
the earlier recognition of "Inevitable Law." The terms often set in opposition
in Christian discourse—"Law" and a "feeling heart"—are actually coexistent
for this speaker, who is consciously resisting their polarization. The refusal to
name that final emotion, to offer conclusion or resolution, marks the transformation Levy attempts in the sonnet form itself. Thus the rhyme scheme
of the poem, complex and skilled though it is, nevertheless refuses to mimic
established sonnet conventions (Shakespearean, Petrarchan, or Spenserian).
Rather than render internal emotional or spiritual turmoil as adaptable to the
logical organization of ideas, Levy challenges herself to use that form for the
representation of an internal order "other" to those conventions, calling into
question the possibility of a "universal" form for representations of internal
psychic, spiritual, or sexual struggle. While one could argue there is nothing specifically "Jewish" about "Sonnet," it participates in Levy's larger project of destabilizing aspects of conventional poetic identity, a project that is
rooted in her awareness of Jewish difference but which she explores from the
broader position of "minority."

In the end Levy remained far more of an outsider within Anglo-Jewish
British literary culture than the poets we will turn to next. Levy focused her
work on critique—of English poetics, the Jewish middle class, restrictive religious law, compulsory heterosexuality, and Christian hegemony. It is perhaps
not surprising that, as the most assimilated Jew considered in this essay,
Levy emerges as the one least tied to specifically Jewish themes and literary
traditions. However, in her move away from a Romantic and sentimentalized
female poetic identity, in her turn to a sparse, less descriptive lyric mode,
and even in her move toward translation later in her career, Levy can also be
cast as a harbinger for the Anglo-Jewish women poets who follow her. Her
complex positioning within British and Jewish literary history becomes even
more fascinating in the comparison between her translations of the medieval
poet Yehuda Halevi and the translation work of the later poets, to which I
turn in the final section of this essay.

Claiming Jewish Literary Authority: Twentieth-Century Voices

Lady Katie (Emanuel) Magnus, Alice (Julia Montefiore) Lucas, and Nina (Davis)
Salaman were all born or married into prominent upper-class Jewish families in
which their education in both Jewish and English subjects was made a priority.

As a group they demonstrate a remarkable movement to create a new figure of the Anglo-Jewish woman writer: a scholar/teacher with connections to male Jewish and academic Hebrew circles; a woman who commands the authority to transmit Jewish learning and to create poetry based on a classical Jewish and Hebrew literary heritage, and who is at the same time immersed in the traditions of British culture, poetics, and language. The ways this group reshaped the role of the Anglo-Jewish woman poet are a result not only of particular personal histories; larger social and historical shifts also made possible a new vision of the Anglo-Jewish woman poet. By the end of the nineteenth century, England saw the emancipation of Anglo-Jewry from civil disabilities, increased interest in women's education, and the influence of the "New Woman" movement affecting Jewish and non-Jewish society alike.

Class identity and education also differentiated these later poets' experiences as well as their access to Jewish education: the Mosses and Aguilar came from lower middle-class backgrounds and often wrote for a living, or at least to augment their family's earnings. Although they always maintained the goal of presenting Jews and Judaism in a positive light, they sought to insert their Jewish voices into the English literary tradition in a way that would be marketable. These earlier writers, in part due to their lower-class identity, in part to the limitations of Jewish and women's education at the time, obtained their Jewish learning where they could, often relying on male tutors and publications like Morris Raphall's *The Hebrew Review*.[23] In their writing, not surprisingly, they often made the education of the Jewish woman a primary issue. Amy Levy also seems to have supported herself through her writing, though her middle-class background may have made the earning potential of her writing less urgent. Her access to the elite establishment of Cambridge University also separates her experience of education from that of the Mosses and Aguilar, though we have less sense of the extent of Levy's Jewish learning.

Lady Katie Magnus was described in 1913 as "a devoted teacher in Israel, a satirist, and a keen observer of the tendencies in modern life; all her characteristics are blended in the most lovable and original way, showing a strong sense of humour."[24] This evaluation holds up as remarkably apt a century later; Magnus combines the satire and modernity we saw in Levy with a far deeper interest in Jewish themes. She has been most celebrated in Anglo-Jewish literary history for the series of articles she published in the 1880s for the *National Review*, which were later anthologized in the volume *Jewish Portraits*. In this remarkable series of essays, Magnus speaks in the easy, cultured persona of the educated upper-class Englishwoman, often using irony and sarcasm and demonstrating a detailed knowledge of Jewish literature and religion. Her essays cover topics that would be obscure to a mainstream English audience ("Charity in Talmudic Times," "Jehuda Halevi," "Manasseh Ben Israel") as well as Jewish themes they might find more familiar ("Heinrich Heine," *Daniel Deronda* and His Jewish Critics," and "Moses Mendelssohn"). In all her work, Magnus attempts to render the potential otherness of Judaism, Jewish historical figures, and Jewish texts accessible for non-Jewish readers (or noneducated, assimilated Jewish readers). She presents Jewish culture and law with a cosmopolitan and often ironic wit, describing the Talmud, for example, as the "one work of the world which has suffered about equally at the hands of the commentator and the executioner,"[25] or referring to medieval Jewish liturgists as having "a decided tendency to clutch at the halo."[26] But where Levy often ends at the point of satire and critique, Magnus's larger aim is to inspire a new recognition for or interpretation of Jewish characters and topics that ultimately leads readers toward appreciation—of Jewish poetry, of Jewish history, and of Judaism itself.

Magnus's own poetry likewise demonstrates these two strands—the exhibition of a much deeper kind of Jewish textual literacy than we have seen previously, as well as a willingness to offer an urbane critique. *A Book of Verse* (1905) collects poetry that had been previously published in the *Westminster Gazette* and *Jewish Chronicle*. In it, Magnus brings together poetry from Jewish literary and scriptural traditions, in sections titled "From the Book" or "From the Talmud." In later years, this rendering of poetry from Talmudic and biblical sources would be continued by Lucas and Salaman. Magnus's personal lyrics are less directly Jewish in theme, yet many, as in the poem "Unorthodox" from the 1905 volume, use the questions that concerned Jews as a larger metaphor. Thus "Unorthodox" begins with a standard question of lyric longing:

> Shall we be ever again together—
> We who so long were never apart?
> What like will it be, that new Forever?
> Haply the finding a waiting heart. (1–4)[27]

Magnus draws on conventional poetic themes of both English and Hebrew traditions as she merges figures of romantic and devotional love at the moment she names "that new Forever"—perhaps a reference to the coming of messianic times. The poem concludes in the second stanza with the more explicitly religious imagery of the jewels that border the High Priest's breast plate in Exodus, as well as "New Earth," an apparently Christian reference to the New Jerusalem in Revelations (significantly put in quotation marks):

> What says the Vision? "New Earth" revealing—
> Borders of agate, gates of red gold;
> Are we ungracious to pray, low kneeling,
> "Only renew our days of old"? (5–8)

By the end of the poem, Magnus juxtaposes a vision of messianic redemption, in which some readers might read Christian references, with a quotation from the Day of Atonement liturgy, which resists images of "the new" in favor of a prayer for restoration to past glory—a choice that points directly at the differences in Jewish and Christian theology. Magnus writes deceptively simple lyrics, but even this cursory glance at "Unorthodox" suggests that her poetry demonstrates the complexities of claiming an "other" voice in a Christian British poetic tradition.

Alice (Julia Montefiore) Lucas was a contemporary of Magnus, a poet and translator whose versions of medieval poetry were widely accepted in many Hebrew-English prayerbooks of her day and long after. Born and married into prominent Anglo-Jewish families, Lucas was active in literary, educational, and philanthropic Jewish work all her life. Her publications include translations of German poetry and Jewish history; deemed a "fine Hebraist," she also translated poetry from classical Hebrew and Talmudic sources.[28] Much of this work culminated in Lucas's most audacious and important collection of her own poetry and translations from classical Jewish sources, *The Jewish Year: A Collection of Devotional Poems for Sabbaths and Holidays Throughout the Year* (1898). This fascinating volume is modeled on the single most popular book of poetry in the Victorian era, John Keble's *The Christian Year* (1827). Lucas's volume is designed as a collection of devotional poems "for the use of English Jews," and contains translations from medieval Hebrew poetry, poetic renderings of "talmudic legends," reworkings of poems from the prayerbook, and original works by Lucas herself, organized thematically through reference to the weekly Sabbath Torah portion.[29] Like Magnus, Lucas displays a far deeper knowledge of Hebrew and Jewish texts than her Anglo-Jewish predecessors. She also takes on liturgical authority to create a book designed "for devotional purposes . . . as an adjunct to the prayer-book, to be used at home, in the Sabbath school, perhaps occasionally in the synagogue, as an aid to religious meditation" (xvi–xvii). In choosing to respond to what Lucas terms in her preface a "famous literary precedent" (i.e., Keble's work), Lucas recognizes the power of Christian literary examples and suggests ways in which Jewish worship could emulate and adapt to Christian models—in this case the idea of a daily hymn (xviii).

Most interesting of all is the author's inclusion of her own poetry (acknowledged as "original" in the table of contents) along with translations of Halevi, Solomon ibn Gebirol, the Talmud, Abraham ibn Ezra, Nachmanides, and Alkabets. That is, Lucas, and later Salaman, has no qualms about including her own devotional poetry in such a list of "Judah's bards." Indeed, of the seventy-five selections in *The Jewish Year*, twelve are Lucas's own poems. One of her original poems, "Not Worthy," is linked to Genesis 32.10, in which Jacob speaks to God regarding his own unworthiness for the many blessings he has already received and offers a further prayer for God's continued protection as Jacob meets his brother, Esau. Lucas's poem first creates a dramatic monologue in the voice of Jacob, opening with what seems a straight translation of the biblical verse in Jacob's voice. But through the next three verses, Lucas transforms the voice into a more traditional lyric speaker, a devotional "everyman," which clearly aligns Jacob's identity with that of a different "pilgrim's" voice. The final stanza reads:

> I am not worthy—yea, but greater far
> Is Thy great love than my unworthiness,
> Thy love, that cannot pitiless
> Our sorrows and our sins behold,
> That comes to pardon and to bless,
> And gives us peace as in the days of old. (19–24)[30]

As with Magnus's poem cited earlier, Lucas understands her poetry to be in a direct line with "the days of old" not only in the theological or devotional sense but also in her literary claim to the text and voice of a biblical Jewish patriarch. Thus Lucas links her own identity as a Jewish woman in prayer to that of Jacob at the banks of the Jordan, and chooses to write her own poem about this shared religious positioning.

Lucas pursued this link to aspects of Judaism considered more "masculine" in her 1908 collection *Talmudic Legends, Hymns and Paraphrases,* which she used to explore the Talmud and obscure moments in Jewish history as sources of poetry; the last section also includes a series of reworked "Psalms and Hymns." Thus, like Aguilar, Lucas seeks to render religious and textual experiences of Judaism accessible in English, though she claims a much more direct relationship to original sources, displaying a confidence in Jewish learning not usually associated with women. And while we saw a similar

Jewish textual confidence in Magnus's work, it is worth noting that Magnus was more interested in rendering Jewish history and figures accessible to non-Jewish readers. Lucas, on the other hand, directs her writing toward Jewish readers, providing English versions of the great works of Hebrew literature and liturgical aids to Jewish worship.

Magnus and Lucas demonstrate their Jewish learning without apology, claiming the right to engage with classical Jewish learning at all levels, including the most elite texts of the Talmud. Nina (Davis) Salaman, the last poet in this trajectory, was perhaps the most important scholar, the woman most recognized for her erudition by her community and subsequently one of the most important, and most overlooked, Jewish women poets of the century. Her father, Arthur Davis, was a Hebrew scholar who collaborated with Herbert Adler on a *machzor* (festival prayerbook); he was noted for his commitment to educating his daughters. Salaman's final work was a translation of poems by the great medieval Hebrew poet Yehuda Halevi, published by the Jewish Publication Society of America and in print as late as 1974—the work through which generations of readers came to the poetry of Halevi in English.[31] Yet this exemplary accomplishment for a woman of her day was only one of many for Salaman. In later life Salaman was the learning partner of the Cambridge scholar Israel Abrahams and worked closely with the writer Israel Zangwill.[32] She had been elected as the first woman president of the Jewish Historical Society of England when, in 1922, illness precluded her taking up the role; nevertheless, her election suggests the degree of respect accorded to her scholarship.

Salaman also wrote her own poetry, which was published in three volumes: *Songs of Exile* (1901; under her unmarried name, Nina Davis), *The Voices of the Rivers* (1910), and *Songs of Many Days* (1923).[33] This last volume demonstrates the ease with which Salaman could move between Hebrew and English literary traditions, as well as her explicit naming of a tradition of diaspora Hebrew poetry, in which she includes herself. The final section of *Songs of Many Days* is titled "Eight Translations"—a group of Hebrew poems from the sixteenth century to the present, chronologically arranged and including the classical Hebrew poem "Lekha Dodi," a work by Abraham Hazan, a poem by the Italian Jewish poet Rachel Morpurgo, a lyric by Heinrich Heine, Isaac Edward Salkinson's preface to his Hebrew version of *Paradise Lost*, Naftali Herz Imber's Zionist national anthem, "Hatikvah," and Chaim Nachman Bialik's gloss on Isaiah 40.7. To conclude this illustrious list, moreover, Salaman offers a poem titled "Psalm in the Silence," with the simple description "Translated from the Hebrew of the Author." This last act of poetry, the insertion of a translation of her own Hebrew verse into this historical sweep of canonized Hebrew poetry, is a noteworthy move in the history of Anglo-Jewish women poets.

Indeed, "Psalm in the Silence" falls squarely in a Hebrew tradition of poetry that refuses to enact a conversion or resolution—though perhaps also resonating with Levy's far less Jewish "Sonnet" in this refusal. Like so many biblical psalms, the poem begins with the acknowledgment of God's silence—"My God, thou art exceedingly silent unto me"—and follows the classical pattern of poetic parallelism as a structuring device, ending with the following lines:

> O Lord, wilt Thou be always silent?
> Wilt thou hold Thy peace unto the utmost length of days?
> Blessed be the Lord who hath upheld me
> Through trust in him.[34]

The two synonymous statements of God's silence, a classical formal device of Hebrew poetics, are followed by a synthetic couplet, which links the blessing of God to the idea that the speaker's undying trust is all that she has to "uphold" her. Not only remaining faithful to the structure of Hebrew verse, Salaman's use of the phrase "[b]lessed be the Lord" (and earlier in the poem "Blessed art Thou, oh Lord") also calls on a familiar formula of Hebrew blessing, one that positions Salaman within the authoritative rabbinical and scholarly voices of Judaism. Salaman demonstrates the literary and religious confidence to use the poetic voice that had been the domain of so many male poets and rabbis before her, and in their language—which she then translates for her English or Jewish readers who do not know Hebrew. If we return to the idea and line with which this essay started, namely the idea that Anglo-Jewish women poets always had to grapple with the notion that "we are not what [Judah's bards] have been," I would argue that Salaman reverses that formula, suggesting in this last poem that indeed she does write directly in line with "Judah's bards," with the Psalmist(s) themselves. Publishing after World War 1, after the passage of female suffrage, after the complete enfranchisement of Jews in England, after a century of successful women poets in England, Salaman is light years away from the world of the early Victorians with which I began.

"Judah's [Female] bards" Meet Judah's Bard: Anglo-Jewish Women Poets and Yehuda Halevi

Surveying Anglo-Jewish women poets chronologically, we see evidence of a line of women poets whose literary strategies not only are reflective of their personal poetic style but are also linked to changes in civil rights, educational practices, class identities, and women's access to education, both Jewish and secular. However, a chronological survey cannot always reflect the interactions among these writers across time. Indeed it is highly likely that all the later writers knew of those Anglo-Jewish women who preceded them; in addition, the latter three figures, Magnus, Lucas, and Salaman, probably crossed each other's paths in Jewish social, literary, and philanthropic circles in Jewish London between 1900 and 1920; Amy Levy, too, collaborated with Magnus on a number of projects and knew her socially. In their time, none of these women was *sui generis* but rather evinced awareness of their Anglo-Jewish predecessors and drew on their shared knowledge as part of their literary activity.[35] To give an example of such interaction, I conclude this essay by exploring a fascinating set of overlapping literary "events" shared by three of these writers with regard to the poet most considered "Judah's bard," Yehuda Halevi. In so doing I hope to highlight their important work in Hebrew translation, and also to speculate on what new insights this approach can offer into the literary history of Anglo-Jewish women.

Yehuda Halevi wrote in the late eleventh–early twelfth centuries and has been revered throughout Jewish history as one of the most important Hebrew poets. His poetry is deeply devotional but also uses a number of secular themes; as in much Hebrew and biblical poetry, heterosexual romantic figures gesture toward both secular and religious meanings simultaneously. Thus Halevi relies on the common figure of the male lover addressing a female figure in much of his poetry, and this feminizing of the divine in many places is coincident with Hebrew literary traditions that identify the female presence of God as the Shekhinah, the object of the poet's desire. In other Hebrew poetic conventions, the male figure is associated with God, and the feminine object associated variously with the Jewish nation, the city of Jerusalem, or the land of Israel as a desired symbol of divine union. Indeed Nina Salaman notes in her introduction to her translations of Halevi that "while some of Halevi's poems were intended for use in prayer and others were not so intended, the great mass of his work is impregnated with religious feeling. This is seen even in his love poems. . . . Often such a poem, in its opening words, indicates a human relationship; we read on and find that the lovers are God and Israel."[36] Of course, some of Halevi's poetry may have been addressed to an actual woman, most likely his wife; some also lovingly address male friends and colleagues in the fashion of other medieval poets like Rumi or Hafez.

These questions of poetic subject and object become increasingly important in the translations and interpretations of Halevi poems by Jewish women. Indeed the monumental importance of Halevi in the tradition of Hebrew poetry meant that any writer who sought to claim authority in Jewish literary scholarship, poetics, and translation would necessarily confront his legacy; major figures in Jewish thought and literature ranging from Abraham Geiger and Heinrich Heine to Charles Reznikoff translated Halevi. When Amy Levy, Katie Magnus, Alice Lucas, and Nina Salaman engaged with Halevi's works, they necessarily made claims to a certain kind of Jewish poetic authority and likewise inserted their own work into a long trajectory of (usually male) Jewish poets, scholars, and rabbis. Yet examining their respective interactions with Halevi also reveals important contrasts in these women's approaches to and understandings of classical Jewish texts.

Lady Katie Magnus's essay on Yehuda Halevi was one of the many on Jewish topics in *Jewish Portraits*. Her essay puts Halevi in the context of the contemporary poets of *piyyutim,* noting that not all his contemporaries were as powerful artists as Halevi. The essay clearly seeks to introduce Halevi to a contemporary English audience and relies on biographical material as a way to make him come alive to Victorian readers who might otherwise be unfamiliar with his work. Among other contextualizing details, Magnus notes that affection and tenderness among the male writers in Halevi's circle were unusually profound: "There is, in truth, a wonderful freshness of sentiment about these gentle old scholars. They say pretty things to and of each other in almost school girl fashion. 'I pitch my tent in thy heart,' exclaims one as he sets out on a journey."[37] In validating the affection among men that marked Halevi's circle, Magnus normalizes such statements of same-sex affection in ways that might resonate with a Victorian readership familiar with works like Tennyson's *In Memoriam* or all-male traditions like the academic circles of Oxford and Cambridge. Magnus's essay works to make Halevi both revered and accessible, introducing this important figure of Jewish literary history to a mostly non-Jewish audience.

Amy Levy's Halevi translations seem to have been written in conjunction with Magnus's essay on Halevi. Levy also worked on translations of Heinrich Heine's poetry for another essay in Magnus's book. That Levy was collaborating with Magnus is important in itself; Linda Hunt Beckman has suggested that this relationship may have tempered Levy's critique of Anglo-Jewish culture and brought her into a more positive relationship with her own Jewish identity.[38] While most critics have downplayed Amy Levy's interest in Jewish religious or devotional texts or practice, her Halevi translations, read along-side other poems in her corpus, like "Sonnet," suggest that there are some markers in Levy's poetry that can be read as participating in a Jewish liter-ary tradition: in her linking of sexualized and devotional images, figures of lament and captivity, and the idealization of a city (Jerusalem/London) as a source of emotional sustenance. Levy's translations of Halevi confirm her interest in Jewish literature, even as her unique approach to his work high-lights other recurring themes in her poetry.

Levy did not translate Halevi from the original Hebrew but rather from the translations into German by one of the major agents of the Reform move-ment in Judaism, Abraham Geiger.[39] While it is likely that this choice was motivated by Levy's greater knowledge of German, it also seems possible that Levy would have been drawn to Geiger's work in reforming and rethinking Jewish orthodoxy.[40] Her translations strike a very modern tone—so modern, indeed, as to transform conventional religious and heterosexual symbols in the original text and to link these medieval poems with her own much more contemporary poetic voice.

When Levy approached the poem that she (and later, Salaman) titled "Parted Lovers," she removed most of the biblical references and transformed a classical Hebrew poem into a contemporary lament for a lost female lover.[41] Levy's version of "Parted Lovers" reads as follows:

> So we must be divided; sweetest, stay,
> Once more, mine eyes would seek thy glance's light.
> At night I shall recall thee: Thou, I pray,
> Be mindful of the day of our delight.
> Come to me in my dreams, I ask of thee,
> And even in my dreams be gentle unto me.
>
> If thou shouldst send me greeting in the grave,
> The cold breath of the grave itself were sweet;
> Oh, take my life, my life, 'tis all I have,
> If it should make thee live, I do entreat.
> I think that I shall hear when I am dead,
> The rustle of thy gown, thy footsteps overhead.[42]

Levy, perhaps in conjunction with Geiger, compressed many different ele-ments of what is a much longer Halevi poem. Levy has rendered very few of these references literally, as well as shortening the poem considerably. Yet she seems to be playing with many of the tensions between devotional and romantic verse in her translation, just as Halevi's original moves between references to divine and human love in his poem. When Levy writes, "Thou, I pray," in line 3, she too engages in this devotional/romantic play. Her poem reads as a secular work that takes a traditional address to God and transfers it to this more earthly context; no other markers in the poem (note the uncapitalized "thou" at the start of the second stanza) indicate that this is a religious poem. Instead, Levy's point is to use the language of devotion to heighten the sense of urgency in this text about lovers who must part. The ambiguity of the voice and object suggests links with Levy's other lyric experiments with same-sex address. It is exactly this translation that Nina Salaman would subsequently cite as a particularly problematic approach to Halevi's poetry.

Comparing Levy's and Salaman's translations is difficult, as Salaman worked from the Hebrew original, and she (or perhaps Heinrich Brody, the editor of the volume) cited the relevant biblical references along the left side of her English translation, with the Hebrew text on the right facing page in the Jewish Publication Society edition. Just looking at the two translations suggests very different poetic aims: Salaman's is seventy-six lines long, following literally the length of the original Hebrew, compared with Levy's twelve lines. While Levy compacts and contracts a number of images and ideas from the original poem, perhaps the most telling difference in their translations comes in the line Levy translates as: "I think that I shall hear when I am dead, / The rustle of thy gown, thy footsteps overhead." Salaman renders that verse as: "Would that after my death, unto mine ears should come / The sound of golden bells upon thy skirts." On the left side of the poem, Salaman has also included the references from Exodus (28.33–34 and 39.25–26) that describe the golden bells that will decorate the high priest's tunic: "On its hem make pomegranates of violet, purple and scarlet stuff, with golden bells between them. . . . Aaron is to wear it when he ministers, and the sound of it will be heard when he enters the Holy Place of the Lord and when he comes out, and so he will not die" (Revised English Bible translation). Including these references suggests the work is not a heterosexual love poem but rather includes devotional and religious symbolism, making it resonate with biblical reference to the high priest's vestments in the Jewish Temple.

But Salaman also includes a somewhat unusual footnote to the line that references the "golden bells," writing: "The poet refers to the bells on the skirts which are still worn in old fashioned countries of the Orient and also in Spain."[43] This footnote suggests that the "golden bells" might not be a reference to the clothes of the high priest, despite the biblical citation, but is instead (or also) a reference to the clothing worn in Halevi's time and place. Salaman thus emphasizes both a biblical and historical understanding of the poem in her work. Levy, on the other hand, is much freer in her translation, leaving out all references to bells and instead noting "the rustle of thy gown," an image that specifically invokes the clothing of a modern woman. Thus Levy has taken what, according to Salaman, was an intentionally intricate image of the high priest's (male) vestments and a medieval Spanish woman's skirt and transformed it into the more contemporary, and unambiguously female, image of a "rustling gown."

Also interesting with regard to this comparison is that Salaman specifically refers to Levy's translation as representative of bad translation practice in her introduction to the volume. Salaman quotes both her own and Levy's translations of these lines from "Parted Lovers" and writes: "It has always seemed to the present translator at once unfair to a poet and displeasing to his reader to divest verses of their own peculiar dress. . . . To do these things may be attractive, but the oriental flavor is lost, and the poet is made to speak with the voice of a modern western writer, while clearly he was neither western nor modern."[44] Salaman's comment and her own translation suggest that her guiding principle for translation of classical Hebrew sources is that they should conjure the biblical references as well as the poet's historical context. Thus in her poem Halevi's loved object is intended as both a specifically Jewish religious symbol and as a more generic reference to a female figure. It is easy to see how a translation like Levy's, by transforming the golden-belled skirts to "the rustle of thy gown," functions to "divest [the] verses of their own peculiar dress." Indeed it is clear that Levy's translation practice has no interest in historical context or biblical connection; instead her poem seeks to take the emotional essence of the Halevi poem and make it speak not only to a contemporary audience but also, more radically, as a woman addressing a female love object.

In fact Levy may indeed have aimed to "divest" the Halevi original of its "own peculiar [gendered] dress" so that it could emerge as one of Levy's poetic explorations of same-sex love. And this move makes even more sense when we put the Levy translations in the context of Magnus's note that the men in Halevi's circle "say pretty things to and of each other in almost school girl fashion," reminding us that such same-sex address is in fact often a hallmark and legacy of devotional medieval poetry—a fact that would not have been lost on Levy in her collaboration for the essay with Magnus. Levy's poem, so transformed from Halevi's original, is reminiscent of themes that other scholars have noted in many of her love lyrics to women—love lyrics that are most often marked by themes of unrequited love, death, dream states, or lament, such as those included in the "Love, Dreams and Death" section of *A London Plane Tree and Other Verse*.

If Salaman and Levy can be seen as two poles on a translation spectrum, it is worth noting that Alice Lucas also did many translations of Halevi in her collections, clearly seeing his work as a central source in the heritage of classical Hebrew poetry. Her translations find a middle ground between Levy's focus on contemporary themes and Salaman's more scholarly historical approach. Lucas's translations, especially those in *The Jewish Year*, strip the poems of specific historical markers so that they can speak more universally to her audience of practicing Anglo-Jews, but she has no interest in the more daring moves that Levy makes in her translations. For Lucas, Halevi's poetry is part of a larger set of "aids" to Jewish prayer and religious practice; in her introduction to the volume she writes: "Written in the dark ages of Jewish life, these hymns are illuminated by a divine optimism that may well serve to strengthen our own often wavering faith, and lead us too to find in our religion, that peace and happiness which blessed the singers of those days in the midst of sorrow and persecution."[45] Aiming to make Halevi's work speak to contemporary Jewish seekers, Lucas's poems take on a more universalized lyric voice than either Levy's or Salaman's.

We can see this in a comparison of Lucas's translation of the poem "Though I Sit in Darkness" and that of Salaman. Salaman is clearly the more scholarly in her approach, translating the last lines as follows:

> So will He yet light up my gloom,
> And uphold him who raiseth my fallen state,
> And make the light of mine assembly shine forth.
> Then the chosen one yet shall boast herself:
> "Behold the light of the Rock or my praise
> *Is mine, though I sit in darkness.*" (19–24)[46]

Characteristically, Salaman includes with the last line a reference to Micah 7.8, linking Halevi's verse to its biblical source. In comparison, Lucas translates the same poem:

> Thus will He turn my night to day,
> And when I fall, my footsteps stay.
> He will my people's light restore

And make them glad as heretofore.
He is my light for evermore
Although I sit in darkness. (19–24)[47]

Lucas's rendering of the poem reduces complex biblical terms and removes the more mystical symbolism that Salaman retains. Thus Lucas's rendering of Halevi resounds with the familiar rhythms, images, and diction of conventional English (Christian) devotional verse. Faithful to the concepts in the Halevi original, Lucas nevertheless transforms the poetry into something that finally feels very English, whereas Salaman's versions make much stronger claims to historical, scholarly, and textual accuracy.

What do we learn from this complex interplay around Halevi among Salaman, Lucas, Magnus, and Levy, and what does it mean for an account of Anglo-Jewish women poets in this period? These poets have strikingly different approaches to their translations, and those differences enable us to infer their quite different ideas about what Jewish literacy might mean in the early part of the twentieth century. Levy calls on the poetry of a classical Jewish past in ways that augment and support her own lyric practices; for her, Halevi—via Geiger—is a source of poetic feeling that can ultimately be disconnected from anything specifically Jewish, religious, or medieval. Levy's translation emerges as the most contemporary and radical, despite the fact that she wrote well before the other two poets. But it is not adequate, I think, to simply cast Salaman or Lucas as more "conservative" writers without contextualizing that impulse as well. For what we see in this overview of Anglo-Jewish women writers is the impact Jewish literacy had on their work. Skilled in Hebrew, knowledgeable in Jewish classical texts and Talmud, and playing important roles in publications and institutions of Jewish learning and literature, the later generation of women writers makes startlingly authoritative claims to a kind of Jewish learning not usually associated with women in this period. While their predecessors like Grace Aguilar may have aspired to the knowledge and skill in Hebrew learning that Lucas and Salaman display, they did not have the privileges of class and education that enabled later women writers to engage in Jewish cultural practices that had been traditionally male for centuries.

Writing by Anglo-Jewish women was also connected to the changing needs and experiences of Anglo-Jewish society. For the Moss sisters and Aguilar, writing before Jewish and women's emancipation, the very idea of representing a Jewish perspective in English literature was a radical move, one to which Aguilar repeatedly attested her commitment. For her, having a "Jewish" literature in English was a way to combat temptations besetting Jewish women to convert, intermarry, or assimilate. Levy, reaping many of the benefits of both Jewish and female emancipation, was more interested in creating what she termed a "minor" poetry that could use "University English" to represent a number of new perspectives and voices, including— at least occasionally—a Jewish one. But her literary goals were not directed toward "saving" Jewish women or increasing Anglo-Jewish literacy in Jewish texts; rather, they were concerned with participating in and creating new literary forms in English poetry that could also expand the range of possible literary voices and minority perspectives. In her poetry and essays, Magnus was also more interested in offering a new vision of Jews and Judaism to a mainstream British readership, while giving Jews a sense of their illustrious past as they moved into the twentieth century. Lucas and Salaman, finally, were significant for their bold entry into realms of Jewish scholarship and translation that had until then been reserved for men. That their poetry and translations are still well represented in many liturgies, prayerbooks, and poetic collections suggests that they broke through the barriers that had separated men's and women's access to Jewish learning and literary authority for centuries.

Anglo-Jewish women poets in the long nineteenth century have been neglected in both Jewish studies and British literary studies. Indeed, it is tempting to apply to this group of poets the evaluation Magnus made of the group of medieval Hebrew poets she compares unfavorably to Halevi: "One sees them now as victims, and now as spectators, but never as actors in that strange show."[48] Yet Anglo-Jewish women poets were neither "victims" nor "spectators" in English and Jewish literary history but rather actors who made vital contributions to both literary cultures—as well as the bridges between them. Their work offers a fascinating window into the changing relationships between Jewish and English literary traditions, as well as demonstrating the variety of ways Jewish women displayed their spirituality and their religious learning.

Acknowledgments

This paper could not have been written without a fellowship from the Oxford Centre for Hebrew and Jewish Studies in Oxford, England, in 2001, where I did most of the primary source research; the Mills College Women's Studies Department also offered generous research support. I am grateful to Nadia

Valman for her supportive editorship of this project, as well as to Michael Galchinsky for all of his crucial research on Anglo-Jewish women writers. Many thanks to Daniel Harris for his precious gifts of scholarship and so many out-of-print works of Anglo-Jewish women writers.

Notes

1. Misses Moss (Celia and Marion), *Early Efforts: A Volume of Poems by the Misses Moss of the Hebrew Nation, Aged 18 and 16*, 2nd ed. (Portsmouth: Whittaker and Co., 1839). Further citations from their verses cited in the text are from this edition.

2. Grace Aguilar, *The Magic Wreath of Hidden Flowers* (1835; repr. Brighton: W.B. Mason, 1839). Emma Lyon, *Miscellaneous Poems* (Oxford: J. Bartlett, 1812). For more on Emma Lyon, see Michael Scrivener, "Following the Muse: Inspiration, Prophecy and Difference in the Poetry of Emma Lyon (1788–1870), Anglo-Jewish Poet," in *The Jews and British Romanticism: Politics, Religion, Culture*, ed. Sheila Spector (New York: Palgrave Macmillan, 2005). Scrivener's reading does analyze the connections between Lyon's verse and her Jewish identity, suggesting Lyon uses "a rhetorical Judeo-Christian approach" (107).

3. J. B. Selkirk, *Ethics and Aesthetics of Modern Poetry* (London: Smith Elder and Co., 1878), 161.

4. I am in debt to Nadia Valman for this insight.

5. See two important anthologies of nineteenth-century women's poetry: Angela Leighton and Margaret Reynolds, eds., *Victorian Women Poets* (Oxford: Blackwell, 1995); and Isobel Armstrong, Joseph Bristow, and Catharine Sharrock, eds., *Nineteenth-Century Women Poets: An Oxford Anthology* (Oxford: Oxford University Press, 1996).

6. It seems likely that a private edition—which had "a rapid sale" according to the 1839 volume "Advertisement"—was issued in 1838, which accounts for the authors' ages listed as eighteen and sixteen, rather than twenty and eighteen, which they would have been in 1839. The Moss sisters have been more known for their work in historical romance and journalism; indeed, in 1855 Marion Moss (Hartog) started what Michael Galchinsky terms "the first Jewish women's periodical in history, the *Jewish Sabbath Journal*." Michael Galchinsky, *The Origin of the Modern Jewish Woman Writer: Romance and Reform in Victorian England* (Detroit: Wayne State University Press, 1996), 107. For more on the Mosses' fiction, see also Nadia Valman, *The Jewess in Nineteenth-Century British Literary Culture* (Cambridge: Cambridge University Press, 2007), 115–29.

7. Galchinsky, *Origin of the Modern Jewish Woman Writer*, 107.

8. Lord George Gordon Byron, *Hebrew Melodies* (London: J. Murray, 1815); Henry Hart Milman, *The History of the Jews* (1829; repr. London: George Routledge and Sons Ltd, 1892).

9. David Rothstein, "Forming the Chivalric Subject: Felicia Hemans and the Cultural Uses of History, Memory and Nostalgia," *Victorian Literature and Culture* 27.1 (1999), 49–68 (49, 66).

10. For more poems focused on female and child deaths and martyrdom, see Hemans's "The Suliote Mother" (1825), "The Image in Lava" (1828), and "The Indian with His Dead Child" (1830), in *The Poetical Works of Mrs. Hemans* (New York: Worthington, 1887),

as well as Letitia Landon (L.E.L), "A Moorish Maiden's Vigil" (1836), "Infanticide in Madagascar" (1838), and "A Suttee" (1839), in *The Victorians: An Anthology of Poetry and Poetics*, ed. Valentine Cunningham (Oxford: Blackwell, 2000).

11. See, for example, Barrett Browning's "Cry of the Children" (1843).

12. "The Hebrew's Appeal: On Occasion of the Late Fearful Ukase Promulgated by the Emperor of Russia," in the 1863 edition of Aguilar's *The Spirit of Judaism*, ed. Isaac Leeser (Philadelphia: No. 1 Monroe Place). Further citations from the poem are from this edition and appear in the text. Leeser reprinted Aguilar's prose work, *The Spirit of Judaism* (first published in 1842), in 1863 and added thirty-two "poetical effusions" of Aguilar's that had been previously published; this poem was reprinted from its 1844 publication in *The Occident and American Jewish Advocate* (vol. 2, no. 6). In that issue, Aguilar notes that it was actually first published in 1843, in *The Christian Lady's Magazine*, having been rejected by the British Jewish journal *The Voice of Jacob*.

13. See Cynthia Scheinberg, *Women's Poetry and Religion in Victorian England: Jewish Identity and Christian Culture* (Cambridge University Press, 2002), ch. 5, for more on Aguilar's use of Christian symbolism for explicitly Jewish purposes.

14. For more on Aguilar's relationship to Romanticism, see Scheinberg, *Women's Poetry*, 155–63.

15. For more on Aguilar's "Song of the Spanish Jews," see Cynthia Scheinberg, "Victorian Poetry and Religious Diversity," in the *Cambridge Companion to Victorian Poetry*, ed. Joseph Bristow (Cambridge: Cambridge University Press, 2000), 166–70.

16. Grace Aguilar, *The Jewish Faith: Its Spiritual Consolation, Moral Guidance, and Immortal Hope*, ed. Isaac Leeser (1846; repr. Philadelphia, 1864), 264–65.

17. On Levy's Jewish education, see Linda Hunt Beckman, *Amy Levy: Her Life and Letters* (Athens: Ohio University Press, 2000), 12–19. See Levy's "Middle Class Jewish Women of Today" (1886) and her depiction of Judith Quixano in *Reuben Sachs* (1888) for her critique of the lack of education provided to Jewish women, in *The Compete Novels and Selected Writings of Amy Levy, 1861–1889*, ed. Melvyn New (Gainesville: University Press of Florida, 1993). See also Susan David Bernstein, "Introduction," in *Reuben Sachs*, ed. Susan David Bernstein (Peterborough ON: Broadview Press, 2006), 11–43.

18. Deborah Epstein Nord, "'Neither Pairs nor Odd': Female Community in Late Nineteenth-Century London," in *Signs: Journal of Women in Culture and Society* 15.4 (1990), 733–54; Alex Goody, "Passing in the City: The Liminal Spaces of Amy Levy's Late Work," in *Amy Levy: Critical Essays*, ed. Naomi Hetherington and Nadia Valman (Athens: Ohio University Press, 2010). Critics have used various methods for reading her lyrics addressed to women, some claiming she is merely taking on a "man's voice" to preserve the heterosexuality of her poetry, others asserting clear evidence of Levy's lesbian address. Given her interests in challenging conventions, it seems apparent to me that she sought to create a lesbian poetics, albeit one that could be interpreted ambiguously by readers who resisted the same-sex address.

19. See her essays, "The Ghetto at Florence" (1886) and "Jewish Humour" (1886), in *The Complete Novels and Selected Writings of Amy Levy*, for some subtle indications of Levy's ideas about Judaism. See also Hunt Beckman, *Amy Levy: Her Life and Letters*; Scheinberg, *Women's Poetry*, 190–233; and Valman, *The Jewess*, 175–93.

20. See Levy's essay "Jewish Humour," in *Complete Novels and Selected Writings*, 524.

21. For example, I have argued that her dramatic monologue "Magdalen" rewrites the Christian scriptures to create a defiantly Jewish Mary Magdalene. See Scheinberg, *Women's Poetry*, 218–27.

22. "Sonnet," in *Complete Novels and Selected Writings*, 367; first published in *Xantippe and Other Verse* (Cambridge: E. Johnson, 1881). Further citations are taken from this edition of *Complete Novels*.

23. Morris Raphall's *The Hebrew Review and Magazine of Rabbinical Literature* was published from 1834 to 1836, offering a weekly series of translations from the Mishnah, important later rabbinical sources, summaries of Talmudic precepts, and historical information. Aguilar also published at least one poem in the journal; her "Lament for Judea" appears in no. 73, vol. iii (Friday, June 17, 1836). For more on *The Hebrew Review*, see Galchinsky, *Origin of the Modern Jewish Woman Writer*, 210.

24. Mrs. Meyer A. Speilman, "Jewish Women Writers," Presidential Address to the Union of Jewish Literary Societies, 1913.

25. Katie Magnus, "Charity in Talmudic Times" (first published in the *National Review* in 1888), reprinted in *Jewish Portraits* (New York: Bloch, 1925), 133–34.

26. See Magnus's "Jehuda Halevi," in *Jewish Portraits*, 3.

27. Katie Magnus, "Unorthodox," in *A Book of Verse* (London: George Routledge and Sons, 1905), 65. Further citations are taken from this edition.

28. See William Rubenstein, ed., *The Palgrave Dictionary of Anglo-Jewish History* (Basingstoke: Palgrave Macmillan, 2011), 622.

29. Alice Lucas, *The Jewish Year: A Collection of Devotional Poems for Sabbaths and Holidays Throughout the Year* (London: Macmillan, 1898), xv. Further references to this edition will appear in the text.

30. "Not Worthy," in *The Jewish Year*, 17–18.

31. Heinrich Brody, ed., *Selected Poems of Jehuda Halevi*, trans. Nina Salaman (1923; repr. Philadelphia: Jewish Publication Society, 1974).

32. For the most recent scholarship on Salaman, see Shira Koren, "Nina Salaman: The Fusion of Old Judaism with the Modern Western World," *Women in Judaism: A Multidisciplinary Journal* 9.1 (2012), 1–17.

33. Nina Salaman, *Songs of Exile by Hebrew Poets* (London: Jewish Historical Society of England/MacMillan, 1901); *The Voices of the Rivers* (1910; repr. Cambridge: Bowes and Bowes, 1923); *Songs of Many Days* (London: Elkin Matthews, 1923).

34. Salaman, "Psalm in the Silence," in *Songs of Many Days*, 58.

35. See Galchinsky, *Origin of the Modern Jewish Woman Writer*, 151–55.

36. Nina Salaman, "Introduction," in *Selected Poems of Jehuda Halevi*, xxiv.

37. Magnus, "Jehuda Halevi," in *Jewish Portraits*, 12.

38. See Hunt Beckman, *Amy Levy*, 77.

39. Abraham Geiger, *Divan des Castiliers Abu'l-Hassan Juda ha-Levi* (Breslau: Verlag von Job, Urban Rern, 1851).

40. Abraham Geiger (1810–1874) was one of the fathers of the Reform movement in Germany. Levy's interest in Geiger is beyond the scope of this essay; however there seem to be some distinct similarities between her ideas about the dilemmas facing contemporary Jews and Geiger's work. See Michael Meyer, *Response to Modernity* (Oxford: Oxford University Press, 1988), 89–99.

41. It is possible that Melvyn New titled this poem "[Parted Lovers]," because Salaman used this title (without the brackets); the excerpts in Magnus's essay, from where New extracted them, are not titled.

42. Amy Levy, "[Parted Lovers]," in *Complete Novels and Selected Writings,* 405. New notes that these translations were first published in the Magnus essay discussed above, and offers initial comparisons between them and Salaman's in his note (555).

43. Salaman, *Selected Poems of Jehuda Halevi,* 47.

44. Salaman, "Introduction," in *Selected Poems of Jehuda Halevi,* xxvii.

45. Lucas, *The Jewish Year,* xvii.

46. Salaman, *Selected Poems of Jehuda Halevi,* 131.

47. Lucas, *The Jewish Year,* 2.

48. Magnus, "Jehuda Halevi," in *Jewish Portraits,* 2–3.

3

WORLDLY EXILE

Mina Loy's "Anglo-Mongrels and the Rose"

RACHEL POTTER

The poet Mina Loy (1882–1966) was born Mina Gertrude Löwy, the eldest child of Sigmund Löwy, a Hungarian Jewish tailor who immigrated to London in the late 1860s, and Julia Bryan, an English Nonconformist Christian who was reared in Croydon. The couple married in 1882 because Julia was pregnant, and their marriage, from Loy's descriptions of it, seems to have been an unhappy one. Sigmund followed Jewish custom by leaving Mina's religious upbringing to her mother, and she was therefore raised as an Evangelical Christian. The nature of her Jewish paternity, however, featured importantly in her writing. She wrote about her family life in a number of unpublished prose works, including "The Islands in the Air," "Goy Israels," and "The Child and the Parent," as well as in her most substantial long poem, "Anglo-Mongrels and the Rose" (published in installments from 1923 to 1925). In the unpublished writings, the mother often became "The Christian," the father "The Jew," and the parents "Mr and Mrs Israels." The recurrence of imagery and phrases across these different texts reveals that Loy worked on this material throughout her life.

"Anglo-Mongrels and the Rose" had a complicated publishing history, as it came out in sections in separate journals and books in different geographical locations between 1923 and 1925. Initially under the title "Anglo-Mongrels and the Rose," Loy published the first section, "Exodus," in the spring 1923 "Exiles" edition of the New York magazine the *Little Review*.[1] She went on to release a separate poem called "English Rose," which consists of the first three stanzas of section 2 of the final poem, in her first collection of poems, called *Lunar Baedeker,* published in Dijon in 1923. Then, under the title "Anglo-Mongrels and the Rose," she again issued "English Rose," but this time in New York in the autumn–winter (1923–24) edition of the *Little Review.*[2] The final sections of the poem—"Enter Esau Penfold," "Ova Begins to Take Notice," "Opposed Aesthetics," "Marriage Boxes," "Psychic Larva," "Christ's Regrettable Reticence," "Enter Colossus," "Ova. Among. The. Neighbours.," "Ova Has Governesses," "Jews and Ragamuffins of Kilburn," "The Surprise," "Illumination," "Contraction," "The Gift," "Ova Accepts the Popular Estimate of Humanity," "Religious Instruction," and "The Social Status of Exodus"—came out in Robert McAlmon's Paris-based *Contact Collection of Contemporary Writers* in 1925 under the title "The Anglo-Mongrels and the Rose."[3]

In the 1958 edition of Loy's selected poems, *Lunar Baedeker and Time-Tables,* edited by Jonathan Williams, a shortened version of the poem appeared under the title "Anglo-Mystics of the Rose."[4] This included the following sections: "Enter Esau," "Ova Begins to Take Notice," "Ova Has Governesses," "Christ's Regrettable Reticence," and "Religious Instruction." The poem was published in its entirety under the title "Anglo-Mongrels and the Rose: 1923–1925" only in Loy's collected poems, *The Lost Lunar Baedeker,* edited by Roger Conover in 1982.[5]

There are a number of aspects of this publication history that are of interest. The initial appearances of "Exodus" and "English Rose" as stand-alone poems, both under the title "Anglo-Mongrels and the Rose," invite us to consider them as semi-autonomous entities. A different question is why, in all these versions of the poem's title, the "Anglo-Mongrels" is always plural and the "Rose" always singular. Of interest too is Williams's editorial replacement of "mongrels" with "mystics," a decision that created a very different poem, one focused far less on the issue of Jewish paternity. We do not know why Williams wanted to change "mongrel" to "mystic," but it seems possible that he wanted to underplay the word's racial undertones.[6] In this he would not have been alone, as the antisemitic register of this word, and the more general nature of Loy's engagement with Jewishness, have continued to trouble readers. Elisabeth Frost and Aimee L. Pozorski have interpreted Loy's use of the word in relation to her wider interest in eugenics, although Frost argues forcefully that Loy ironized rather than endorsed the racist connotations of the word "mongrel."[7] Marjorie Perloff, in an essay that considers the internal poetic dynamics of Loy's prosody and language, claims that "in her portrait of her father Sigmund Löwy Loy seems to accept all the anti-Semitic stereotypes of her time and place," stereotypes that include the ideas of the Jew as a "shrewd, money-grubbing Jewish immigrant" and of a man "with the reputed 'Jewish' artistic bent."[8] But Perloff also points out that both the Jewish father and the Christian mother are stereotyped and satirized in the poem and that Loy produces a poetic "polyglossia" which is both a product of her cosmopolitanism and of her "Anglo-Mongrel" ancestry. For Perloff, Loy's mixture of different registers and discourses disrupts any straightforward representation of identity, and it is language itself which is "mongrelized" in Loy's poem: "what is entirely Loy's own poetic signature is that her rose images, far from producing an imagist or symbolist landscape, jostle with conceptual nouns, puns, and aggressive rhymes, in a curious 'mongrelization' of linguistic registers." Perloff connects this linguistic mongrelization to Loy's Jewish and Christian parentage: Loy invents an "intricately polyglot language—a language that challenges the more conventional national idiom of her . . . contemporaries."[9]

Keith Tuma, in a different reading of the poem, argues that Jewishness in "Anglo-Mongrels and the Rose" is a form of religious, rather than racial, difference. It should be "read as a 'religious' poem," in which "nearly all forms of 'orthodox' religious doctrine—Jewish and Christian—are renounced by Loy on behalf of an experience beyond intellect which she believed to be a direct sensual and intuitive apprehension of divinity."[10] Tuma insightfully identifies Loy's construction of sensuality and intuition as Freudian in orientation: it is "Freud or Freudianism that gives her the language—the discourse of instinct—she needs to validate her experience against the competing religious practices of her father's Jewish ancestors and her mother's Christianity."[11]

In effect, Frost, Perloff, and Tuma all claim, in distinct ways, that Loy's antimimetic modernist poetic style plays with Jewish stereotypes. But Perloff also argues, in a way that is important for my essay, that Loy's construction of Jewishness might be located in language itself, most notably in the connection of Jewish exile and a cosmopolitan linguistic "mongrelization." I want to explore this link further and to argue that Loy's "Anglo-Mongrels and the Rose" is a modernist version of what Wai Chee Dimock calls "a universe of tongues" that undermines ideas both of sovereignty and of literature defined by nation.[12] In Loy's hands polyglot language is opposed to a tepid intellectual nationalism and exile stands opposed to English xenophobia, but they are also, as in Dimock's argument, entwined. In Loy's poem this dialectic is one that plays itself out on the body of a young woman.

Exile in "Exodus"

Loy's "Exodus," as a standalone poem, places a Moses figure called Exodus in late nineteenth-century Budapest and London, in a way that is similar to James Joyce's positioning of Leopold Bloom, his modern Odysseus, in Dublin in 1904. A language of biblical imagery, particularly one of miracle, is invoked and reworked: Baby Moses lying in his basket beside the river becomes Exodus reclining on the "shores of the Danube"; God's appearance in the flame of a burning bush echoes in the "burning track / of lengthening sun shafts"; and Moses's staff is a "swagger stick / tempting."[13] The light of divine revelation and enlightenment is a key motif in "Anglo-Mongrels and the Rose," but one that is present in this section of the poem in its absence: while we first encounter Exodus lying under starlight and it is the "sun shafts" that prompt him to travel, he is paralyzed by spiritual ignorance and gazes on an "unrevealed universe."[14] Loy will run with the metaphor of light as revelation in "Anglo-Mongrels and the Rose," and it is important to the "Illumination" section that Tuma reads as central to the poem. In this first part of the poem, Exodus is a stunted Moses, a character stuck at the beginning of Moses's biblical journey toward articulacy and agency.

Such textual echoes suggest that Loy is partly posing a question in this poem: What do biblical ideas and images of exile, the promised land, and revelation mean for a disinherited, late nineteenth-century Hungarian Jewish man? The echoes act as a framing device that invokes both this biblical history and a rich literary tradition of Jewish wandering. The infamous Wandering Jew, the punished man doomed to wander in the wilderness forever for his crimes against Christ, was a popular figure in nineteenth- and twentieth-century literature. The legend of the Wandering Jew is the tale of a "man in Jerusalem who, when Christ was carrying his Cross to Calvary and paused to rest for a moment on this man's doorstep, drove the Saviour away, crying aloud, 'Walk faster!' And Christ replied, 'I go, but you will walk until I come again!'"[15] The legend had undergone many interpretations, some anti-semitic, seeing the Jew as antichrist and the diaspora as the punishment of the Jews for their refusal to recognize the divinity of Christ. Other readings produced a more positive evaluation of the Jew as outcast. This latter version had gained currency in the mid-nineteenth century. Most famously, Eugene

Sue's serialized novel, *Le Juif errant* (1844–45), saw the Jew as a reflection of his Fourierist and Saint-Simonian socialist beliefs, a champion of the working man able to articulate the protest of all laborers against their oppressors. Courbet's painting *The Meeting* (1854), in turn, represented a portrait of the artist-as-Jew, whose social homelessness reflected that of working men in general. As George Anderson documents, by the end of the nineteenth century the Wandering Jew became a "symbol of the Jewish people." He summarizes: "Along with the rise of Zionism, near the close of the nineteenth century, one finds Ahesuerus [the Wandering Jew] identified with all Jews deprived of their homeland; on the reverse side of the coin, because of this identification, he becomes a target at which the anti-Semitic element of the world's Gentile population can aim its missiles."[16]

These nineteenth-century accounts shifted the nature of Jewish wandering, from the biblical demand to escape from slavery to the modern-day pressures of racial persecution and economic migration. The figure of the wandering Jew, as both a biblical outcast and economic migrant, was also an important one for many modernist writers, but the ideas both of wandering and exile shifted ground. Joyce's Bloom and Djuna Barnes's Felix Volkbein in *Nightwood* (1936) connect Jewishness to an exile that is both internalized and symbolic of a general existential predicament. Loy's disinherited Exodus forms part of this modernist imaginary. While Exodus inherits an economic stimulus to travel, he also, unlike his nineteenth-century predecessors, situates mystery in the mind. Like Moses, Exodus must learn his fate through revelation, but where Moses discovers his destiny through the angel of God, Exodus confronts it by way of natural stimulus: "the primary / throb of the animate / a beating mystery."[17] This throb is located both in the natural landscape and in the human body, so the unknown here is partly connected to Exodus's lack of biological and anatomical knowledge. If mystery has come down to earth, so has the language used to describe it. But the shift from angels to the positivist language of physical things is complicated by the new kind of beyond opened up by Freud's theory of the mind: Exodus's "infantile impacts with unreason / on his unconscious," so that one route to revelation would be the psychoanalyst's couch or what Loy, in a different part of the poem, describes as new "dictionaries / of inner consciousness" (113, 148). If mystery and revelation now lie partly in the unconscious, such ideas chime with comments Loy made in essays throughout her life about Freud's ideas as a new religion.

The poem, however, does not simply suggest that the unknown is situated in the unconscious rather than God. Instead, by including these different linguistic registers, as well as describing the need for a new language of inner consciousness, it presumes that new knowledge resides in the linguistic juxtapositions that only poetry can create. With regard to the idea of exile, for instance, the poem constructs it as biblical deliverance from oppression, an ancestral desire "to emigrate," an instinctual need to move, and it is also the gap that separates biblical deliverance from instinct, a gap that sees Moses in Freud and by way of Freud (112, 113). Mystery lies in the connections it produces, and the distance it exposes, between different kinds of linguistic registers. It is poetry that allows these different tones and styles to coexist, an idea that not only is implicit in the words and structure of "Exodus" but also forms part of the narrative of "Anglo-Mongrels and the Rose" as a whole poem. It is for this reason that, as the poem progresses, it focuses on the development of a female artist out of a complicated Anglo-Jewish household.

"English Rose" to "Mongrel Rose"

Exodus, in his desire to assimilate, confronts and idealizes the "English Rose." "English Rose" originally appeared as a standalone poem comprised of the first three stanzas of the final poem. It is a description not of a character but of an ideological symbol, the British "paradox-Imperial" whose global reach is a "World Blush," a "British Empire-made pot-pourri / of dry dead men" which whirls itself "deliriously around the unseen / Bolshevik" (121, 122). Here, the unknown is given a political slant, biblical angelic mystery and the Freudian unconscious replaced with the political threat of Bolshevik anti-imperialism. When Ova's mother rises up from a hedgerow, she is an embodiment of a political symbol, a stubborn capitalist bred on romantic novels whose racism is barely held in abeyance.

But if the poem's stage is one in which Jewish exile confronts racist British imperialism, it then moves to descriptions of a number of infantile beginnings: Exodus, Ova, Esau Penfold, and Colossus are all described in swaddling clothes. Esau Penfold, whose name signals a biblical, suppressed, and traditional (fold/old) literary identity, "enters" the poem and the world as an "infant aesthete" who has been "singled out" by a privileged imperialistic British culture, in which African explorers and anthropology professors compete with Tibetan treasures for Esau's attention. Colossus's entrance is an altogether more monumental event (134). He is the "male fruit" of a Celtic coupling, whose natural and "criminal" propensity to transgress has him pissing into the "reverent pastor's hat" (151). Given what we know about Loy's failed relationship with her first husband, Stephen Haweis (partly a model of Esau), and her devastatingly passionate relationship with her second husband, Arthur Cravan (partly Colossus), it is not hard to imagine which model of childhood or artistic orientation she privileges. But both beginnings also involve a lot of anxious women pandering to the needs of male babies and serve as a contrast to that of Ova, who is grotesquely pulled out of her mother's body in an obscure Kilburn terrace, subject to "insensitive maternity," and begins to "take notice" of its imprisoned infanthood by way of light.

Gender, class, religion, *and* artistic orientation determine the nature of these different beginnings. Ova is imprisoned both by her mother's "ineludable claws of dominion," her ability to turn Ova's infantile impulses "to shame," the dripping "psychic-larva" of her anger and disgust, and the stunted artistic impulses of her class: "the arrested artists / of the masses" (136, 147, 142). While Esau Penfold is schooled in "antique" beauty, Ova, having no artifacts to look at, must "coerce" the "Spirit of Beauty / from excrements and physic." There is implied causality in the depiction of Ova's embrace of a Christian God. It is out of her emotional and artistic isolation that Ova discovers "the gentle Jesus" who offers an absolution that Ova internalizes (148, 149). The description of Ova's "Christian / introspection," coming as it does immediately after the account of Colossus's aggressively externalized transgressions, implies that women's route to artistic expression is complicated by the necessity to negotiate this Christian emphasis on women's shame (152).

Religious, racial, class, and gender barriers are precisely the places where Ova develops as an artist. Ova is born with a "mongrel heart" both in the sense that her inheritance combines a conflictual Anglo-Jewish ancestry and in that her birth is doglike: she makes her appearance in the world by being torn from her mother's loins, and is then "lapped" by insensitive maternity (132, 130). Given the intellectually stunted and repressive nature of Ova's home life, her progression to spiritual and artistic enlightenment will require an intuitive and wilful assertion of independence. But while "personality" is "mostly / a microcosmic / replica / of institutions," it is significant that Ova, with her "Jewish brain," is not straightforwardly a piece of Anglo-Christian "tepid flesh," not simply a product of a "bland" and repressed English society (153, 154, 156). Instead, reared in a "home" saturated with the "shocks of intimate impact / of the instinctive / murderer and pamperer / of Jesus," Ova grows up being buffeted by national, religious, and racial conflict. When, after an unfair punishment, Ova "decides to travel," the poem comes full circle (163). For if the poem begins with reference to biblical exile out of oppression and mid-nineteenth-century economic emigration, then Ova's decision to travel both forms a part of this history of Jewish wandering and constitutes a modern female version of it. The implied connections in this poem involve the idea that because of her "mongrel" inheritance she commits herself "to justice," a justice that will supersede the "accidence of circumstance" (170). She will head for the "horizon of liberty," a horizon in which she will be able to dodge the "breeders' determination" and trust to the "terms of literature" (170, 171). Just as Joyce's *A Portrait of the Artist as a Young Man* suspends the narrative at the point where its protagonist is poised to depart, Loy's poem does not follow Ova in her journey toward liberty and literature. The implication, in both Joyce's novel and Loy's poem, is that the text itself is that thing.

If poetry is cast as a site of justice and liberty, then what kind of freedom, specifically, does Loy's poetic language open up? "Anglo-Mongrels and the Rose" refers to aesthetic decadence by way of Esau Penfold and Dadaist transgression by way of Colossus, and suggests that Ova's artistic orientation—and by implication Loy's poem—accords with neither. Peter Nicholls and Elisabeth Frost have noted the Poundian echoes in "Anglo-Mongrels and the Rose," seeing Esau as a kind of Mauberley figure. Not only are there Poundian rhymes in lines such as "which was all of aspiration / the grating upon civilisation," but Loy ironizes both literary decadence and Dadaist transgression.[18] Hers is a poem whose parts clash and do not synthesize.

In addition to its poetic echoes, however, it is Loy's prosody that is distinctive and arresting. Marjorie Perloff notes that her stanzas are "intentionally ungainly" in the sense that "syllable and stress count, line length, spacing, and stanza length" are more variable than is usual in free verse.[19] For this reason she ingeniously identifies Loy's metrics as a "variant on *skeltonics*," named after the Tudor poet John Skelton. Loy's stanzas cohere by way of "a network of elaborate rhyming, chiming, chanting, and punning."[20] John Wilkinson also sees her prosody as deliberately clumsy, describing it as a kind of "stumbling": "Loy's syllabic intricacy is such that her lines risk falling over their own feet." This stumbling is produced through "[s]hort lines, the emphasis on conjunction, and extreme intricacy of internal rhyme as a kind of syllable-shuttling."[21]

In her essay "Modern Poetry," Loy specifically identified modern poetry with a polyglossia arising from the United States as the place of a "thousand languages." She also suggested that modern poetry was defined by "the gait of the mentality" of the poet. Nicholls notes the shift from Symbolist dancing to Loy's "gait" as one that brings verse down to "the more deliberately mundane figure of walking." For Nicholls the ungainliness noted by Perloff and Wilkinson embodies a deliberate stance on the world: she creates a "pedestrian encounter with words whose ungainliness and imperfection incite new rhythms and cadences which root them in a human world with all *its* acknowledged grubbiness and rough edges."[22] This helpfully reveals how the poem's rough rhythmical "gait" embodies its earthbound perspective, in which the messiness of the everyday is the proper subject matter for poetry. Loy saw the contemporary writers she admired in terms of the transnational reach and rhythms of their language experiments. In her poem "Joyce's Ulysses," she links Joyce's linguistic experimentation to the biblical confounding of human language: "guttural gargoyles / upon the Tower of Babel." In "The Starry Sky of Wyndham Lewis," artists and immigrants are conflated in a spatial image: "Enviable immigrants / Into the pure dimension." And in "Gertrude Stein," poetic language is the product of scientific experiment: "Curie / of the laboratory / of vocabulary."[23] Loy's own distinctive prosody, seen through her own lens, arises from the rhythms of worldly exile and physical alienation. The "justice" opened up by this poetry is one that specifically accords space to grubby objects or those who are ostracized.

The world captured by Loy in "Anglo-Mongrels and the Rose" is also distinct from her previous poems because she brings together the different styles of her early oeuvre, uniting the caustic satire of "The Effectual Marriage or the Insipid Narrative of Gina and Miovanni," "Sketch of a Man on a Platform," "Giovanni Franchi," and "Lion's Jaws," with the lyrical intensity and ambiguous registers of "Love Songs." Loy is brilliant at satirizing characters as cultural stereotypes. Just as the "Raminetti" of "Lion's Jaws" is both Marinetti and a prototype male avant-garde polemicist, so Exodus is a version of Loy's father and a stereotypical Jewish exile. Her satirical writing inhabits the rhythms and diction of these cultural stereotypes and exposes widely held cultural attitudes. The following is typical: "perfection / being an obligation / shoved on to / the next generation" (168). Some stanzas juxtapose introspective insights and images of desire in ways that incorporate the rhythms and imagery of "Love Songs." Consider the following from "Anglo-Mongrels and the Rose":

> A twilight turbulence
> of routine in coma
> shot
> with stranded rockets
> of curative colour (157)

Wilkinson notes in his discussion of "Love Songs" that Loy offends "against the most basic precepts of verse writing by starting a line with a customarily forceless conjunction such as "of" and "with."[24] Here, limp conjunctions dominate the stanza and force attention onto both the disruptive "shot" and the line-ends. Loy, in her "Aphorisms on Futurism," stated that artists should "LOVE the hideous in order to find the sublime core of it."[25] In this stanza a sublime beauty arises out of the mindless tedium of everyday life. The "routine in coma" is both a succinct and witty description of Ova's life and the bedrock for the colors and energies that both "cure" the illness and disrupt the routine. This is classic Loy, allowing her to expose and ridicule the repressive elements of her culture, and incorporate the jolt in perspective, as well as the signs of beauty and imagination that escape the routine. In "Anglo-Mongrels and the Rose," as well as "Love Songs," these signs often incorporate a rush of light which captures ephemerality and speed. A sublime vocabulary is thus reworked to incorporate Loy's interest in the bodily. In "Aphorisms on Futurism" Loy wrote that "the Future is only dark from outside. / *Leap* into it—and it EXPLODES with *Light*."[26] But Loy's leaps into the illuminated unknown do not discard the comatose routines or physical foundation from which they arise. In "Anglo-Mongrels and the Rose," Loy's Anglo-Jewish "mongrel heart" is the inescapable basis for her artistic revelations and leap into light.

In "Anglo-Mongrels and the Rose," Loy creates a more wide-ranging and sustained version of the poetic polyglossia central to her style generally. Ova's cosmopolitan artistic sensibility is indistinguishable from her Anglo-Jewishness, femaleness, and class, all of which present Ova with barriers to expression she must wilfully supersede. It is partly for this reason that the barrier and the threshold are significant metaphors for the poem's meditation on the phenomenal world and language acquisition. Ova is born split: she is "bifurcate fat." The implication that some kind of internal hereditary division manifests itself in a fleshly fashion is carried through the poem's imagery. When "Ova Begins to Take Notice," her "will" has "two elongations" which crave for the visual stimulation of light and color (135). Infantile desire, meanwhile, negotiates fleeting glimpses of unattainable words, colors, and objects. It is the "shadow" into which joy recedes, the "non-being" into which a crimson ball rolls, the light that is extinguished as Ova is "carried away," the sudden "self-identification" that is "lost" through parental "annihilation" (137, 136). Ova's acquisition of language arises in these borderline spaces. A heard word that is an echo of a word, "iarrhea," connects to a receding visual image, a disappearing ball:

> And instantly
> this fragmentary
> simultaneity
> of ideas
>
> embodies
> the word
> A
> lucent
> iris
> shifts
> its
> irradiate
> interstice (141)

Loy often made lists of alliterations and assonances like this. There are lots of them in the unpublished writings in her archive, and they were clearly important for the process of her writing, but they also dominate her poems. Here Loy, in characteristic fashion, addresses the serious issue of infant language acquisition by way of an obscene joke. Language, the portentous, biblically inflected "the word," is revealed by way of shit. Beautiful and intense language, the lucent radiating iris, is collected out of the truncated diarrhea, a nice instance of Loy finding the sublime in the excremental. But the joke has a serious point to it. Not only does Loy collect together some of her favorite images—those of speed and light—she also reveals the "gait" of her own mentality. The stanza beginning, "A / lucent" both gleams with light and forces movement. The iris, incorporating both the eye and the flower, is described in movement—it "shifts"—and the words, isolated in their lines, also move fast down the page. The movement takes place in the iris's "interstice," and the poem, too, moves in its spaces, between words and on the page. It presents itself as an image on the page, a restrained version of a Futurist word-picture. Space is important to how we see and read these words. The "word" is both a synthesis of heard words and the visual world, and the moment when words and the phenomenal world attach to each other. But this is also about the instant Ova becomes an "I"; a separate body and mind whose distinctness from others is performed by language; and an eye that sees the boundaries of the visual world and seeks to see beyond them. Yet this drive to see beyond is one that Ova must fight for as she is repeatedly pulled back within parental boundaries. She sometimes stumbles because these parents are keen to trip her up.

This stanza stages the provisional nature of the word's relationship to the world, and the undecided position of Ova, or more generally an Ovum, within this relationship. The Ovum is, at some level, the source of language, but it is also a piece of biology that only becomes an "I" by virtue of a word. If Loy's rhythms tumble and stumble, they do so partly because the acquisition of language is a chancy and jagged process. "Anglo-Mongrels and the Rose" began with reference to biblical miracle and Exodus's lack of light. Here Loy presents a version of a modern-day miracle: an isolated ovum acquires language out of her own clotty fat and excrement. An earthbound poetic language is both the product of this miraculous process and the form in which this miracle can be expressed.

Anglo-Mongrels/The Rose

I want to conclude this essay by picking up on a question posed at the beginning but not fully addressed so far: Why the plural "Anglo-Mongrels" and the singular "Rose"? Readers have, for obvious reasons, assumed that Ova is the Anglo-Mongrel, but who are the others? Given that the Exodus section, containing no reference to Ova, was published initially under the title "Anglo-Mongrels and the Rose," it would be reasonable to assume that he also is an Anglo-Mongrel, and a reading of the poem bears this out. If Ova is born split, so is Exodus. Exodus must master the "German" of imperial Austria and the Hungarian "Magyar tongue," the language that was also the most widely spoken non-Indo-European language in Europe (111). This contestation over language and identity incorporates a power struggle, and the link between language and power runs through the poem. Exodus is "lashed with tongues" rather than "knouts" when he reaches his English paradise, but he is also an instant master of "business English," a pidgin English that, through the international power of capitalism, transcends national borders (113). Exodus is defined through his inarticulacy but understands the rhythms of a "Hebrew" inheritance. The bound and bordered Englishness Exodus confronts in

"English Rose" is fragile, a national identity inherently at risk from its own transnational capitalist energies (115).

Exodus, then, is an Anglo-Mongrel by virtue of his status as an immigrant; he is "in between" languages and cultures. So what about that singular Rose? The rose in "English Rose" as a standalone poem is a national symbol. When Loy added to the poem, the Rose also became a stereotyped English virgin to accompany the stereotyped Exodus and Ova. Part 3, by far the longest section of the final poem, is called "Mongrel Rose," and the title clearly signals a shift, from an "English" to a "Mongrel" Rose. Ova's mother is central to this change. While she partly *is* the English Rose in part 2, in part 3 this label falls away entirely and she is instead referred to as "the mother" or the "woman." There is one further reference to her as a Rose, but the imagery has become doglike: she is a "rabid rose" with "savage" irritations who laps her baby (145, 146). Within the terms of the poem, Ova's mother ceases to be an English Rose when she gives birth to Ova. This would mean that the Anglo-Mongrel is a much more mobile category than some readers have assumed. In a description of the family life of "the Penfolds" and a family called "The EXODI," Ova's mother has become part of a family defined in its exile (144). She, too, at some level, is an Anglo-Mongrel.

But then, Loy's point seems to be that everyone is; in other words individuals are born split because of parental religious, national, or racial differences, or they are split because they must master distinct language systems (as Exodus must), or because they migrate to a different culture, or because, in the case of women, they cease to conform to a particular model of femininity once they become sexualized. This latter point was central to Loy's thought throughout her life as she consistently criticized the insidious connection of women's sexualized bodies with shame. The images of this physicality are often animalistic. In "Three Moments in Paris," the woman lapses into her "animal" state while avoiding the "cerebral gymnastics" of her fellow men, and other women trail their "animal" selves behind them (39). In "Virgins Plus Curtains Minus Dots," the virgins are "bait" to the stars (38). In her writing about her parents, Loy often suggested that, despite the ideological battles and cultural differences between her mother and father, they concurred in their belief that sexual women were impure. In unpublished writings the battle between the Jewish father's fantasies of cultural inclusion and the Christian mother's brittle resistance to such fantasies is made more intense by the stain—a biological stain—of the child, variously named Ova, Mina, or Goy. But Ova's mother in "Anglo-Mongrels and the Rose" is also, within the ideology of English nationalism and female virginity, stained and shamed by the biological birth of Ova.

Along with her critique of English nationalism, then, the sinister ideology of women's purity, which Loy often insisted extended across Christian and Judaic traditions, fuels the style and orientation of her poetry. The polyglossia and refusal of prosodic elegance in "Anglo-Mongrels and the Rose" form part of a narrative about the birth and development of a female modernist artist. Here is a poem that is deliberately uncouth, that, like its female protagonist, extracts "beauty from excrement." Its prosodic rhythms are physical and earthbound, its language is polyglossal and transnational, and its narrative is self-reflexive of how these poetic features are a modern and female take on a world not bound by national borders.

Notes

1. Mina Loy, "Anglo-Mongrels and the Rose," *Little Review* 9.3 (Spring 1923), 10–18.

2. Mina Loy, "Anglo-Mongrels and the Rose: English Rose," *Little Review* 9.4 (Autumn–Winter 1923–24), 41–51.

3. Mina Loy, "The Anglo-Mongrels and the Rose," in *Contact Collection of Contemporary Writers,* ed. Robert McAlmon (Paris: Contact Editions, 1925).

4. Mina Loy, *Lunar Baedeker and Time-Tables*, ed. Jonathan Williams (Highlands: Jonathan Williams, 1958).

5. Mina Loy, *The Lost Lunar Baedeker*, ed. Roger Conover (Manchester: Carcanet, 1982), 109–75.

6. The circumstances around the shift are hard to unravel. Huge thanks to Roger Conover, who pointed out to me in an email exchange that Loy was still alive when the 1958 selected poems were published, and evidently looked over the proofs: "JW [Jonathan Williams] told me she looked at the proofs, but from the correspondence it appears to me that her daughter Joella actually signed off on them, so it is difficult to know how involved ML was." Email, Roger Conover to Rachel Potter, 2008.

7. Aimee L. Pozorski, "Eugenicist Mistress & Ethnic Mother: Mina Loy and Futurism, 1913–1917," *MELUS* 30.3 (Fall 2005), 41–69 (41); Elisabeth Frost, "Mina Loy's 'Mongrel' Poetics," in *Mina Loy: Woman and Poet,* ed. Maeera Shreiber and Keith Tuma (Orono, ME: National Poetry Foundation, 1998), 152.

8. Marjorie Perloff, "English as a 'Second' Language: Mina Loy's 'Anglo-Mongrels and the Rose,'" in *Mina Loy: Woman and Poet,* ed. Shreiber and Tuma, 139.

9. Ibid., 139, 145, 140, 133.

10. Keith Tuma, "Mina Loy's *Anglo-Mongrels and the Rose*," in *Mina Loy: Woman and Poet,* ed. Shreiber and Tuma, 184.

11. Ibid.

12. Wai Chee Dimock, "Introduction: Planet and America, Set and Subset," in *Shades of the Planet: American Literature as World Literature,* ed. Wai Chee Dimock and Lawrence Buell (Princeton, NJ: Princeton University Press, 2007), 8.

13. Loy, "Anglo-Mongrels and the Rose," 116.

14. Ibid., 114, 115.

15. See George K. Anderson, *The Legend of the Wandering Jew* (Providence, RI: Brown University Press, 1965), 11.

16. Ibid., 248, 332.

17. Loy, "Anglo-Mongrels and the Rose," 113, 114. Further references to this edition will appear in the text.

18. Peter Nicholls, "'Arid Clarity': Ezra Pound and Mina Loy," in *The Salt Companion to Mina Loy*, ed. Suzanne Hobson and Rachel Potter (Cambridge: Salt, 2010), 134.

19. Perloff, "English as a 'Second' Language," 136.

20. Ibid., 137.

21. John Wilkinson, "Stumbling, Balking, Tacking: Robert Creeley's 'For Love' and Mina Loy's 'Love Songs to Joannes,'" in *The Salt Companion to Mina Loy*, ed. Hobson and Potter, 155, 154.

22. Nicholls, "'Arid Clarity,'" 140–41; emphasis in original.

23. Mina Loy, *The Lost Lunar Baedeker*, 22, 24, 26.

24. Wilkinson, "Stumbling, Balking, Tacking," 154.

25. Loy, "Aphorisms on Futurism," in *The Lost Lunar Baedeker*, 272.

26. Ibid.; emphasis in original.

4

BETTY MILLER AND THE MARRANO SELF

SARAH SCEATS

In the introduction to the 1985 republication of Betty Miller's novel *On the Side of the Angels*, Sarah Miller recounts how in the late 1940s her mother advised an aspiring young niece of her husband's on how to become a writer: "conform with the outside world, do all the rituals of domesticity of being a wife and mother—but keep the true faith to yourself and hide every trace of it. In other words, my mother advised Renie to become a 'Marrano'—the Jews of fifteenth-century Spain forced to convert, or face death or exile, but who while outwardly conforming went on secretly practising Judaism."[1]

If in her practice Betty Miller (1910–65) employed these Austen-like tactics—for writerly concealment is as much a function of femininity as of Jewishness—most of her fiction seems equally "Marrano." Her writing emanates from the world of the English middle classes, providing "stereoscopically clear" depictions of wives and mothers recounted as though from the inside, from one of the class's privileged members.[2] Even in the one novel that deals centrally with being Jewish, *Farewell Leicester Square*, there is a narratorial distance and coolness of tone that suggests a certain detachment. Detachment is not the same as disowning, however, and I will argue that Miller's writing is profoundly concerned with struggles to achieve a coherent identity within the middle classes: explicitly Jewish identity in *Farewell Leicester Square*; female identity in *On the Side of the Angels*; and also, more problematically, conflicts between "female" and male" mindsets and between what might loosely be termed mind and body, intellect and sensuousness, in these

81

novels and in *The Death of the Nightingale*. Much of her writing may be seen as exploring the conflicts and ambivalences that characterize perceptions of self in the mid-twentieth century. Her characters' questioning sensibilities owe something to modernism and to Freudian psychology (it may not be coincidence that her husband was a psychiatrist), but her fiction has a flavor of its own. Most of the novels are situated shortly before, during, or just after World War II, although only *On the Side of the Angels* deals directly with the matter of wartime. The novels feature recurring preoccupations about who or what we are and how best to live, and are saturated with a peculiarly heightened consciousness of conflict and uncertainty. Jewishness has something to do with this; so too does gender. But, more indefinably, there is the question of sensibility.

Miller's writing focuses consistently on the whole person—on thoughts and feelings certainly, but also on physicality and its significance: eating, drinking, bodily experiences, and felt impressions. Attention to the senses is evident both in her highly detailed impressionistic descriptions and in the occasional linguistic intoxication of her prose style. Indeed, she was taken to task by contemporary critics for what they seem to have considered a self-indulgent sensuousness in her writing. Her early mentor, St. John Ervine, for example, wrote to her: "you overwork your words, and you yield too much to your sensuousness. . . . Simplify yourself, girl." Even Rosamond Lehmann commented, "Sometimes too stressing of sensuous impressions . . . [her writing] is if anything a little overdone for my taste."[3] But sensuousness in Miller's writing is not simply a matter of purple prose; it is a central element in her characters' experience of the world, in their self-perceptions, and in their states of turmoil. This emphasis on the sensuous (and sometimes sensual) is more or less evident in all her fiction, but in three of her novels it is at the thematic core, intimately bound up with understanding the world and conflicts within identity, and it is these three that I discuss in this chapter: *Farewell Leicester Square* (1941), *On the Side of the Angels* (1945), and *The Death of the Nightingale* (1948).

Farewell Leicester Square is explicitly concerned with Anglo-Jewish identity in the 1930s. The novel polarizes the oppressive comfort of ethnic belonging and a chill English middle-class exclusiveness, the evocation of the Jewish milieu emphasizing a mildly claustrophobic sensuousness: warmth, flesh, smell, color, sound, and, of course, food. For the protagonist, Alec Berman, the dining room is a "warm haven" but includes the sometimes unnerving presence of his father, whose irritation and stern affection (and, for a child, painful expressions of that affection: cheek-pinching and tossing-in-the-air) the young Alec dreads.[4] The close-knit quality of the family is potent, evoked not only in relation to the father's control but also through the mother's devotion and the children's squabbles and occasional transforming generosities, and this quality continues into their adulthood. Its very potency causes a breach when Alec leaves home to take up an apprenticeship in the film business, for the closed circle of this Jewish family unit is shown to be brittle in the context of the wider world. Its supposed self-sufficiency is threatened by Alec's prospective connection with the outside world; his father issues an ultimatum, and this precipitates Alec's departure and a severing of contact with his whole family.

The closed circle is not threatened by incomers, however, or at least not by Jewish ones. If anything, the reverse is demonstrated when Alec's elder sister becomes engaged and her fiancé comes to stay at weekends; the Friday supper is upgraded by the presence of a maid. In contrast to Alec's yearning to reach outside the family and the faith, Jack Goldberg is described in terms that suggest a stolid, unwavering commitment to both. If his appearance, as perceived by Alec, suggests a slightly flashy stereotype, this only underlines the contrast between his affirmation of a fixed, unquestioning identity and Alec's more open, searching, and conflicted sensibility.

Jack's presence at the Friday suppers functions to strengthen the family's cohesion and sense of tradition with the elaboration of a familiar and regular routine: "Preliminary helpings of chopped herring, redolent of onion and vinegar; slices of the sweet twist loaf; golden-brown triangles of fried plaice; savoury fish balls; well-seasoned salad of diced celery and beetroot; stewed pears soaking in cream; and a rich cheese-cake, the final crumbs of which were finished up with a cup of good milky coffee" (25). After the food comes the "lengthy choral grace" (25) reinforcing ancient traditions, and then the evening is spent in conversation that consolidates connection, accompanied by chocolates and toffees and finished off with lemon tea and little cakes. The whole event is a ritual. The Friday evening meal is, of course, a fixed point in observant Jewish life, and through her atmospheric evocation, Miller indicates both the family's adherence to their faith and their perpetuation of ethnic traditions. The meal also has a structural function in the novel. The narrative is more or less bracketed by two such suppers: the one I have described here, when Violet and Jack are cementing their relationship and Alec is setting his sights on the film business, and another at the end of the novel, marking Alec's homecoming after the failure of his marriage. Ethnicity, aspiration, and boundary-breaking are outlined through the first meal, and suffering, reconciliation, and (Jewish) comfort suffuse the second.

I will return to discussion of this final meal, but first I want to consider Alec's life outside the fold. The central part of the novel is almost entirely concerned with his struggle to accommodate his Jewishness within a chosen English middle-class lifestyle. The narrative centers on his attraction to film, to the magnate Richard Nicholls, or at least to what he represents, and more specifically to Nicholls's unglamorous and very English daughter Catherine, whom Alec first glimpses when he importunes Nicholls in search of a job. It is this early sight of Catherine and her brother Basil, young people who have absolute assurance almost as a birthright, that first ignites both Alec's desire and his sense of foreignness, or as we would probably now put it "otherness."[5] When he later meets Catherine at Basil's house, it is their world that he moves into. Having left his family behind, he marries Catherine in part to escape from his sense of being an outsider to this world and an exile from that of his childhood. The scene of his impassioned declaration to her is prefaced by a sharp memory of his mother and father at the dining table and an irresistible nostalgia for the festivity of Friday nights. This memory provokes a "paralyz-ing loneliness[. . . .] A pain of regret for his mother, for that old life. For the sense of being one in a community again; for that protection, that solidarity, that oneness . . ." (132). It is his own sense of Jewishness that he misses, but he also longs for the ease and comfort of physical belonging, something that he does find, for a while, married to Catherine. There is a representative scene in which he comes home to lunch and is greeted by the intangible smell of "home" (156), which Miller describes as appealing to him almost as an animal summons and as affording him a moment of pure joy.

Alec is drawn as a character of exquisite sensibility and sensuous aware-ness; this is what ostensibly makes him a successful creator of film. The sen-suous memories of his childhood home are described as things "one would remember always" (8); he carries them with him. He has a vivid physical con-sciousness. In his early days as a film apprentice living in digs, for example, there is an episode at the Lewisham public baths in which he is lying in the soapy water in a dreamy state of suspension. The narrator notes that "adjust-ment became so perfect that the smallest action was superfluous" (49); he is totally relaxed, slightly floating, aware only of his body in its perfect state. Roused by the attendant, he has to drag his attention back to intellectual function, and it is only then that he observes he has lost weight and specu-lates that he eats too many cold meals, tinned food, bread and butter. These observations precipitate him into hungry and once again physical imagination of his single hot meal of the week, the Sunday dinner provided by his landlady: "Two slips of underdone meat, boiled greens, dark roast potatoes, Yorkshire pudding: and another plate with a pale crust of pie cupped over some sugar-stewed fruit. The gastric juices spurted suddenly, painfully under his tongue, as he thought of the joint inside the oven, trickling salt red wine from its sinews as it browned and spat. His jaws began to ache slightly, under the ears . . ." (50; ellipsis in original).

There are two points of particular interest in these passages. It becomes clear that Alec's perceptions are mediated through his body and sensuous apprehensions; elsewhere in the novel, too, it is apparent that Alec needs to gain a *sense* of things before he can articulate them to himself. This is one of the ways in which he is contrasted to the cold, over-refined, upper-middle-class figure of Basil, who "sought, never the direct experience, but its abstraction. Refinement: essence. For him, the actual was always the vulgar" (99). For Alec, it is clear, the actual is vital. This quality, it is implied, is part of his Jewishness and his physicality, integral to his sensibilities, as well as informing his aesthetic. The second and related point of interest is Miller's use of food. What makes Alec's mouth water here is traditional English food: the archetypal Sunday dinner, with all that connotes, a far cry from Friday night challah and gefilte fish. Through food Miller thus reinforces the focus of Alec's aspiration, but also perhaps intimates future isolation, for the roast dinner that causes him to salivate, provided by his landlady, is left outside his door, and he eats it in his room, alone.

It should be noted, however, that in Alec Miller is not creating a simple sensualist. If Basil represents an extreme of chilly refinement, then the other extreme is personified in Brian, the location manager. Amiable, tactless, and lacking in social skills, Brian is constantly observed by Alec and the narrator in terms that suggest an unconscious submission to the imperatives of appetite. Watching him drive, for example, Alec notes that he has "the mouth tender, unformed, of an acquisitive and frustrated baby" (80); when he hears paper rustle, he looks up with eager expectancy like one of Pavlov's dogs (84); when smoking their pipes, the "hollow sternness" of Basil's face is contrasted to Brian, whom Alec finds faintly disgusting, like a baby with a dummy in its mouth (98). Brian is also the only character to display a leering sexual suggestiveness, whereas Alec is portrayed as enjoying a communicative sexuality.

Alec, then, is perhaps *l'homme moyen sensuel*. But he is shown as a man who struggles to reconcile the warring elements within himself, and this struggle is exacerbated by his being both English and Jewish, identities that seem polarized by everything around him. Miller keeps him perpetually exercised by the problem, unlike his friend Lew, with whom he discusses antisemitism over a Chinese meal. While Lew is content to shrug it off for the occasion and concentrate on the food—mixing the dishes, incidentally, on his plate—Alec cannot let it rest, pushing away his food and picking away at the *"intolerable"* difficulties of being Jewish, with its "ridiculous, impossible complications on top of the normal complications of merely being alive" (180; emphasis in original). Lew, who has remained within the bosom of his family, maintains a survivalist stance—bleakly ironic in a novel written in 1935. He is as troubled as Alec by the problem of belonging, but until reminded of it he remains anaesthetized, or as he puts it "acclimatized" (182). Like Basil and Brian, Lew is thus another of the types against which Miller defines—or perhaps refuses to define—Alec: he is not abstract and refined; not a sensualist; not a man who prefers to avoid the internal dilemma of his identity and status.

Alec's wife, Catherine, voices the criticism—not uncommon where unthinking prejudice is in evidence—that Alec's sense of not belonging is of his own making; in effect that he is projecting his own feelings as a self-hating Jew.[6] Miller's narrator maintains a neutral position; the marriage founders amid accusations and implications from Catherine that Alec's hypersensitivity is responsible for the gulf between them. Readers may be drawn to sympathize with both or neither. Catherine's determination to remove their son from a situation in which he might develop a similarly conflicted sense of identity seems cruel but has a certain logic, even to Alec, who earlier observes that insensitivity may be "the hall-mark of superiority," and ruefully accepts that his complicated feelings may be born of insecurity (159). Indeed, Alec's brief but dramatic illness in the wake of Catherine's declaration could even be seen as a kind of weakness, at least in the terms of Catherine's world. What seems obvious is that, notwithstanding Alec's continuing conviction that the ideal of their union was right, Catherine is portrayed as all of a piece, and Alec as ambivalent and contradictory—altogether too complicated for her. It should be said that Catherine is not portrayed entirely unsympathetically, for she too is given a point of view, not only through her dialogues and her silences with Alec but in self-revelation with Basil, through the narrator's observations, and by means of reported thought: *"Stop it, she was crying in herself, stop it, oh, stop it, you fool, can't you guess what I'm trying to spare you?"* (247; emphasis in original).

I referred earlier to Miller's use of food not just in relation to sensuousness but as a thematic vehicle, and it is worth noting that much of Alec and

Catherine's relationship is played out—and given meaning—within a context of meals and drinks. Most if not all of these occasions are inescapably English and middle-class in flavor. Most revealing, perhaps, are domestic scenes, especially "tea time." Indeed, on the very first occasion that Alec and Catherine take tea together—described as a "joyful" (104) relief on a wet afternoon at Basil's house—Miller foreshadows their future relationship: "Catherine was serving the tea [. . .] Alec watched. Enjoying keenly that which was missing so often in his life—the ritual of being served by a particular woman [. . .] feeling [. . .] he was surrendered to her: that she took from him the burden of his own independence" (105). Catherine here appears subservient (she is "serving" the tea) but in fact is in control (he feels "surrendered"); the relationship is maternal, she is strong and nurturing. The promise of this cozy picture is compromised, however, for Miller makes Catherine deliver a shocking wound to Alec's sensibility when she answers his query about who now owns her childhood home, saying vaguely that it belongs to "some awful dago" (107). The casual racism in her vocabulary first mortifies and then enrages the silent Alec, who for "dago" hears "Jew" (107).

On other occasions, too, what might be comforting domestic occasions become prickly; the intimacy of mid-morning tea and biscuits with Catherine, for example, is cruelly deflected by the clicking of her knitting needles. Even nursery tea, with its possibilities of regressive comfort, is undermined, for Alec censures the luxury of the food on offer, acutely aware of the distance between himself and his son. That distance is emphasized by two snippets of conversation: an exchange between Catherine and Alec about the difficulty of finding a cook who can do more than "good plain" food (217), and the revelation that the child has a friend called Timothy Hope-Sewell. The first leaves Alec feeling blamed for being exotic, foreign, craving "old tastes, old sensations, long ungratified" (218), and the second triggers a desire in Alec for his son to "have a Jewish friend, be surrounded with Jewish people, people with whom he was at ease; secure" (222). In other words, Miller keeps the sense of Alec's troubled identity on the boil even—and perhaps especially, given the nature of his sensuous and vulnerable sensibility—in scenes where minor, normally banal, domestic consumption takes place.

The novel ends, as I have said, with a reprise of the Friday supper. Alec, separated from his wife and son, feels empty and free: he has lost what he most wanted and so has faced the worst that can happen. He returns to the family home where his mother is very ill—to be welcomed by his sister with hot soup and salt-beef sandwiches, and a reconciliatory conversation with his father over breakfast the following morning. His mother begins to recover. The novel looks set for a happy ending, of sorts. The final passage of the novel describes a supper very similar to the first, if a little more luxurious due to the addition of grapefruit, smoked salmon, and a beribboned, tiered cream cake. There is another difference, Alec notes, and that is the empowerment of the younger generation, who gently undermine the authority of his once-feared father, though everybody still participates in the grace. The recapitulation and updating of the Friday supper has a number of functions. As well as providing an inclusive resolution, it both reasserts the basis of Alec's internal conflict and offers him solace. The family is still a closed circle, albeit more tolerant than it was of what lies outside, and it is still antipathetic to the integration Alec holds to as an ideal. But it also both embodies continuity, the persistence of faith and tradition, and enfolds a degree of change and growth. Finally, the meal offers nourishment for body, spirit, and feeling. Alec's wounded emotions are tempered by a belief that he can no longer be touched by anything, but Miller's final words before the grace are that it "smote sharply upon Alec's awareness" (309); he is not perhaps so deprived of feeling as solaced by a return to the familiar.

The internalized conflict between Jewishness and Englishness in Alec's characterization is by far the most obvious concern of the novel, both in terms of the individual dilemma and as a critique of insidious antisemitism at large. That this overt concern touched a nerve is perhaps reflected in the fact that the manuscript (originally titled *Next Year in Jerusalem*) was rejected by Miller's publisher in 1935, and the book was not published until 1941. The more coded or abstract conflicts in identity that Miller deals with are less obviously sensitive, and she offers a psychosomatic model of the self that sits well with the later twentieth-century reclamation of the body, disturbing only in its insistence on internal war between opposing characteristics.[7]

I have already referred to a conflict between intellectual function and what generally passes as knowledge on one hand, and what is felt, sensed, physically experienced on the other, aspects of perception that have been understood as a split between mind and body and which are sometimes characterized as relating to "male" and "female" elements within the self. The other two novels I want to discuss take up this aspect of identity more directly. *On the Side of the Angels,* set in and around a military hospital during the war, accentuates a gendered opposition, with the sensuous, intuitive, "feminine" sensitivities focalized specifically through a young mother, Honor, and the rational, ordered, "masculine" mindset shared among several characters, including Honor's sister, Claudia. The sisters' mode of being is represented in their physical appearance: Claudia belts her dress at the waist as though to separate herself off from the world and remain intact (echoing, perhaps, the uniformed males all around her); Honor, by contrast, has a full and fecund body, formless in the aftermath of childbearing and always threatening to spill over in response to the needs of the baby.

The novel's plot connects directly with this opposition. Honor's husband, Colin, somewhat to her dismay, strives desperately to curry favor with the woman-hating commanding officer to whom Honor represents all that is distasteful and threatening. Claudia's boyfriend, Andrew, is invalided out of the army and takes up a skeptical position on the sidelines, while Claudia herself falls under the spell of a fake commando, the apparently macho Herriot. Stable identities are undone and reformed in the context of war. Herriot, for example, in "normal" life a thoroughly respectable bank manager, dutiful husband, and father, succumbs to the excitement of the idea of war and assumes the identity of a hero. We have little access to his inner life other than through his conversation, but the implication is that war for him, like an irresistible appeal to a gambler's lust, touches an "uncivilized" streak, releasing him from normally socialized behavior. Part of his appeal to both Claudia and Andrew is precisely this amorality, though in Andrew's case largely because it confirms his sense that war is an expression of civilization's internal strife, the mirror—though he doesn't put it this way—of the battle between an individual id and superego.[8]

Stresses of the kind seen within the character of Alec Berman, when tradition, ideals, emotions, and bodily sensation all seem to be pulling in different directions, are represented in Claudia's conflicted relationship with femininity. In this respect she is contrasted to her sister, Honor, who is dreamily maternal and wholly dependent on her husband, whom Miller describes unequivocally as the "lynch-pin around which all her thought, her emotions, her smallest daily actions revolved."[9] Faced with the military, Honor is ashamed of her own rich femaleness, characterized as "inchoate, ununiformed" (39), and yet she has an extraordinary capacity of empathy and vision, observing and drinking in her sister, for example, with a sort of negative capability (95). In return she is replenished through an unboundaried contemplation of the natural world, "a silent interchange in which her whole being was gradually irrigated and renewed by the life of the leaves and plants and grasses about her" (164), and by the "sweet," "consoling" pleasures of breastfeeding (144). In sum she is an archetypal feminine female, a caring, nurturing "earth mother" of thoroughly traditional hue, as is summed up in the description of her darning: "Slipping the wooden mushroom into the heel of a sock, she began to darn; pricking the long needle in and out: resuming that essential maintenance and repair work, emotional no less than practical, which derives from the feminine desire to preserve at all costs the *status quo*" (168).

Compared with this, Claudia is not feminine. She is certainly portrayed as an attractive and sexual woman, but she has none of Honor's nurturing, maternal sensibilities. She is represented as perpetually irritated by her small nephew Peter and lacks empathy for him. Just as Miller uses food to convey emotional exchanges in *Farewell Leicester Square,* so here she suggests Claudia's sharpness in her reactions to the little boy's eating. Over tea with him and Honor at the outset of the novel, she feels uncomfortable under his gaze, telling him "severely" (17) to eat his food as he warily sniffs the boiled milk and examines his honey sandwich. Later she is so repelled by the sight of him experimentally unwinding his slice of Swiss roll that she leans across and cuts it smartly with her knife, leaving him speechless with "complete outrage" (18). In a scene much later in the book, she overrides his expressed desire to cut up his own food, briskly doing it for him without explanation (205). Neither does she like to see Honor's baby lying and kicking naked. She is drawn rather toward the inhuman, to tidiness and order, appreciating the bleak neatness of the cemetery (for which we may read the uncomplicatedness of death) and experiencing sudden shame at the sight of her own body hair (28). There are elements of Kristevan abjection here: Claudia is repelled by her sister's maternal fecundity and troubled by her own female body; she withdraws from the signs of Herriot's maleness; she cannot bear mess, especially where food is concerned; and she approves the ordered aridity of the cemetery. In so craving a "clean and proper body," she tries to disown a part of her self.[10]

It is Claudia's fiancé, Andrew, who first begins to see conflict in her, which he identifies as part of a general self-deception about how civilized we are—for contemporary humanity, he claims, is deeply and destructively at war with its own desires (78). Himself complicated and defensive, he effectively pushes her toward Herriot, wanting her to discover what really drives her. Herriot in turn identifies what he sees as a "state of perpetual civil war" (99) within her, for he too believes that she continually struggles to suppress what she really wants, merely for the sake of convention. This struggle is partly about sex, for some of Claudia's rigidity is virginal, and her relationship with Andrew is, it seems, primarily driven by intellectual and emotional connections. Indeed Claudia is represented in some sense as the battleground through which the two men—and what they represent—are engaged in combat. Herriot (a bank manager, though this is, conveniently, not revealed until the end) represents—indeed is drawn to—the Dionysian; he is an energetic seducer, with apelike hair on the backs of his hands hinting at bestiality. He is associated with the excitement of danger, an excitement that briefly arouses Claudia, before she ashamedly persuades herself that such wilful indulgence is "debased" (64). His arguments are dangerous: he punctures Claudia's cherished beliefs and questions her claim to hate violence, accusing her on the contrary of doing violence to her own nature. Physically, Claudia finds him hard to resist; indeed she moves into an almost sleepwalking acceptance. The pull exerted by Andrew is on a different plane; apart from her loyalty to him as fiancée, she is fiercely reluctant—or unable—to let go of what he represents, to which she is bound: intellect, skepticism, painfully acute awareness.

The intense conflict within Claudia represented by these two men is articulated from her sister's point of view: "Honor saw a creature caught in the trap of its own nature, hounded by impulses so contrary that it took every available ounce of will-power and energy to control them" (201–2). Honor first feels pity for her sister but is then filled with respect; she comprehends something of what it costs Claudia—like Alec in *Farewell*—to maintain the struggle. When at the end of the novel Claudia and Andrew compare notes, they both feel themselves to be prisoners of unrelenting consciousness. Like Alec they are described as defeated, though theirs is a failure to escape their "higher nature" (236)—he by joining the army, she by going with Herriot to London. They do, however, find in each other some form of mutual protection and settle for self-acceptance and the difficulties this involves. They are the ones, incidentally, who are on the side of the angels.

A desire to escape is a feature of almost all Miller's novels. If thematically such an impulse reflects the intolerable nature of the conflicts within identity that Miller is exploring, in plot terms the impulse is often focused on a conflicted desire to escape a parent. This is the case with Miller's final novel, *The Death of the Nightingale*. If *Farewell Leicester Square* presented the young Alec Berman as driven by the need to distance himself from an imperious and disapproving father, who in part represents the ethnic identity that he finds difficult to defy or reject, in *The Death of the Nightingale* there are two would-be escapees from parental domination: Léonie and her suitor, Matthew O'Farrell. Despite being Irish, Matthew enlisted and fought with the RAF during the war, in large part to escape maternal pressure to live up to his martyred father. At the opening of the novel, he is estranged from home. Léonie is torn between her relationship with Matthew and the repressive desires of her father, Newman Cain. She has been brought up by Cain and Mrs. Paull, his housekeeper and one-time lover (who, it turns out, helped him confiscate the baby Léonie from his unfaithful wife). So close has Cain kept Léonie that she seems to have no volition distinct from him, and it is only at Matthew's insistence and with the aid of Mrs. Paull that she is ultimately enabled to leave home to get married.

Like Claudia in *On the Side of the Angels*, Léonie is a person through whom battles are fought. In the novel's back story, she is the prize in the struggle between her mother and Cain; in the central plot she is pulled between Cain and Matthew; and in general she mediates between the opposed impulses of rationality, order, and control on the one hand and the forces of life and nature on the other. As a character she is represented not as wrestling with the elements within her own identity, like Claudia, but as being unwillingly pulled one way and the other by external forces. The dilemma she faces is encapsulated in a passage of free indirect speech that mirrors her lack of agency: "If only it was [sic] possible simultaneously to satisfy both Matthew and Cain, to solve the antagonism of which she was the unwilling focus!"[11] While she is deeply attached to her father, she is also stifled at home with him, and she recognizes the danger in his self-control, achieved, she perceives—in words that might have been attributed to Herriot or Andrew in *On the Side of the Angels*—through "an act of prolonged and slow-motion violence" (27). At the same time she recoils from the scenes of drinking and violent play that Matthew describes, and periodically withdraws from a feeling of overexposure in his company. The polarization is manifested, too, in her reactions to the natural world; she experiences a "shock of delight" (13) on feeling the healing warmth of a calf's flesh, but she is repelled by the crude physicality of animals in the zoo.

Opposition between the impulses of the natural world and the refinements of human thought and creativity is a major trope in this novel. It might even be said to be labored. Matthew is largely associated with the physical world. He enters the novel by proxy, through his dog, Robber, a bounding, undisciplined creature with which he is portrayed as having a close physical bond that imbues him with a sense of natural harmony (109). The importance of animal nature is emphasized in this connection; the dog is even given something approaching a point of view: "Robber, the dog, inhaled an obscure ammonia-smelling splash on the wall: startled, he glared, ears flexed, at a rattling truck: intent suddenly, pulling on his leash, he sought unerring between the haunches of another dog the root of knowledge, of all personal data" (21). Later in the novel, when Matthew revisits his mother and his childhood home, it is his body that remembers:

he is overwhelmed by the smell of the woolen blanket; his face recoils from the "terrible known softness" of his mother's cheek (91); his fingers recall where the light switch is located. In the garden, listening to his mother's tale of Cain's past involvement in her life, he watches a cat preparing to pounce on a bird and feels his own muscles tensing in empathy (204).[12] It is partly in subsequent reaction against Cain that he decides he must have a life in harmony with outdoor living things and goes ahead with plans to start a farm with his friend the wing commander. He even announces to the wing commander that what Léonie most needs is contact with animals and "ordinary things" (156).

Cain, by contrast, is characterized from the beginning as an indoor man, a refined intellectual of a high order. He craves routine, is uncomfortable with thresholds, open doors, animals, weeds, rain. He experiences an almost visceral revulsion in the presence of Matthew's dog. His ideal environment is the Reading Room of the British Museum, where each reader sits in a halo of light from the desk lamp, so deep in thought as to appear almost disconnected from the body and its limitations. For added emphasis, this scene of disembodiment is juxtaposed with one of absolute bestiality among mandrills at the zoo (131). Cain is aware of his physicality; he takes exercise, but specifically to subdue his body and keep it healthy. Matthew observes that he eats in such a way as to distance himself from the reality of such animal activity. It seems to Matthew that Cain would like to deny his dependence on food, a perception that gives the strange impression that in his case carbohydrate is transformed directly into thought, and that his bodily presence is only ghostly (47). Cain also approves the mortification of the flesh practiced by the saints (76). Named perhaps to reflect his liability for the death of fellow academic Kevin O'Farrell, he is also responsible for the murder of something in himself.

While Cain's existence as a creature of intellect and the spirit seems diametrically opposed to Matthew's association with the "forces of life" that resist control (14), it becomes apparent that Cain is a far more complex character than he first appears. Of course a person cannot be as removed from his or her body as Cain seems to be unless there is some extreme repression going on, and Miller's use of the word "uncanny" (11) in relation to Cain's response to plants and animal life is revealing.[13] In the novel's earlier events, Cain is seen as suffering a psychosomatic illness (56), and Matthew's mother, Rose, describes a vivid recognition of the young Cain as wrestling with his own demons: "you're fighting against your own real nature all the time" (195). The events in Ireland (when Cain becomes obsessed with Rose and betrays her activist husband, Kevin, to the authorities during the Troubles) are in Rose's view at least partly occasioned by Cain's fascination with Kevin's "terrific vitality," and she characterizes argumentative discussions between the two men in terms of wrestling and embrace (101). In these retrospective passages Cain is represented as subject to passionate desire, even while he clings to the notion of duty. When Léonie is a small baby, he feels impelled to avoid the sight of her breastfeeding, so closely does he empathize with the baby: "Cain, having once seen the sight of the small blind creature fastened leech-like at [Ginette's] breast, chose thereafter to absent himself from the room on such occasions; since he could not but recognize in this shameful avidity an impulse, current in himself, that all his life he had sought unsuccessfully to dominate" (63). The years-long attempts to subdue the body, the relentless intellectual focus and cultivation of abstraction, are thus framed as responses to unbearable and ardent need.

Whereas the conflict on which the novel pivots appears to be centered on Léonie, the real turbulence is within Cain himself. While on the one hand he struggles to become detached, wholly rational, and self-sufficient, on the other, like a frantic baby, he seeks to possess the source of love.[14] This happens first in relation to Rose, with the tragic consequences of Kevin's death and its repercussions. Later, when Cain's wife, Ginette, falls in love with someone else and wants to leave, he desperately tells her that husbands and wives cannot divorce because they are part of each other forever, and when she denies him, he seizes the baby. When he realizes that he cannot dissuade Léonie from marrying Matthew, he tries to persuade Mrs. Paull to take her away once again, and when he can no longer prevent Léonie's marriage and her departure to the farm, he offers the gift of his house for them to live in, on condition that he can remain as a lodger. The sheer desperation of these actions hints at the power of the hunger that drives him, and his awful fear of loss. Even the thought of abandonment is enough to fill him with a dread of the "degradation" he will experience: "the helpless rage, the sorrow; the vindictiveness that rising from the depths of his nature would overwhelm" (142). And each time that he is thwarted, he is described as instantly becoming old. Like the previous characters I have discussed, Cain suffers a defeat, a failure to reconcile the warring elements in himself, to draw together the polarized aspects of self. In his case, however, unlike those of Alec Berman, Claudia, and Andrew, the failure is due to an attempt to ignore the conflict within. The futility of his effort to subdue the uncontrollable is realized in a distressing recurring dream in which a great slab of stone is levered up by a single blade of growing grass (123–24).

The novel is perhaps more nuanced than my focus on the polar opposition of mind and body would suggest. Cain, for example, like Alec, loves his home, which through the years has come to seem almost as though it conforms to the shape of his own body, his desires. His domestic life is filled with pleasing rituals: mealtimes with Léonie; working together with her; working alone in his library; Sunday walks. He most particularly enjoys, and looks forward to, his afternoon tea, with cake baked by Mrs. Paull. The house itself is described as offering a welcome, and sensuous, continuity: "The dining-room was at the other end of the passage. A long room, overlooking the cypress trees of the churchyard, it had at all seasons of the year, a mellow date-like smell, as of old furniture, of preserves and spices, of table-linen packed freshly glazed in a paper-lined drawer" (41). The passage is typically sensuous, appealing to sight and smell, but it also draws together both the physical world (the trees, the food) and a sense of order (the linen carefully packed in the drawer), with even a passing allusion to the disembodied and spiritual in the view of the churchyard. The "reassurance" (41) that the room vouchsafes, overtly to Léonie but implicitly to Cain, has to do with both its appeal to the senses and its unchanging, habitual associations.

Comfort and habit cannot heal the angst of a tortured soul, however, nor reconcile the opposing elements in individual or social identity. In all of these novels, Miller seems to be suggesting that the attempt to resolve the struggle between conflicting aspects of identity and profound and contradictory desires is doomed to failure, even involving a death of the self or a part of the self. To recall Freud for a moment, what is repressed *will* return, one way or another. Miller's novels sketch some of the catastrophic consequences that may result from refusal to recognize aspects of the self, of specific selves and of all selves, and these range from broken marriage to personal disintegration to war, which is repeatedly attributed to the ignorance and repression of profound and uncivilized "inclinations and desires" by "civilization" (*Angels,* 78, 77). If Miller offers a solution, it is implicit: there is no solution but consciousness, the "daytime insomnia" (236) that so wearies Claudia. For Miller it is of the essence to struggle: spiritually, intellectually and emotionally, however much the struggle is concealed within a conforming Marrano self.

Notes

1. Sarah Miller, "Introduction" to Betty Miller, *On the Side of the Angels* (1945) (London: Virago, 1985), xviii.
2. The description of Miller's characters as "stereoscopically clear" belongs to Rosamond Lehmann, cited by Sarah Miller in the introduction to *On the Side of the Angels,* xiv.
3. Cited in Sarah Miller, "Introduction," xi, xiv.

4. Betty Miller, *Farewell Leicester Square* (1941; repr. London: Persephone, 2000), 9. Subsequent references to this novel are given parenthetically in the text.

5. Alec's position as an English Jew within English culture does not make him an obvious (post)colonial subject, but there are certainly parallels.

6. I have written elsewhere about Alec in relation to the notion of the self-hating Jew: "Divided Loyalties: Betty Miller's Narratives of Ambivalence," in *In the Open: Jewish Women Writers and British Culture,* ed. Claire M. Tylee (Newark: University of Delaware Press, 2005). See also Kristin Bluemel, "The Urban Geography of English Antisemitism and Assimilation: A Case Study," in *Antisemitism and Philosemitism in the Twentieth and Twenty-First Centuries*, ed. Phyllis Lassner and Lara Trubowitz (Newark: University of Delaware Press, 2008), 175–95.

7. According to Maud Ellmann, in the 1990s the body became a "shibboleth" of literary theory, "the last bastion of materiality" against a perceived excess of theoretical signification. Maud Ellmann, *The Hunger Artists: Starving, Writing and Imprisonment* (London: Virago, 1993), 3.

8. In other words, a battle between instinctive urges and conscience-driven socialization. Sigmund Freud, *New Introductory Lectures on Psycho-analysis,* trans. and ed. James Strachey, International Psycho-Analytical Library, no. 24 (London: Hogarth Press, 1974).

9. Betty Miller, *On the Side of the Angels* (1945; repr. London: Virago, 1985), 46. Subsequent references to this novel are given parenthetically in the text.

10. Julia Kristeva, *The Powers of Horror: An Essay on Abjection* (New York: Columbia University Press, 1982).

11. Betty Miller, *The Death of the Nightingale* (London: Robert Hale, 1948), 54. Subsequent references to this novel are given parenthetically in the text.

12. There is a further metaphorical resonance here with the tale his mother tells of Cain's actions in denouncing her husband's involvement in the Troubles. Matthew's empathy with the cat, and recognition that cats will always catch birds (213), suggests at least an acknowledgment of Cain's position.

13. The implication is of some disavowed aspect of Cain's self that he sees horrifyingly mirrored in the natural world, though in the end we see not so much a return of the repressed as the atrophy of human emotion. Sigmund Freud, "The Uncanny," in *The Standard Edition of the Complete Psychological Works of Sigmund Freud,* ed. and trans. James Strachey, vol. XVII (London: Hogarth, 1953), 219–52.

14. Cain's ambivalence and passion call to mind the intense, almost violent feelings of the infant as characterized by Melanie Klein. See Juliet Mitchell, ed., *The Selected Melanie Klein* (London: Penguin, 1991).

5

"ALMOST AN ENGLISHWOMAN"

Jewish Women Refugee Writers in Britain

SUE VICE

In this essay I discuss some examples of the wide range of writing by Jewish women who fled Nazi Germany for Britain before the war. I focus here on both fictional and testimonial material by three such refugees, who came to Britain from Germany under varying auspices—Karen Gershon on a *Kindertransport* train in 1939,[1] Eva Figes on a private initiative of her parents in 1938, Judith Kerr under circumstances similar to Figes's in 1936. Their writings are significant not only for their historical or sociological dimension but also because they defamiliarize the usual form taken by women's autobiography. Like female *Bildungsromane* of a recognizable kind—for instance, Lorna Sage's memoir *Bad Blood* (2000), about family secrets and adolescent alienation—these works trace an ostensibly familiar pattern. But they are at the same time about unfamiliar matters. The secrets here are historical ones, and adolescent alienation is the lens through which exile and war are viewed. It is this clash between the familiar pattern of the lives of young girls growing up in Britain and their refugee status that is distinctive in all the texts I discuss. It produces an effect that is almost uncanny,[2] precisely by combining the well-known with the outlandish. In a further extension of the techniques of traditional auto-biography, several of the texts try to match form to content through the local means of narration or in broader generic experiments.

I have taken the title for this essay from Charles Hannam's *Almost an Englishman* (1979). Hannam's account resembles Karen Gershon's memoir,

A Lesser Child (1993), which I mention below, in being a nonfiction autobiographical narrative that is nonetheless written in the third person. As Hannam notes in his introduction about his refugee experience, "It was all so far removed from the person I am now that I could not use the personal pronoun and I began to write about myself as 'Karl' in the third person."[3] Hannam was born Karl Hartland in Essen in 1925 and came to Britain on a *Kindertransport* train in 1939. *Almost an Englishman* describes his life in Britain at school and in the army, and his efforts to reconcile "*all* aspects of my personality, the Jewish, the refugee and the English part."[4] The act of narrative itself does not effect this reconciliation so much as reveal the discrete elements that go to make up Hannam's British identity. I chose to quote—and modify—Hannam's title to highlight the difference between women's and men's experiences of such a problematic reconciliation, and of the refugee experience more generally.

Karl's shedding of his refugee status and his assimilation into British life, as Hannam describes it, is always a facet of his masculinity. For instance, in his quest for Englishness, Karl wishes to "go into the army and do a man's job." Karl takes his anglicized surname from "Hannam, the quiltmaker who had bequeathed his fortune to the Elmfield village school in the eighteenth century . . . a tribute to the school which had set Karl on the road to being a new man": that is, a British man.[5] In her novel *The Bread of Exile* (1985), Karen Gershon describes the "camouflage"[6] that the protagonist, Inge, adopts, in which femininity is an integral part of a national or even "racial" role: "a gym tunic and other clothes that translated her into an English schoolgirl."[7] By contrast Karl's camouflage is emphatically masculine, and calls upon more precise and public signifiers of class and integration: "He wanted to disguise himself with a perfect Oxford accent, a pipe and a commission in His Majesty's Forces, a lovely uniform and perhaps the spread wings of a pilot on his chest."[8] However, it is not only the performance or internalization of Englishness which is at stake in the writings by women I discuss in this essay but what turns out to be a more existential awareness of subjective division—represented at the very least by the presence in each text of an English-speaking adult narrator and a German child.

Karen Gershon: Versions of Autobiography

Karen Gershon was born Käthe Löwenthal in Bielefeld, Germany, in 1923, and in 1939 arrived in Britain with her older sister Lise on a *Kindertransport* train; the oldest sister, Anne, came separately. Gershon's parents were deported to the Riga ghetto and killed there. Gershon died in Britain in 1993.⁹ The genres of Gershon's autobiographical prose range widely in an effort to convey the costs of external and subjective exile.¹⁰ Her edited volume *We Came as Children: A Collective Autobiography* (1966) is an anthology of anonymous comments on the *Kindertransport* experience nearly thirty years on. In her prefatory comments Gershon includes herself in the anthology: "Nearly ten thousand of us came with the children's transports, most, like myself, through Youth Aliyah,"¹¹ although she does not make clear whether she has quoted herself elsewhere in the anthology as well as acting as its editor.¹² A second edited volume, *Postscript: A Collective Account of the Lives of Jews in West Germany Since the Second World War* (1969), follows the same format, although without Gershon's own implicit "autobiographical" presence.¹³

Gershon's novel *Burn Helen* (1980) is an experiment in indirection of a different kind. Although it is not ostensibly about the refugee experience, it is an unusual allegorical autobiography in which the protagonist, Helen, knows that she is dying of chronic poliomyelitis. Helen, like Gershon, is an orphan, although her parents died in the Blitz, and it is her daughter-in-law Kim whose father is a Jewish refugee from Berlin. Helen's plight offers a way of imagining the daily presence of death and loss in British life, but—in a pattern we will see in all these works—it transfers the historical to the personal and to bodily trauma. There are other, more incidental links between Helen and Gershon. For instance, Helen remembers that her mother used to say of her three daughters, "Susan's for talking to, Belinda's for doing things with and you are for cuddling,"¹⁴ a variant of which appears later in Gershon's memoir *A Lesser Child,* with the addition of Kate's characteristic "lesser" view of herself in relation to her sisters: "When the girls were in their teens, their mother took to saying that in Anne she had someone with whom to discuss her problems, that Lise was a comfort to her, and that Kate was for cuddling—a role which Kate thought belittling and did not want."¹⁵

Gershon's second novel, *The Bread of Exile: A Novel* (1985), is about the experiences of Inge, a young woman who arrives in Britain on a *Kindertransport* train, between 1938 and 1942. Gershon's memoir of her childhood in Germany, *A Lesser Child: An Autobiography* (1993) is written in the third person and was originally published in German. As Gershon put it in the foreword to *A Lesser Child,* "This is an autobiography, as truthful as I could make it; only, I was unable to write about myself in the first person. Kate was my childhood name."¹⁶ The sequel to *A Lesser Child,* the first-person *A Tempered Wind: An Autobiography,*¹⁷ was written in 1992 and published posthumously nearly twenty years later. It is, as the subtitle reveals, the most clearly autobiographical of Gershon's works. *A Tempered Wind* is written in the first person in English, with a close fit between the adult narrator and the teenaged character Kate, and concerns Gershon's life as a refugee in Britain up to the end of the war. *A Tempered Wind* accounts more clearly than any other of Gershon's autobiographical writings for the process of artistic development by which it came to be written. The last line describes the young Kate's decision not to complete a university degree since such a course of action "was irrelevant to what I wanted to do with this life which my parents and the British people had preserved for me: to begin another family—which I did, and to write—which I continue to do."[18]

In each of Gershon's texts, it is the relation between the narrative and focalizing subjects that changes radically, and each is an experiment in a specifically narrative kind of autobiography. By this I mean that explicit evidence of the "autobiographical contract"[19] between author and reader—which in Gershon's nonfiction work is reflected in the use of the term "autobiography," the presence of a foreword (in *We Came as Children*), or the reprinting of family photographs (in *A Lesser Child*)—is supplemented in her novels by a more formal device, that of the way in which the narrator represents the text's central character or voice.

In *The Bread of Exile,* it is only the author biography that overtly links the author, Karen Gershon, with the fictional character, Inge. The blurb states that "Karen Gershon *herself* came to England with a children's transport in 1938, hoping to move to what was then called Palestine. However, the war kept her *in this country*" (my italics). The words I have emphasized show, respectively, the distinction between the fictional Inge and the author Gershon—which nonetheless relies on their shared experience—and the novel's British readership. Indeed, it is tempting to see even this biographical note as an instance of Gershon's characteristic divided position, since it reads as if written from a third-person, British viewpoint when it was clearly composed by Gershon herself.[20] However, the narrator of *The Bread of Exile* is of a distinctive kind, hinting within the novel itself at a relation between herself and the character Inge. It is this as much as information about the author that makes the novel appear autobiographical. However, it does not make it any less fictive. For instance, Inge is accompanied on her journey to Britain by her brother Adolf, known as Dolph, rather than by the sister who traveled with Gershon. Dolph's role is partly to be the object of Inge's hero worship, equivalent to that which Kate lavishes on the older Anne in *A Lesser Child;* but he is also a symbolic presence as Inge's "alter ego" (74), a free, active, masculine figure, yet one who does not master English—or Englishness—as his sister does. His age corresponds to Gershon's own, as he is fifteen in 1938, while Inge is only thirteen, again as if they were the two parts of a single subject.

These two characters point to a difference between masculine and feminine shapes of assimilation, a notion that Gillian Lathey discusses in her survey of wartime children's writing, *The Impossible Legacy.* Lathey uses the examples of Karl in Charles Hannam's memoirs and Anna's brother Max in Judith Kerr's novels to argue that young men are more likely than women to "deny" their origins through abandoning the German language and enthusiastically entering British public and institutional life in ways often not open to women.[21] However, the respective features are not always consistent, and Gershon's fictional Dolph does not conform to this pattern. Indeed it is precisely the English language that represents Britishness for the young women exiles I discuss here. Gershon, like Eva Figes and Judith Kerr, produces an "English" subject in the very act of writing. The texts' *énonciation* (their utterance in the present by a first-person narrator) is in English, although the *énoncé* (what is represented) is German. Englishness thus supersedes Germanness, even when German words are directly quoted, as specimens to be instantly translated.

Throughout Gershon's *The Bread of Exile,* the narrator knows more than Inge. She is party to the mental habits of different national groups, knows what people other than Inge are thinking, and understands how personal and historical events will turn out. She has a retrospective, omniscient view, and is as much identified with the British context of Inge's new life as with her refugee notions and misunderstandings. The elements of this construction both suggest and deny a connection between narrator and character. The narrator's viewpoint is not limited to Inge's perspective during the war, but her knowledge is such that it seems the narrator must be the older Inge, although this is never stated. Instead this link is figured by the kind of literary self-consciousness common in autobiographical fiction. The trope of writing, or even wishing to be a writer, as a device implicitly accounting for the text's existence appears in many autobiographically styled novels, whether or not these are based on the author's own life.[22] For instance, Judith Kerr's novels about (her own) experiences as an exile from Nazi Germany, *When Hitler Stole Pink Rabbit* (1971) and *A Small Person Far Away* (1978), focus respectively on the protagonist Anna's childhood wish to become "famous," like her writer father, and on the beginning of her career as an author. In *A Small Person,* the time of writing the text is forecast as Anna reflects on being a refugee: "I could write about it all, she thought. But the thought was so cold-blooded that she shocked herself and tried to pretend that she had not had it."[23]

In *The Bread of Exile,* such self-consciousness takes a form related specifically to Inge's refugee status and her interest in English—not just because she is destined to be a writer, as in the more usual kind of *Künstlerroman,* but because her first language is German. This is clear in an instance where Rudi, another *Kindertransport* refugee, replies to Inge's letter expressing unhappiness at using the English name "Jill" in place of her own: "He wrote that she was making a mountain out of a molehill (another item for her collection)" (67).[24] The once-foreign phrase is blended seamlessly within the narrator's free indirect discourse. Free indirect discourse in itself enacts a close relationship between narrator and character, and here this is extended as the narrator both uses and comments on Rudi's phrase, and thus on Inge, her younger self.

However, the link between narrator and character in *The Bread of Exile* is clearest when narration does not rely on a temporal disjunction between past and present linguistic knowledge but takes place in present time. Rudi is arrested for acting suspiciously, and Inge learns that her letters have been read by the police: "It was not until afterwards that she felt gratified that he should have kept her letters, and wondered if they could possibly mean as much to him as his meant to her—she being only Inge—and tried to remember what she had said in them that had been read by strangers—*wildfremde:* there is no equivalent word for it in English, perhaps the English never feel wildly estranged" (68). There is a shift here from free indirect discourse in the past tense, to a collapse of past and present: "there *is* no equivalent word for it in English." In this instance narrator and character overlap. It is hard to tell which one is responsible for the last comment, "perhaps the English never feel wildly estranged": it could be either, or both, the newly arrived Inge, still bemused by British habits, or the adult narrator at the moment of writing, reflecting on her knowledge of alien mores after forty years. Either way, the need to translate the word into an English equivalent acts as a way of distancing Germanness, despite—or because of—the claim that there is no such English sentiment.

The autobiographical hinge between Inge and the narrator seems incontrovertible in a final instance, where it is unambiguously the moment of writing that unites them. Inge's brother cannot be known in Britain by his full name, Adolf, for obvious reasons, and she amends it still further: "This was when she got into the habit of spelling his name with a ph so that *even now to write Dolf,* as it once was, *looks wrong*" (163; my italics). It is made clear here, although not stated, that it is Inge at a time in the future, "now," who is writing the text in which she appears, and at this moment assesses what she has written: it "looks wrong." Inge's memoir, written by her adult self about her first years in Britain, is Gershon's fiction on the same subject. It is clear that only fiction and not memoir will do for someone who is riven by a gulf between past and present consisting of altered nation and language as well as the losses of the Holocaust. By contrast, *A Tempered Wind,* as a nonfiction memoir narrated in the first person, suggests continuity and self-presence. This is the case even though it describes the refugee Kate's subjectivity in terms very similar to those used by Inge: Kate too is convinced of her own inferiority and beset by an incomprehension that the adult narrator high-lights and corrects. Fiction, in its construction of character versus narrator, preserves the distance between refugee child and writing adult, the young Inge who collects everyday phrases and the adult who uses fluent English.

Eva Figes: Children's Perspectives

Eva Figes was born Eva Unger in Berlin in 1932, and came to Britain with her parents and brother in 1939. She died in 2012. She published thirteen novels and several nonfiction works, but here I will focus on her two memoirs, *Little Eden: A Child at War* (1978) and *Tales of Innocence and Experience: An Explo-ration* (2003). The memoirs make an unexpectedly stark comparison, since although they deal with largely similar material—the young Eva's experiences as a wartime evacuee in Cirencester in *Little Eden,* the older Eva's memories of herself as a young girl in *Tales*—their means of representing the war are very different. While Figes goes back to the "sanctuary of the past"[25] of Gloucester-shire in *Little Eden,* the return to her German childhood in *Tales of Innocence* is much bleaker.

The title of *Little Eden* conveys the surprising notion that, for the aptly named Eva, life in wartime Cirencester was a miniature paradise from which, at the memoir's end, she undergoes "the inevitable expulsion" when her fam-ily leaves for London against her wishes: "But the gates of my happy child-hood had clanged shut behind me; I had become adult enough to recognise the need to conceal unbearable emotions for the sake of others" (140). How-ever, this moment registers not simply the inevitable loss of childhood plea-sure and surety, but a historically inflected loss. Eva has already experienced emotions that the older Eva describes here as "unbearable"—she has a recur-ring dream about leaving her grandparents behind in Berlin, and feels herself tainted by the "secret disease" of Jewishness (74)—so that her attachment to life at Cirencester and to an eccentric boarding school seems in its extreme nature to be in response to this. As Figes (as I shall call the adult narrator) puts it, Eva (the child) was to "acquire the passion of a convert offered a land of myth, legend and moral certainties where there had been only nothingness before" (79). Although Figes claims that the fifteen months in Cirencester were a "respite" from the "private war" Eva underwent in Britain, this "passion" appears throughout the memoir in the form of Figes's interest in the history of Cirencester, which often masks only imperfectly her anxiety about the devastation and murder occurring in Nazi Europe. The instances in which Figes details local history represent her adult voice alone, not the child Eva's, and benefit from her later research into such sources as "reports of the meetings of the Cirencester Rural District Council in 1940 and 1941" (34), and even earlier material about the English Civil War.

It is as if the adult's researches have given form, however obliquely, to the child's more nebulous fears. Such instances take the form of irruptions and reminders of death. One concerns the nineteenth-century restoration of Cirencester church, of which Figes observes that "the floor [was] covered with rather dull red tiles after it had been surfaced with six inches of concrete to seal in the stench of old corpses" (46). Another effort to talk about the British past sounds as if it is about a different kind of subject altogether. Figes's observation, "When it comes to pain, human superstition does not change very much," turns out to be a comment on remedies advertised in nineteenth-century newspapers—"That was in 1841. In 1941 . . ." (104)—but serves only to remind the reader of the lack of progress marked by the century's passage and the particular kind of "pain" and "superstition" extant in mainland Europe in 1941.

Even when it is not obliquely about Eva's own experiences, the historical material in *Little Eden* performs a disavowing function,[26] protecting Figes from considering the "harsh reality" (14) of contemporary events in Europe. This is partly because of Figes's relish for the "Strange, almost bizarre, but true" (56) nature of some British reactions to the war. Figes records a journalist's argument in the *Wiltshire and Gloucestershire Standard* that fox-hunting was an integral part of the war effort (57); and quotes a letter to the local paper from a scion of Cirencester county life, "Mrs D," who had refused to billet soldiers in her huge house, in which she insisted, "During the last war my housekeeper, Mrs. Pearson, taught the Cirencester W.I. to make jam . . . I hope [my housekeeper's] method of sealing jam has not been forgotten, but in case it has I will describe it again" (41).

In general, Figes values but also maintains an observer's distance from the notion that "England's superiority was at all times felt to be more than merely moral. It had something to do with character, a sense of humour, and the capacity to produce and imbibe cups of tea in a crisis" (65). This analysis is clearly that of the adult narrator, but the child Eva's comic misperceptions similarly register a combination of the absurd with the serious. In one episode, Eva, her mother, and her six-year-old brother go to visit Eva's father, now serving in the British army, and the little boy "yelled at the top of his voice, 'Daddy! How many Germans have you killed?'" Figes notes, "I had sensed that his remark was inappropriate, though I was not sure why. Possibly there were no Germans in Gloucestershire who had to be killed" (21). This moment condenses Eva's residual sense of herself as German—earlier she noted of her father's enlisting in the British army that it was "far from clear to me why we had changed sides" (20)—with anxiety about death, since although she herself is a "German in Gloucestershire,"[27] she need not fear "having to be killed." By contrast, the terrible juxtaposition of death and domesticity in Nazi Germany, where, for instance, nursery life is deployed to shield children from such events as *Kristallnacht* in November 1938, is quite without any kind of humor: "My nursemaid, who later died of cholera in a concentration camp, organised a sing-song in a back room away from the street while the smashing and looting, the beating and killing, went on four floors below at street level" (14).

In *Tales of Innocence and Experience*, the "sharp, hilarious"[28] tone Figes adopted in *Little Eden* is replaced by something rather different, and the humor at the expense of a child's view becomes instead an overvaluation of childhood itself. Its principal technique is an extension and reversal of the disavowing interest in local history that we saw in *Little Eden*. In *Tales*, the narrator is a grandmother (Figes)[29] for whom all kinds of experiences are filled with reminders of historical atrocity, in particular the fairy stories of her German childhood: "Evil has come out of the story books and is now history" (25). But, while arguing for the sudden historical resonance of the fairy-tale tropes of wolves, witches, forests, and endangered children, Figes in *Tales* makes a bid to evade historical time altogether. She does this partly by focusing on generational time, seeing herself alternately in the figure of her granddaughter or her grandmother in herself; and by implying that the "horror" (74) implicit in the fate of characters in fairy tales, and the roles of victim, bystander, and perpetrator during the Holocaust years, have comparable roots.

Figes emphasizes the ahistorical nature of early childhood and its "timeless hour" (25) with the envy of one whose early years were cut across by a different kind of temporality. Figes's childhood seems to her as unreal as a fairy tale: "Once upon a time I was a child who lived happily from moment to moment, hour to hour" (53). Now "the gift of timelessness" (120) can be restored to her only by her granddaughter, who is not "a child of war" but one of peace (143), and for whom "[t]he moment is everything" (119). This desire for "timelessness," although understandable in a former refugee, smacks of an impossible retreat from reality, and a conflation of developmental with historical innocence. For instance, Figes's observation of her granddaughter's perception of the world as "fresh every morning," including objects seen "as if for the first time" (119)—a necessarily ahistorical view—allows the grandmother to recapture her childhood and to "enter [the bubble of] my lost world, forgetting how it burst" (120). Figes refers ostensibly to the "bursting" caused by exile and the losses of the Holocaust, but also to the inevitable "ontological absence," in Dominick LaCapra's phrase, of "the passage from nature to culture . . . the entry into language": in other words, the loss of infancy. LaCapra urges vigilance in relation to such slippage between historical and what he calls "structural or existential" trauma. He argues that in such cases "one moves too quickly and without sufficient mediation from a historical loss or lack to a traumatizing hole in being or a constitutive absence."[30] In *Tales* Figes often makes the two realms indistinguishable, as she continues: "The long journey behind me, I find myself back where I started, a homesick child" (120). Although Figes also refers to herself as a historically "traumatized" child (121), here the phrases do double duty. The "long journey" is both that of exile and of life itself, while "homesickness" is felt both for a lost country and for early childhood.[31]

Eventually Figes does acknowledge that the two kinds of trauma, historical and existential, are separate, but she makes the former synecdochic of the latter. The Holocaust is invoked as an extreme version of an inevitable fall, "a violent expulsion from childhood, sudden and premature, which leaves an indelible mark" (159). Returning to the trope of Eden from her earlier memoir, Figes describes this "expulsion": "I imagine Eve, fully formed but still a child at heart, dreaming of Eden after the expulsion, gradually adapting to the harsh wilderness years, but forever homesick for the earthly Paradise she had lost . . . I know how she felt. My childhood ended suddenly with an exodus, abrupt, inexplicable" (159–60). Figes clearly likens both the end of childhood and the acquisition of adult knowledge to the biblical Fall. However, the location of Eden is unstable in Figes's accounts. In *Little Eden* it is a short period of life in Britain as a refugee and an evacuee, while in *Tales of Innocence* it is situated earlier, in the Germany before the "exodus" of the winter of 1938. The precise moment and nature of the fall, and entry into the "wilderness," changes too. Figes describes at least three different instances, which range in time and between exile and knowledge of genocide, and include not receiving an answer to her question about a window display of brown uniforms in Berlin (*Tales*, 160–61); leaving Berlin and her grandparents (*Little Eden*, 15–16; *Tales*, 111); and seeing a newsreel about the liberation of Belsen at the age of thirteen (*Little Eden*, 131, *Tales*, 122). But, despite these crossovers, the two memoirs tell different stories. *Little Eden* does separate historical from existential trauma, albeit camouflaging instances of the former, while *Tales*, written from a later vantage point on the same history, "generalize[s] structural trauma so that it absorbs historical trauma."[32]

Parallel to the conflation of childhood with historical innocence and experience in *Tales* is a constant interchange between fairy tale and history. There are two starting points for the equivalence that Figes draws. The first is the notion of the forest that surrounded her childhood home. This exists on two levels, as a physical aspect of the past—on a return journey to Germany, Figes finds that the forest has become a park (150)—and as part of a symbolic fairy-tale landscape, peopled with little girls in red hoods, woodcutters, and wolves. As Figes puts it, in reply to her granddaughter's question about where the forest is, "The forest, I think but do not say, represents darkness, that which cannot be civilized . . . its shadow will always lurk on the edge of human consciousness" (56). The other starting point is the fact of Figes's own wartime escape and survival, which is as "grim but redemptive" as a fairy tale. In the middle of retelling the moment from "Snow White" when the huntsman does not kill the little girl but leaves her in the forest to perish, Figes reveals the overlap of that story and her own: "It's a wonder that the child survived, an accident really" (37). The huntsman too partakes of this overlap, and is described, in an echo of the historian Christopher Browning's phrase, as "just an ordinary man."[33]

"Snow White" is the first in a series of well-known fairy tales, ranging from "The Sleeping Beauty" to "Hansel and Gretel," that are retold by Figes to bring out their relevance to her own story and to aspects of the Holocaust. This method reaches its apotheosis in Figes's imbrication of the story of "The

Wolf and the Seven Kids" with the story of her paternal grandmother. First, Figes reads out to her granddaughter the story, in which a wolf eats all of the old goat's children except for one kid who hid in a clock case. But all the kids are retrieved from the wolf's stomach, and he is thrown into a well, inspiring Figes to add, "The well, I think but do not say, has been poisoned ever since" (65). The next chapter moves without transition to Figes's speculations about her grandmother, who survived in hiding in Germany, then managed to flee to Sweden in 1944, but died a few months later. Its opening sentence is *in media res*: "Where did she hide, all those years?" (66). Figes tells her grandmother's story in words that again have a double resonance: "I try to see her . . . growing thin enough on meagre handouts of food to fit into a narrow space no larger than the clock-case which had stood for decades in one of the old-fashioned rooms . . . even as the wolf was baying at the door . . . after her son had been swallowed up into the night and spewed out weeks later" (66). The "clock-case," as an image derived from the fairy tale, is a way of imagining both Figes's grandmother's prewar life—the weight of which prevented her leaving Germany—and her years in hiding; while the imprisonment of Figes's father in Dachau is retold in the fairy tale's terms of introjection and rescue.[34]

The reader might ask what the bald facts of Figes's grandmother's and father's experiences gain by being redescribed in such a metaphorical way. This episode in *Tales* seems to be an instance of "moving too quickly and without sufficient mediation," to repeat LaCapra's phrase, between general and specific trauma. Indeed, it is the episodes in *Tales* where this movement takes place between history and fairy tale, rather than between history and life patterns, that are more effective. It is clear that the fairy tale reminds Figes of the Holocaust, not the other way round. We also read about the grandmother's fate in *Little Eden*. Here the story is told in a different way, from the perspective of twelve-year-old Eva. When the family learned of the grandmother's survival in 1944, Eva "looked forward to having a grandmother of my very own" (132). This was despite Eva's prewar perception of her grandmother's "apparent immunity to the charms of small children": "She was capable of ignoring me altogether while she ate pineapple and a boiled egg for breakfast, and I fidgeted in a chair opposite her, licking salt" (132). Eva even felt responsible for her grandmother's death, having informed her in a letter that she wished to be an actress: "I felt guiltily convinced that the shock of having a granddaughter on the stage had been too much for her" (133). This account in *Little Eden*, although focusing on apparently irrelevant details, is "historical," whereas that in *Tales* is literary—because family relationships, war, and death are represented from a child's perspective, one that may be narcissistic but that is also sharp-eyed and evaluative. In *Tales* such matters are represented from an adult's viewpoint, which generalizes and distances. This change is a generic one, from historically based memoir to cultural "meditation."[35]

Although it generalizes historical trauma, *Tales* is interesting as a memoir for just that reason. While Karen Gershon's fiction is autobiographical, Eva Figes's autobiographies are generically hybrid, and *Tales* in particular resembles other works that attempt to represent the Holocaust as one part of a metaphor. Like Georges Perec's part-autobiographical novel *W or the Memory of Childhood* (1975) and Anne Michaels's novel *Fugitive Pieces* (1996), *Tales* is structured in alternating chapters about the past and the present, linked by associative textual patterns. Figes's reliance on the biblical story of Eden has something in common with Dan Pagis's well-known poem "Written in Pencil in the Sealed Freightcar" (1976), purporting to be a note scribbled by Eve as she and her sons are deported. Both represent the violence done by history to biblical and other myths, if not to literature itself.

Judith Kerr: Learning to Write

Judith Kerr was born in Berlin in 1923. She left Germany with her parents and brother in 1933, and arrived in Britain, via Switzerland and France, in 1936. Although Kerr's autobiographical novels constitute a trilogy, and have been republished in one volume,[36] the means of narration and implied readership is different in each. However, the kind of displacement of historical events onto subjective experience that we have seen in Gershon's and Figes's writing is present in all three of Kerr's works.

It is partly true that the changes of implied readership in Kerr's novels follow the age of the protagonist Anna, who, like Kerr, was born in 1923. *When Hitler Stole Pink Rabbit* is about the years 1933 to 1935, which Anna's family spent in Switzerland and then France. Anna's childlike perspective is matched by a clearly adult and sometimes didactic narrator who steps away from the past to point out, in the present, such facts as "the children had cassis, which is blackcurrant juice," and "The main celebration in France is not at Christmas but on New Year's Eve."[37] The sequel, *The Other Way Round* (1975), concerns 1940 to 1945. It is set in Britain, where Anna, who is in her early twenties by the book's end, is able to speak fluent English without an accent. Here the narrator overtly refrains from providing the kind of information she did in *When Hitler Stole Pink Rabbit*. In some instances this constructs or relies on a reader with enough historical knowledge to understand Anna's mistakes—for example, about the kind of work her physicist cousin, Otto, has been commissioned to undertake in the United States: "Atoms, thought Anna—what a pity. It did not sound as though Otto's research would be very important" (126). Here the gap between Anna and the narrator is less explicit—"It did not sound" is Anna's perception, not a narratorial overview—but the reader's knowledge of the future may identify Otto's work as connected with the Manhattan Project and the development of the atomic bomb, making Anna's error both funny and ominous. The second volume in Kerr's trilogy, *The Other Way Round*, could be described as a "crossover" text suitable for both a child and an adult readership.[38] Even its title, referring to the reversal of roles by which Anna and her brother help their parents feel less like refugees, "the other way round" from the pattern in the past (219), suggests a transitional state.[39]

The third volume in the trilogy, *A Small Person Far Away*, is, as Gillian Lathey points out, described on the jacket of the first edition as Kerr's "first novel for adults,"[40] although not on subsequent reprints. *A Small Person* is set in 1956, at the time of the Hungarian uprising, and Anna, "nowadays" a "well-heeled young Englishwoman" (5), travels from London to Berlin to visit her mother. Whereas *When Hitler Stole Pink Rabbit* moved away from the child protagonist to clarify matters over her head, character and narrator are barely distinguishable in *A Small Person*. This is accomplished through a mixture of direct discourse and free indirect discourse, as in a scene when Anna returns, with her mother's companion Konrad, to a restaurant where she used to have drinks as a child:

> [Konrad] smiled. "*Himbeersaft.*"

> "That's right." Raspberry juice, of course. That's what German children always drank. (47)

Here it is Anna, rather than the narrator, who effects the necessary translation into English more elegantly than in the "cassis" instance cited earlier—in a way similar to the adult Inge's translation of "*wildfremde*" in Gershon's *The Bread of Exile*, combining a sensory with a linguistic childhood memory.

 In all three of Kerr's novels, the war and the experience of exile are related "the other way round": that is, from the self-absorbed perspective of the protagonist, Anna. The features of her viewpoint take different forms in each volume. Childlike incomprehension in *When Hitler Stole Pink Rabbit* is replaced by the deliberate detachment of adolescence in *The Other Way Round*, and a fear of the return of the past in *A Small Person Far Away*. Lathey argues that the eponymous stuffed toy of the first volume "symbolizes the aspects of Anna's childhood stolen by Hitler and his regime,"[41] and I would add that the pink rabbit is, as well as this, representative of the only way in which nine-year-old Anna can comprehend the war: as locally and individually related to herself. The same is true of a games compendium the children had to leave behind in Berlin, of which Anna's brother, Max, "gloomily" remarks, "I expect Hitler plays with it now" (196). This notion, although comic, represents and enacts a view of the war from an oblique position: that of a child, and of a refugee who "evaded" the Holocaust. In both roles Anna and her brother are on the periphery of wartime events.

In *The Other Way Round*, the narrator draws ironic attention to Anna's habit of blocking out thoughts of Germany and the war, both deliberately ("the more she thought about her shorthand the less time she would have to think about anything else" [48]) and automatically (when Anna begins a romance with her art tutor, the narrator notes, "Even the war was going better at last" [68]). Finally, in *A Small Person Far Away*, Anna's preoccupation with her lost German self elides the war altogether. Like Eva Figes's explicit comparison of developmental with historical innocence and experience, Germanness in Kerr's novel stands for an irretrievable infancy. Anna remembers asking her mother what happened to people when they died, "long ago when she was still a German child" (86). When she returns to Britain from Germany, Anna visualizes "the small person who had once been herself . . . running up some steps, shouting, '*Ist Mami da?*'" (216), thus showing the inextricability of childhood from the German language. Yet the abrupt end of childhood, and the reversal of family relationships so that parents have to rely on their children, is not identified here with the war. So strong is Anna's association of Germanness with infancy itself that she says doubtfully to her husband about the birth of their first child, "I suppose it won't speak any German" (230).

Conclusion

The most striking similarity in all these examples of writing by Jewish women who arrived in Britain before the war is the use of textual and narrative techniques to convey exile and loss, as much as their appearance in the text as objects of direct representation. It is this rather than any commonality of cultural or religious identity that unites these works. Although Alan Berger argues that the experience of "never quite belonging" in refugee writings "encapsulat[es] the traditional diaspora experience,"[42] it seems rather that Jewishness itself neither fully precedes nor survives the "translation" of these children from

Nazi Germany to Britain. Indeed, in *Tales of Innocence and Experience*, Eva Figes laments the absence of a Jewish upbringing that might have enabled her to understand her experience: "Children whose parents had not abandoned Judaism might have some inkling, not only of what was happening, but why. I was six years old, still waiting for Father Christmas. I had no notion why he failed to arrive during the winter of 1938" (162). Instead, the internal division in these three writers' varying protagonists and earlier selves is between Germanness and Britishness, often devolving into being recognized in terms of a generalized otherness, as Anna discovers in *The Other Way Round*:

> Anna took a deep breath. "I'm not English," she said.
>
> "Ha! Irish!" cried Mrs Hammond and added reproachfully, "You've got green eyes." (98)

Such divisions, between how a refugee subject thinks of herself and how she is seen, can be turned to positive narrative effect, as Anna's increasing ability both to experience and to watch events in *The Other Way Round* suggests. On a difficult occasion, Anna's detachment becomes personified—"extraordinary! noted the little man in her forehead" (215)—as if there were a new narratorial category, not just an unreliable or intradiegetic but also a refugee narrator.

Most of the texts I have discussed here were published in the 1970s and 1980s, as part of what might be called a first wave of exile writing by those who were children on their arrival in Britain before World War II. Gershon's anthologies and novels, Figes's *Little Eden,* and Kerr's novels form part of this group of writings, which is particularly characterized by *Kindertransport* memoirs.[43] Two of the writers on whom I have focused revisited the past and published autobiographical work in later life. Of these, Gershon's 1993 *A Lesser Child* is a belated memoir, and as such still belongs to the earlier group of exile writings. Eva Figes's 2003 *Tales of Innocence and Experience* is, however, of a different genre. It is both temporally and philosophically distinct from memoirs, whether factual or fictionalized, as an "exploration," as the subtitle has it, of the notion of childhood and exile more generally. Rather than viewing events with the local detail of a child's eye, as she did in *Little Eden,* Figes attempts to trace links between features specific to the Holocaust years—such as "ordinary men" who are nonetheless executioners, living in hiding, betrayal, terrible compromises, trauma undergone by parents—and features common to other cultural narratives, including fairy tales. This enterprise marks a shift from memoir to *post-memoir,* to adapt Marianne Hirsch's term "post-memory,"[44] in which the very processes of memory and looking back at the foreignness of childhood are questioned.

Notes

1. The World Movement for the Care of Children from Germany (known as the *Kindertransport*—literally, "children's transport" movement) brought around 7,400 unaccompanied Jewish children on commissioned trains from occupied Europe to Britain from 1938 to 1940.
2. See Victoria Stewart, "Anne Frank and the Uncanny," *Paragraph* 24 (2001), 99–113.
3. Charles Hannam, *Almost an Englishman* (London: André Deutsch, 1979), 9. See also his earlier memoir, *A Boy in Your Situation* (London: André Deutsch, 1977).
4. Ibid., 12; italics in original.
5. Ibid., 123, 151.
6. The term is Eva Figes's, from *Tales of Innocence and Experience: An Exploration* (London: Bloomsbury, 2003), 129. All further page references appear in the text.
7. Karen Gershon, *The Bread of Exile: A Novel* (London: Victor Gollancz, 1985), 43. All further page references appear in the text.
8. Hannam, *Almost an Englishman,* 33.
9. "Gershon," the author's nom de plume, is the Hebrew name of Paul Löwenthal, Gershon's father, and means "stranger in a strange land." Gershon's married name was Karen Tripp (Peter Lawson, "Karen Gershon," in *Holocaust Literature: An Encyclopedia of Writers and Their Work,* ed. S. Lillian Kremer [London: Routledge, 2003], 416).
10. Gershon is also well known as a poet: see Lawson, "Karen Gershon."
11. Karen Gershon, ed., *We Came as Children: A Collective Autobiography* (New York: Harcourt Brace and World, 1966), 9.
12. It is tempting to read certain entries as Gershon's own when they fit her biography, for instance the following, which fits the detail of her journey with her sister Lise: "My sister [Lise] and I travelled together: I was fifteen and she was sixteen. . . . Because my name comes before hers alphabetically, my number was lower and I was always called first . . . this made me realise that people were not concerned with who we were, our rescue was quite impersonal" (Gershon, ed., *We Came as Children,* 38).
13. In my *Children Writing the Holocaust* (London: Palgrave, 2004), I argue that such "choral narration," or collective autobiography, is a distinctive way of representing textually the collective fate of Jewish children during the Holocaust years. Other examples include Henryk Grynberg's nonfiction anthology *Children of Zion* (1969) (trans. Jacqueline Mitchell [Evanston, IL: Northwestern University Press, 1993]), and Clara Asscher-Pinkhof's short stories *Star Children* (1946) (trans. Terese Edelstein and Inez Smith [Detroit: Wayne State University Press, 1986]). See also Phyllis Lassner, *Anglo-Jewish Women Writing the Holocaust: Displaced Witnesses* (Basingstoke: Palgrave, 2008), 48–74.
14. Karen Gershon, *Burn Helen: A Novel* (Brighton: Harvester, 1980), 90.
15. Karen Gershon, *A Lesser Child: An Autobiography* (London: Peter Owen, 1993), 20.
16. Ibid., ix.
17. Karen Gershon, *A Tempered Wind: An Autobiography* (Evanston, IL: Northwestern University Press, 2010).
18. Ibid., 214.

19. This is Philippe Lejeune's phrase, from his "The Autobiographical Contract," in *French Literary Theory Today: A Reader,* ed. Tzvetan Todorov, trans. R. Carter (Cambridge: Cambridge University Press, 1982), 202. Lejeune argues that based on "internal analysis" alone, autobiography is indistinguishable from autobiographical fiction. However, the identity among author, narrator, and protagonist recorded on the title page of a text changes this and transforms the reader's expectation into one appropriate to nonfiction autobiography.

20. Gershon uses similar phrasing in the foreword to her *Collected Poems,* this time in the first person: "When I came to England, at the age of fifteen . . . I was on my way to what was then called Palestine" (London: Papermac, 1990), 1.

21. Gillian Lathey, *The Impossible Legacy: Identity and Purpose in Children's Literature Set in the Third Reich and the Second World War* (Bern: Peter Lang, 1999), 134.

22. See, for instance, Jenefer Shute's *Lifesize* (London: Jonathan Cape, 1992), a *Bildungsroman* that represents the protagonist writing a diary but is not based on the author's biography; and Sylvia Plath's *The Bell Jar* (London: Faber, 1963), a *Künstlerroman* that is.

23. Judith Kerr, *A Small Person Far Away* (1978; repr. London: Collins, 1995), 123. All further page references appear in the text.

24. Other "items" in Inge's collection include such phrases as "having green thumbs," "toffee-nosed," and "with a flea in his ear," each relying on the narrator's and reader's superior understanding of idiomatic English.

25. Eva Figes, *Little Eden: A Child at War* (New York: Persea Books, 1978), 9. All further page references appear in the text.

26. Eric Santner describes disavowing trauma through irrelevant or inconsequential detail as "narrative fetishism," in "History Beyond the Pleasure Principle: Some Thoughts on the Representation of Trauma," in *Probing the Limits of Representation,* ed. Saul Friedlander (Cambridge, MA: Harvard University Press, 1992), 144.

27. The same jarring effect occurs in Judith Kerr's novel *The Other Way Round,* in which, after the fall of France, a French woman demands of the German-born protagonist, Anna, "How would you like to have the Germans here, in England?"—overlooking the fact that some "Germans," as distinct from Nazis, were there already (London: Collins, 1977), 39. All further page references appear in the text.

28. Lore Segal, *New York Times Book Review,* quoted on the back cover of *Little Eden.*

29. Although I call this narrator "Figes," there is not a complete overlap between the narratorial construct and the author. The book's "Note on the author" demonstrates this in observing that "[Figes] is a grandmother *herself*" (185; my italics), as if there were only a coincidental similarity between author and text. It echoes the phrase "Karen Gershon *herself* came to England" that emphasized the link *and* the distance between the author Gershon and the fictional character Inge in *The Bread of Exile.*

30. Dominick LaCapra, *History and Memory after Auschwitz* (Ithaca, NY: Cornell University Press, 1998), 46–48. Interestingly, Figes focuses on the loss of historical innocence rather than on any kind of Oedipal or adult sexuality in *Tales:* Eve is without Adam, Snow White and Little Red Riding Hood are figures who undergo their fates alone, Gretel is contrasted to Hansel, and Figes's own granddaughter is described only in her relations with women.

31. The generalized meaning of "homesickness" is made even clearer in this later remark in *Tales:* "Those who live to grow old eventually die of homesickness" (171).

32. LaCapra, *History and Memory after Auschwitz*, 47.

33. Christopher Browning, *Ordinary Men: Reserve Police Battalion 101 and the Final Solution in Poland* (New York: HarperCollins, 1992). Like Browning's subjects, the huntsman in Figes's account "had a family of his own, whom he loved and petted at the end of a hard day's work" (*Tales*, 36).

34. See also Freud's analysis of this fairy tale in these terms in his "Wolf Man" case history, in *The Standard Edition of the Complete Psychological Works of Sigmund Freud*, ed. and trans. James Strachey, vol. XVII (London: Hogarth, 1953).

35. The term is Rebecca Abrams's, from her review of *Tales* in the *Sunday Times*, quoted in www.thesundaytimes.co.uk/sto/culture/books/article44168.ece (accessed January 25, 2014).

36. Judith Kerr, *Out of the Hitler Time* (London: Collins, 2002).

37. Judith Kerr, *When Hitler Stole Pink Rabbit* (1971; repr. London: Collins, 1974), 206, 221. All further page references appear in the text.

38. See Sandra Beckett, ed., *Transcending Boundaries: Writing for a Dual Audience of Children and Adults* (New York: Garland, 1999).

39. This volume has been republished as *Bombs on Aunt Dainty* (London: Collins, 2002).

40. Gillian Lathey, "A Child's View of Exile: Language and Identity in the Autobiographical Writings of Judith Kerr and Charles Hannam," in *Keine Klage über England? Deutsche and österreichische Exilerfahrungen in Großbritannien, 1933–1945*, ed. Charmian Brinson, et al. (Munich: Iudicium, 1998), 191.

41. Lathey, "A Child's View," 145.

42. Alan L. Berger, "Jewish Identity and Jewish Destiny, the Holocaust in Refugee Writing: Lore Segal and Karen Gershon," *Studies in American Jewish Literature* 11 (1992), 84.

43. See, for instance, Lore Segal, *Other People's Houses: A Refugee in England, 1938–48* (1965; repr. London: Bodley Head, 1974); Martha Blend, *A Child Alone* (London: Vallentine Mitchell, 1995); and Hannele Zürndorfer, *The Ninth of November* (London: Quartet, 1983).

44. See Marianne Hirsch, "Projected Memory: Holocaust Photographs in Personal and Public Fantasy," in *Acts of Memory: Cultural Recall in the Present*, ed. Mieke Bal et al. (Hanover, NH: University Press of New England, 1999).

6
FORGOTTEN WORDS

Trauma, Memory, and *Her*story in Eva Figes's Fiction

CHERYL VERDON

Eva Figes (1932–2012) belongs to the "1.5 generation."[1] Old enough to have experienced the Holocaust but not to have an adult understanding of it, Figes believed that all the shopkeepers were sweeping up glass to put in new windows on the morning after *Kristallnacht.*[2] She would not realize until much later—in common not only with other 1.5 generation writers but also with many second-generation writers—that imagination can be used to fill "the holes of absence."[3] Those holes irrevocably opened up again when Figes's mother sent her, at the age of thirteen, to a British cinema with the words: "Go and see for yourself."[4] What she saw were the first images from Belsen concentration camp. The term "child survivor" has, in the past, been applied strictly to those who were in the camps. It is now used to include those who went into hiding or fled, just as Figes, at the age of six, escaped with her parents and brother to England.

Speaking on literary innovation and childhood trauma, Susan Rubin Suleiman explores the link between writing that breaks traditions and a writer whose existence "starts out with a fracture." Suleiman cites the gaps in Georges Perec's *W or the Memory of Childhood* (1975) and his remarkable novel *The Disappearance* (1969), in which, writing without a single word containing the letter "e" (a quite considerable feat in French), Perec performs an act of language cleansing that risks appearing frivolous yet cannot help but evoke the racial and ethnic cleansing that formed the basis of the Final Solution and from which he escaped.[5] Comparable to Caliban's turning the master's language upon itself, Perec reappropriates erasure to empower his writing and to create a visual reminder of "the holes of absence" that, according to the French Holocaust survivor, scholar, and writer Raymond Federman, can only be compensated for through acts of the imagination.[6] Like Perec's linguistic purging, Federman's repetitious patter in *Double or Nothing* (1971), where he writes about his family, is a system of distancing that becomes more complex the closer he gets to the autobiographical. His seeming glibness is a foil for the longing to compensate with words for the absence of family members.

In common with the work of these 1.5 generation experimental writers, Figes's novels are also characterized by a language of erasure and excess, which illuminates the fractures in the lives of her characters. Like Federman, who claims that the first word of his own writing was his mother's last word to him—*Chut,* the French for "sh-h"—when she hid him in a closet to save him from deportation, Figes writes about silences and the breaking of silences. The hushing of Figes's mother is evoked with the words, "Rule one: never speak German," in Figes's memoir *Little Eden: A Child at War* (1978).[7] With themes of trauma, memory, and women's history, or *her*story, it is obvious that the past plays an important part in Figes's writing. This essay will consider the ways in which the past informs the innovations in her fiction.

Innovation does not come without risk. While it has earned Figes comparisons to Virginia Woolf and praise from Joyce Carol Oates, innovation can also try the patience of many critics.[8] Anthony Thwaite calls *Nelly's Version,* Figes's 1977 novel about a woman suffering from amnesia, "a protracted tease" that left him feeling headachy and frustrated.[9] Thwaite overlooks the possibility that this might have been Figes's intention and that his "sufferings" attest to the power of the narrative to convey Nelly's own. *Days* (1974) similarly comes under fire for its lack of amusing elements. Peter Ackroyd recoils from the reminiscences of its hospitalized female protagonist, saying: "a frayed or neurotic vision is that much less interesting than an average or healthy one. This offends against the canons of the School of Suicide and Worldly Despair, but it agrees with those of good taste."[10] Timothy Mo is not sold on the white spaces in *Days*. Rather than symbolizing the lack of connection between the past and the present, which troubles its protagonist, they smack of pretentiousness.[11] While Alan Sillitoe praises Figes for taking "real risks" yet remaining "exquisitely readable," most critics believe Figes too often sacrifices readability.[12] Yet, as the remarks by Thwaite and Ackroyd suggest (and these are fairly typical), it is often the bleakness of Figes's message that is distasteful to them. Writing *against* popular tastes or beliefs is always a gamble, and one that Figes always resisted giving up. Even her professed happiness as a grandmother does not cushion her reveries on history and human cruelty in *Tales of Innocence and Experience: An Exploration* (2003).

Figes was consistently able to find publishers for her work, and, along with the negative reviews, that work has often been respectfully reviewed in major publications. However, she has been ignored by literary scholars. Lorna Sage, for example, finds nothing to say about Figes in her important study *Women in the House of Fiction* (1992). Ellen G. Friedman and Miriam Fuchs's essay in *Breaking the Sequence: Women's Experimental Fiction* (1989) is an exception. Such neglect is ultimately inexplicable except in terms of the arbitrariness of academic canonization. Looking over Figes's long but often ignored career, one cannot help but wonder what her place in British literature might have been had she begun writing today instead of in the mid-1960s. Certainly late twentieth-century critics have shown a greater openness to the depiction of women's experience and literary experiment than Figes's earlier commentators did. In addition, there has been within the last twenty years a surge in the quantity of fiction and nonfiction focusing on the Holocaust and its survivors. The situation was different in the 1960s and 1970s, when Figes began publishing her work. Her combination of feminism, Jewish experience, and literary experiment met with critical neglect and some degree of disdain. However, her offenses against critical norms may be seen as contributing to the stature of her work, and in fact anticipate more recent developments in feminist and Jewish writing.

Sue Vice writes that "Holocaust fiction which is unaccommodating to the reader may be more successful in conveying the disruption and unease that the subject demands than more seamless, aesthetically pleasing work."[13] By this criterion, Figes's *Konek Landing* (1969) succeeds with every fracture of its narrative, which moves from prose to poetry to a blur of incomplete utterances when relating scenes of hiding and flight. If there is a way to duplicate the disturbance when terra firma is shaken, this may well be it. Conversely, Figes conveys the stagnancy of women's traditionally prescribed roles through verbal repetitions unabated by any empowering epiphanies of thought or action, thereby bolstering the message of her 1970 feminist polemic, *Patriarchal Attitudes*.[14] If existential doubts continue to be a concern (as they are, to Thwaite's irritation, for the female protagonist in *Nelly's Version*), then this calls for a narrative whose ends are left dangling, *not* neatly tied up. *Nelly's Version* was ahead of its time in its depiction of postmodern and post-Holocaust dilemmas of identity and knowledge.

Whether she is flouting the rules of grammar, punctuation, or realist conventions of plot and naming characters which many continue to expect of the novel, Figes illuminates the lack of power experienced by both Jews and women with her unconventional control of the page. Just as *Patriarchal Attitudes* adopts a broad historical perspective, Figes's fiction is concerned with the past and its legacies. This essay will examine the various forms that the past takes in her multifaceted writing career. Discussing Figes's novels in a chronological order is difficult, because she repeatedly returns to earlier concerns. Yet it is possible to make groupings of the novels that also correspond to Figes's age when she wrote them. For this reason, the texts considered here represent the major developments in her writing when Figes was in her thirties, forties, and fifties, although she also returns to certain themes in these texts at other points in her life. First, I will look at her "trauma novels" from the 1960s: *Equinox* (1966) and *Konek Landing* (1969), and her later development of this form with *The Tenancy* (1993). Then, I will examine her "memory novels" from the 1970s: *Days* (1974) and *Nelly's Version* (1977), and her return to their subjects with *Ghosts* (1989). Last, I will consider Figes's "*her*story novels" from the 1980s: *Light* (1983) and *The Seven Ages* (1986), and their relationship to *The Tree of Knowledge* (1990). In concluding, I suggest that Figes is a writer of many concerns—Jewish, existential, and feminist—and that the past is central to each one of these. All of her writing, from its more traditional to experimental forms, constitutes a dialogue with pasts informed as much by gender as by her Jewish European background.

Trauma: *Equinox, Konek Landing,* and *The Tenancy*

Figes is a difficult writer, both in her subject matter and her style. As a Jew and a woman, she shared the concerns of many writers who saw themselves on the peripheries of the societies they lived in, and who wrote about the relationship of contemporary Jews to the Holocaust and of women to men. Yet, unlike a wide range of writers who take on these issues, from Jenny Diski to Erica Jong, Figes lent no levity to relieve their seriousness. The darkness of Figes's vision has alienated some readers: Eric Korn, who generally admires Figes's work, writes of the "sullen intensity" of some of her novels, while Tom Paulin calls *Nelly's Version* "glum, clumsy, naïve." Lorna Sage, too, dismisses *Days* as a "pared-down, disappointing book that means to be bleak, and becomes inarticulate."[15]

Equinox was Figes's first novel and also the first whose characters come from the peripheries of mainstream English society. It is the story of a marriage under strain from two traumas, both involving children, although twenty years apart. By juxtaposing a woman's depression following the death of a newborn infant with her husband's residual feelings of guilt after escaping to England on a *Kindertransport* train as a child, Figes explores the trauma of survival from female and Jewish male perspectives and illuminates both as a result. First, Liz's loss of a child in a society that still considered a woman's purpose to be marriage and childbearing leaves her comparable to a stateless refugee. Unable to join the ranks of women with children or to return, as if nothing has happened, to the writing career she had before she was married, Liz is the first of many female characters in Figes's fiction who sit at home because there is nowhere else for them to go. Second, Martin's survival is a bittersweet one that, Liz explains, he keeps a secret: "He never talked about his past to anyone, and most people had no idea. [. . .] Even the name [Winter] sounded English enough with just the alteration of one initial consonant, spelling unchanged."[16]

While Liz is the more obviously traumatized figure, Martin does not escape unscathed from the loss of his parents and years in an orphanage. This is evident from his too careful dress and nervous manner. "[Martin] could never look completely casual. His sweater was always just a bit too new, and he wore it with a white shirt and even a tie. It was the one thing that was alien about him, more than the guttural r which might have been only a personal speech oddity and the bony nose, which might have been just an intelligent one. He was swinging from left foot to right as he talked, backwards and forwards in a nervous dance" (44). Compared with Liz's immobility, the movement that characterizes Martin initially suggests that he is the healthier of the two, both physically and mentally, and the more active and in control. Yet, as the narrative progresses, it is apparent that both are damaged figures. Similarly, Martin's composure, which had at first highlighted Liz's emotionality, masks feeling rather than attesting to his contentment. In the course of the novel, as the reader comes closer to the truth, paragraphs become blocks of sentences set apart by white spaces or introduced by quotations from Shakespeare ("Let me not to the marriage of true minds") mixed with truisms of Figes's own making:

> *Marriage* may be described as an interlocking neurosis. She thought about Martin in the first days that she knew him, his veiled hostility to a civilization which had liquidated his parents scientifically, the way cattle are disposed of, his love hate for the English way of life which had allowed him to grow up in security but condemned his

parents to death because their economic self-sufficiency could not be guaranteed. No guarantor, no visa. His amused fascination for her smug, tight little family, whose economic self-sufficiency needed no guarantee. (86–87; italics in original)

Liz subsequently likens his trauma to a sickness that had, through marriage, "ironically cured itself." But saying that "[s]ome of that hostility had worn off" (my italics) undermines how complete the "cure" may have been (87). Martin asserts, "I put it away," meaning that he has chosen not to remember his *Kindertransport* past. But when Liz starts to hear train whistles in the night, these words suggest that his memories are not contained but are rather resurfacing in his wife's mind (156). As Liz's thoughts drift from her ordinary English life to Zyklon B and the Gestapo, Martin's "cure" seems to be at Liz's expense. Yet other motifs of marriage, presented as a form of entrapment for men as well as women, keep this from becoming merely a novel of resentment toward men. In the absence of children, the wife of a survivor suffers the legacy of trauma as a child might. It is an interesting notion, particularly as it predates second-generation writing such as Thane Rosenbaum's *Second Hand Smoke* (1999) and *The Golems of Gotham* (2002), which chart the legacy of trauma for the children and grandchildren of survivors.

There is relatively little dialogue in *Equinox,* and, as Martin's words "I put it away" suggest, silence can be a form of coping with trauma. This would make for an entirely static novel were it not for Liz's reflections on the year that passes after the death of their child. With the chapters designated for months of the year, a progression is hinted at but, beginning as it does with the month of September, it is not necessarily a positive one, because winter is ahead. The characters' names also suggest that theirs is a difficult journey. Liz's trauma comes with the death of their child, but her earlier loss of her maiden name, "Reading," foreshadows her loss of creativity as a poet and procreativity when she becomes Liz Winter. Her writer's block is symptomatic of her inability to put her pain into words. Where silence is a coping mechanism for Martin, it is an obstacle to recovery for Liz.

In erasing his memory, Martin is not only protecting himself; he is attempting to become like the English. In 1978 Figes wrote in the *Observer:* "England does not share the European experience. German troops never marched down Whitehall; men were not rounded up and shot or sent to labour camps; there were no gas chambers on the outskirts of Surbiton or Tunbridge Wells; no partisans, no collaborators and no bitter aftermath of retribution. This enabled a lot of English people to see life after 1945 as a continuation of life before the war."[17] In contrast, the Germans, according to Federman, understand "because they know exactly what is missing [. . . .] The unspeakable. The unnamable. It's easy for them to fill in the holes in my stories, the gaps, the precipices, the void, the silence, the absence. They know the story. It is part of their history."[18]

What Figes does so effectively in *Equinox* is to illuminate one partner's trauma via the other's. Thus Liz comes nearest of anyone English to understanding Martin, but she cannot close all the gaps between them. Following her trauma, new gaps appear which eventually form an emotional schism foreshadowed in her image of herself as "a pod, burst open" when her breast milk comes in after the baby's death.[19] The metaphor suggests the traumatic violence of maternity, from which Liz does not recover. In contrast, like the English who carry on after the war as they had done before it, Martin "bounces back" after the baby's death to an ordinary routine of work and socializing, which Liz finds incomprehensible. Lest anyone think Figes treats Martin unfairly, it is worth remembering that, like the English, he cannot fully understand a story that is not his. There are, nonetheless, several episodes in the text in which Liz shows compassion for Martin's pain. While she is able to identify herself with his trauma, he seems incapable of understanding the extent to which her life has been devastated.

Landscapes and cityscapes are nameless in *Konek Landing*, a highly experimental novel about a man in hiding and flight, literally and metaphorically, throughout his life. He is named, however, and his name hints at the novel's setting during the Holocaust. After initially hiding him in a closet, his mother hands him over to an unknown woman who says he should answer now to "Pavel Zuck" and pretend he had "never even heard of Stefan Konek."[20] Both first names are common Polish ones, and the first retains part of its Polish pronunciation when Figes spells it with a "v." That this might be Poland is also suggested by his next hiding place in a convent. Figes dehistoricizes the Holocaust and also never uses the word "Jew," but indicates Stefan's background through a nun's antisemitic rages at him. In spite of such coded references to the Holocaust, the novel is disturbing because of its lack of clear designations. Omissions make for a blurring of distinctions between places and people, which reflects the erosion of demarcations separating safe from dangerous zones, and good from evil—as the established order is shattered and confused. Such blurring extends to the narration, which frequently moves back and forth in time, memory, and place, thereby undermining any sense of terra firma for the reader. A visual reminder of the dislocation of identifiers (Konek's own and others) is the disruption of the text by white spaces between some paragraphs, sudden movements from prose to poetry, and the breakdown of regular syntax and discontinuity of punctuation, capitalization, and conventional spacing between words. This makes *Konek Landing* the most experimental of Figes's novels and, in many ways, the most difficult, its style and subject matter uncompromisingly aligned.

Compared with other child witness narratives, *Konek Landing* lacks the pornographic violence of Jerzy Kosinski's *The Painted Bird* (1965) but also does not offer the respite that comes when Kosinski's depictions of cruelty and atrocity end. Instead, in *Konek Landing* violence is never literal but pervasive, thereby rendering otherwise uneventful scenes full of tension. In the following passage, the mundane triviality of the actions and situations considered (making toast, a policeman's promotion, a child's exams, a nosy neighbor) paradoxically highlight the awful danger attendant upon them.

> The policeman on the ground floor she told him, having burnt some toast for him to eat, is our main worry. If he sees you going in and out of the house. Promotion is important to a family man, the oldest boy is about to take his exams and I know she worries. Every time I go out she pulls back the curtain of her window, the one that faces the entrance door. You must not go out at all or she is bound to get suspicious and talk to him. I said that you were my nephew and that you had gone away again. I expect she believed me. I'm quite good at telling little lies sometimes. (30)

The novel's vision of survival, distinct from any notion of "peace," as long as the past continues to haunt the present, is particularly nightmarish because there are no happy memories. Much Holocaust fiction includes elements of redemption, whether in terms of language or plot. Whereas there are moments of beauty and intimacy in Anne Michaels's *Fugitive Pieces* (1996), there are none in *Konek Landing* to suggest the existence of any other reality. Even Cynthia Ozick's *The Shawl* (1989) offers hope for the future when a reclusive survivor puts aside her daily letter writing to her child who perished in the camps and takes a retired New Yorker up to her room. The same is true of Michael Chabon's *The Final Solution* (2004) when the return of a pet parrot brings back a Jewish orphan's ability to speak. The impression that trauma has no end is compounded by the final image of Stefan Konek, drugged and set adrift on a raft by the natives of the island on which he is stranded. The fruit placed around him completes the suggestion that this is a burial rite yet also allows the possibility that he might regain consciousness and survive. Were there any trace of happiness in the man's life, the latter might constitute a happy ending. There is none.

In 1993 Figes returned to the theme of trauma in *The Tenancy* but in a very different manner from its two previous treatments. There are no lapses into poetry or sporting with grammatical rules. Its focus is on events in the present, not the past, and as such delivers a traditional, chronologically told story with fully rounded characters and no abstraction. Its depiction of a trauma in the making is frightening, however, because of the mundanity of its details. The tenants of an old London building find life unlivable when a landlord tries to drive them out. Since the landlord is never seen, there is an elusive quality to the causation of events that makes them more nightmarish. Has he sent the skinhead with the vicious dog or are they there of their own accord? Is the loss of electricity deliberate? The tenants think so, but have no proof, and therefore no grounds for legal complaint. Left on their own, they cling to rational explanations and their trust in law and order. All fail them.[21] The novel ends with the three last remaining tenants going to their beds and the building being set alight. While the police find no proof of arson, the reader has no difficulty coming to this conclusion.

The novel, I would argue, functions as a metaphor for the experience of Jews in German-occupied Europe, their homes become no longer places of rest or safety. Events that initially seemed to lack connection are, in fact, part of a plan. Minor inconveniences and restrictions will lead to the ultimate destruction of life. Set entirely in the tenants' building, apart from a few hours in a restaurant on the night that the final tenants are killed, *The Tenancy* conveys a sense of entrapment even more acutely than *Equinox*. Moreover, its reliance on realism (unbroken by the stylistic innovations of *Konek Landing*) suggests a mimetic rather than symbolic relationship with reality. The novel's characters, the tenants, meanwhile, at first doubt their own perceptions or those of other tenants. The police dismiss their complaints even after verbal humiliations become physical attacks and one tenant "disappears" in the night. As the novel progresses, it increasingly alludes to Jews during the

Holocaust who fled, were rounded up, or were killed, and, at the same time, to the contemporary dismissal of the testimony of Jewish witnesses.[22]

Memory: *Days, Nelly's Version,* and *Ghosts*

In *Ghosts* (1989), Figes writes: "Nothing comes back. It all comes back."[23] *Ghosts* marks, in fact, Figes's "going back" to the subject of memory, which is dealt with at greatest length in *Days* (1974) and *Nelly's Version* (1977). Written when Figes was in her forties, *Days* and *Nelly's Version* marked a change of direction for the writer. In the 1970s Figes turned her attention from past trauma to lives in the present that are seemingly disconnected from the past. As the words "Nothing comes back. It all comes back" suggest, the mind has little or no control over memory. Similarly, Figes's female characters are trapped in ailing and/or aging bodies over which they have no control.

Days is the first treatment of these subjects and Figes's bleakest depiction of aging women. Set in a hospital room where a woman convalesces from an undefined illness, the action is reduced to the woman's observations from her bed and occasional memories of the past. Her physical immobility is reflected in her thoughts. Short sentences, many of them fragments, suggest her breathlessness and lack of stamina, were she to vocalize the narrative let alone attempt to move from the bed. Even feeding herself takes considerable effort and the help of a nurse. Observing and remembering are the only activities left to the woman, and even these seem encumbered by her physical weakness. Clinging to the only faculties she has left, she tries to resist her mind being "wiped out" by the pills that the nurses bring her, although her memories are rarely pleasant.[24] Reveries move in this way, from this room to other rooms she has known:

> I used to lie awake before, many nights. Not just in this place. [. . .] I used to lie awake waiting. It was such a quiet suburban road, after midnight one could hear single sounds quite clearly, footsteps crunching gravel, a milkbottle overturned, it rolled down two steps. Dark spaces soon become filled with images. A cat howling for sex. Boys out late, whistling, laughing. Catcalls. I listened for the sound of his car turning into the drive. The engine would die. I waited, knowing also that I could not rest until then. Rage filled me, hatred, as I hit the pillow for comfort, finding none. How could he, knowing I would be lying like this, waiting for the sound of his key in the lock. And the knowledge that he could, knowing this, was the worst of all. (11)

It is hard to follow Peter Ackroyd's criticism that such reminiscences are "not likely to amuse" because they connect with nothing beyond themselves.[25] In fact, there is a clear connection between the woman's present reality (lying sleepless in a hospital bed) and the past (lying awake listening for a partner's return). In both situations the woman has passivity forced upon her by men (the doctors in the hospital and the man whose homecoming she awaits). The chair, left empty for a visitor, remains that way until the novel ends with the narrator's spirit leaving her body and sitting in it. No male visitor ever comes, confirming a pattern throughout the protagonist's life, in which men desert women: first, the narrator's father, then a husband, and her brother. Although the protagonist wishes never to resemble her mother, this is precisely what happens. In *The Seven Ages,* the theme of women duplicating the lives of their mothers is developed over numerous generations; here it is concentrated within two generations of women who are good daughters and wives but are subjected to the bad behavior of men whose role is ostensibly to protect and care for them. The judgment on men is bleak and unremitting.

In *Nelly's Version,* Figes further explores gender relations with the story of a middle-aged woman who checks into an English hotel under a false name.[26] Her "exhilaration" at her deception is, however, short-lived after she looks around the room.[27] Its furnishings are more than adequate and the service of good quality. The hotel is as outwardly respectable as the woman who has just checked in. She seems even to belong there, and this is the problem. She explains: "My elation was extinguished like a guttering candle by the disturbing impression, a conviction I could not dispel, that in spite of everything, and against all reason, I had been in this room before (11). This thought fuels another, more disturbing one that escape "might not be as easy" as she had hoped (12). What she cannot say is from what or whom she is trying to escape. And this much she admits. After she fails to recognize herself in a mirror, it becomes obvious that the narrator of *Nelly's Version* is suffering from amnesia. But in spite of its first-person narration, the novel is not a meditation on self and passing time. As the protagonist's identity is slowly reconstructed, the text more closely resembles a detective story, particularly a traditional English one. In place of the country house, there is a hotel in a typically quiet and seemingly peaceful village, with all the requisite characters: desk clerks, shop assistants, and local police. A subtext of unsolved violent crimes under investigation contributes to the novel's country house murder mystery atmosphere. There is just one catch. Where is the prerequisite corpse? In effect, the narrator is one. Without any memory to give her an identity, she is reduced to a shell of a person or mere body.

When a husband and son appear at the hotel, "Mrs. Dean" appears less mysterious. But the greater enigma that the novel poses is why this woman, or any woman, needs the endorsement of men to authorize her existence. This question is first raised when the woman checks into the hotel: "My instinct, or the expression on the face of the man behind the desk, told me that my arrival, unaccompanied and without prior booking, ceased to be questionable the moment I ceased being just myself, by myself, and became a married woman in the looming protective shadow of a mythical husband who would shortly arrive to join her" (10). This is one of many such reflections in the novel that make the narrator someone who observes as much as someone who is observed. As a result she is never an entirely passive figure. In fact, as the narrative fills with her observations, especially about the shortcomings of the men who define her life, the less she seems merely to be an unidentified body at the center of the mystery and the more she resembles a detective trying to find the perpetrators of the crime. As one would expect from the author of *Patriarchal Attitudes,* it is not necessary to look far. According to Figes, crimes of patriarchal societies have perpetrators and collaborators: men (who perpetuate traditional models for women) and women (who follow those models). "Woman," Figes explains, "presented with an image in a mirror, has danced to that image in a hypnotic trance."[28]

In a novel about memory loss, mirrors should be disturbing. Yet when the narrator looks into one, she is unconcerned by her inability to recognize her own image. She merely dislikes what she sees: a "hesitant woman, without the art of the quick, bitchy reply," who epitomizes female middle-class respectability, its subservience and silence (14). Shutting the mirrored wardrobe expresses her desire to shut away this image. The sound that the door makes contrasts with the silence of the image in the mirror. It "bangs" like a gun (14). Snuffing out the narrator's past proves, however, to be as difficult as ignoring models of womanhood based on serving men as the good daughter, wife, and mother. Without memory, the narrator is freed from these signifiers. Unfortunately, she has nothing with which to replace them. This is what makes *Nelly's Version* so bleak. Even the suitcase full of money in her hotel room provides the protagonist with no way out of her entrapment. She makes a few sensible purchases and that is all.

In *Ghosts,* similarly, an aging woman puts responsibilities before pleasure. She is, in many ways, the most active of Figes's female characters so far discussed. She is seen not once, but twice, cleaning out large houses full of furniture and a lifetime's possessions. One house is her mother's, the other is her own. In both cases, cleaning them out marks an end not only of a woman's habitation in them but also of her life. Aging is thus depicted as a journey of loss, both physical and mental, symbolized by the breaking up of houses and giving away of its contents. Emptying out rooms, conversely, fills the mind with memories. While there is no single traumatic event in the narrator's past, there is also no great moment of happiness. This is a woman whose life is defined by serving others. In a review of *Ghosts,* Jenny Diski wishes the characters had names and that there was more that was particular about them.[29] Yet the lack of particularity is what makes this a recognizable, if not a universal, story—a device that aims to present the protagonist-narrator's situation as one that is not tied to particular circumstances but relevant to a wide range of women's lives. The second most striking feature of *Ghosts* is the ordinariness of the reminiscences. Yet the lyrical quality of the writing does inevitably elevate even mundane domestic images. In the following passage, the text, typically, takes on features of verse, principally through phonological and syntactic parallelism, to present the most quotidian of actions and situations: "In the room, my son sits in my father's chair. He sits as my father would have sat, legs out, ankles crossed, wriggling his right foot. Sometimes I see only the way his foot twists, round and round. I see only resemblances, shadow on shadow, the ghosts in the living. My sense of the actual is changing" (133).

The message of *Ghosts* may be that traditional women's roles—domestic chores, family responsibilities, caring for children and other blood relatives—are not intrinsically inferior to men's roles. There is value and beauty in them, but, given the inequalities in a patriarchal society, they have been denigrated. In her refusal to connect and flesh out the memories in *Ghosts* and *Nelly's Version,* Figes is rejecting the traditional realist text's grounding in a specific and detailed documented world, not simply "in an effort to be 'liberated' and modern," as Ackroyd contends, but to illustrate how women's narratives may need other models.[30]

*Her*story: *Light, The Seven Ages,* and *The Tree of Knowledge*

As a writer, Figes is not known for her sense of humor. This is what makes the first pages of *Light* (1983) so striking. The novel begins, impressionistically enough, with a description of the artist Monet rising to go out and catch the first light on his easel. After two paragraphs in this vein, there is a space, then these words:

> He will be gone for hours, she thought, as she heard the floorboard creak outside her room, and then the rhythm of his footfalls down the staircase. It already seemed like hours since she had first heard him splash about in his dressing room, humming a little tune under his breath, and it would be hours before it was time to get up. No light came through the slats of the shutters, the window was a dim outline. What was the good of him tiptoeing past her room when she had heard him half an hour before through two dressing rooms?[31]

Monet, the great Impressionist, whose delicate brush strokes trap the nuances of light on reflecting pools, is a heavy-footed man whose ablutions resemble that of a whale pursued by Ahab. Known for light, he gets up in the dark. And all that he actually traps is his wife and stepdaughter in the house where he rules. The contrast between Claude's view of the morning and his wife Alice's indicates from the start of *Light* that there are two sides to the story.

What has been accepted as an account of the past (whether pertaining to art in *Light*, to politics and war in *The Seven Ages*, or to poetry and philosophy in *The Tree of Knowledge*) is often only part of the story—a *his*tory that leaves out *her*story. Thus Figes gives us a day in the life of the women in Monet's home, one that she constructs through a wide range of small-scale events and actions. Details, such as Alice's having to get up from dinner to get bread for the table, and Marthe's struggling to get a bite into her own mouth as she wrestles with her dead sister's small children, reflect the hierarchy in this home. As Ellen G. Friedman and Miriam Fuchs observe: "At the heart of Eva Figes's small and graceful masterpiece *Light* (1983) is the contradiction inherent in Claude Monet's dual role of great experimental painter and Victorian patriarch."[32] *The Tree of Knowledge* (1990) also focuses on the contradiction inherent in the life of a male experimenter. Narrated by Rebecca—youngest daughter of the republican and poet John Milton—who is kept illiterate by her father yet forced to "read" and take dictation in numerous languages before she is cheated of a dowry and left destitute, its message is clear. As Ruth Pavey writes, "No one should cry liberty unless they are willing to extend it to the members of their own family."[33]

Where *Light* and *The Tree of Knowledge* each take on a great experimenter, *The Seven Ages* (1986) has much to say about the great experiments of history. From the Reformation to the election of Britain's first woman prime minister, women's lives largely remain subordinate to men's. There is no real reform or change in the social hierarchy for women or, to put it bluntly, as one reviewer does: "[*The Seven Ages*] is a history of pain and loss, of being fucked over; a history of the dark."[34] While its unremitting chronicle of female suffering reduces this novel to "feminist propaganda of the most extreme kind" in the minds of some critics,[35] for others, like Tillie Olsen, this is an essential aspect of its literary daring. "Virginia Woolf would have so welcomed this book," Olsen writes, "representing as it does the direction she hoped literature would take. Here, at last, palpable, embodied, is that accumulation of centuries of unrecorded lives that she wished for."[36] Where Figes turns "attention from the history of 'events' and kingdoms to the history of lives," in effect appropriating for the novel "the trend that has informed the best historical writing in the last two decades," she does so not to supplement conventional histories but to offer an alternative to *his*tory.[37] Major events and time lines frequently blur as a result. *His*tory with its killing campaigns and conquests is subordinated by *her*story with its birth pains and losses. The lives of women are here not to fill out "major" events but rather to take their place.

In what is arguably the most arduous chapter to read in all of Figes's fiction, a group of women assisting at a birth tell stories of other births. The movements in time, from present to past narratives, make this one birth seem like generations of them. Although devoid of the pornographic violence found in many literary and film treatments of childbirth, this scene in *The Seven Ages,* by its length and the magnifying quality of its multiple narratives, suggests that childbirth is a trauma. The physical suffering of the woman giving birth seems unending, and the women assisting have to resort to more and more stories to pass the time.

> Joan was persuaded to sip a little hot broth. She had scarcely swallowed two mouthfuls when she felt a huge hand squeeze her belly hard, as though it was no more than a bag of curds. She spilt her broth, and let out a lusty yell of shock and protest. Margery came to the bedside as the girl lay panting, lifted her shift, and pushed a finger into the orifice. She shook her head, untied the eaglestone and put it at the very top of her thigh.

Holy Mary bore Christ, she murmured, Holy Anne bore Mary, Holy
Elizabeth bore John, Holy Cecilia bore Remy, Sator Arepo Tenet Opera
Rtas Amen. Oh infant, whether alive or dead, come forth.

. . .

Then, said Margery, there was the feud that broke out between Lord
Robert and a neighboring baron, Lord Harvill, I think it was.[38]

Moreover, chapter 2 of *The Seven Ages* suggests that *her*story is essentially an
oral and aural form, reflected in the novel's multiple narrative voices. As Barbara Misztal notes, such accounts are "used strategically not merely to explain
the group past but also to transform it into a reliable identity source for the
group present."[39] *The Seven Ages* illustrates what Misztal calls "the sacralization of memory": "By placing trauma at the heart of counter-memory, what
is remembered gains in moral weight as, in order to preserve the moral order,
it becomes a duty to remember the past horrors."[40] What Figes does is not
to be confused with the Christian tradition of sacralized suffering, but it is
consistent with the Jewish obligation to remember. Although Figes does not
explicitly identify her characters' sufferings with either a Jewish or a Christian tradition, it is striking that throughout her work her characters' trials
are essentially pointless and are not redemptive in any way. Remembering,
however, these novels suggest, is a necessary duty but a painful one.

While some critics view these novels as attempts "to 'undo' a version of
the past," I see them less as a deconstruction than a re-angling of history.[41]
With the words "we cannot undo the past," Milton's daughter Deborah suggests the condition that each of Figes's novels addresses.[42] In light of this, all
that a writer can accomplish is to undo some of the conventions of the novel
in a symbolic unknotting of the gag that has kept other sides of the story
from being told.

It is difficult to sum up Eva Figes's work. Her oeuvre includes realist and
nonrealist texts, novels that are marked by long passages of poetic prose and
others that soberly, even modestly, recount their protagonist's experiences.
It contains contemporary social-psychological fiction and historical novels,
fictions in which Jewish themes are prominent and works in which these
seem quite absent. Her novels are held together—if by anything—by a focus
on trauma, on memory, and on the burden of the past, especially for Jews
and for women. Her work as a whole shows a fascinating interweaving of

Jewish concerns and radical feminism, although it is striking that these are not brought together, to any substantial extent, except in *Equinox*.

Figes's problematic reception—not wholly negative but scarcely universally positive either—is an indication of complex aspects of her work. She is remarkably difficult to pigeonhole—a Jewish writer, a feminist polemicist, an experimental *romancière,* a sober chronicler of women's oppression within realist conventions? Which is she? How can she be all of these? In addition, her feminism is of a particularly unaccommodating sort; her vision of male-female relationships is unremittingly bleak.

It is tempting to attempt an interpretation of Figes's work that brings together its disparate strands. It is, then, worth noting that her Jewish and feminist concerns have this much in common: they speak of those whose lives have been ravaged by the past, and of those whose memories are inescapable and, yet, unbearable. The novels do so in a variety of manners that all attempt to capture and express disruption and pain, be it that of a *Kinder-transport* child, the abused daughter of a great man, the tenants of a house under siege, or a woman whose identity is shattered by the forces of patriarchy. The midwife protagonist and principal narrator of *The Seven Ages* hears women's voices from the past—"forgotten words . . . I hardly know from where."[43] Figes's work as a whole is a medium for such "forgotten words," the stories of the traumatized that have to be told and remembered if there is to be any escape from history's dismal nightmare.

Notes

1. Susan Rubin Suleiman coined this term to differentiate child survivors from the first-generation Holocaust survivors and second-generation children of survivors in a plenary lecture at "The Future of Memory: An International Holocaust and Trauma Studies Conference," at the University of Manchester, in November 2005.
2. Eva Figes, *Tales of Innocence and Experience: An Exploration* (London: Bloomsbury, 2003), 93.
3. Amiya Kumar Patra, "Writing the Silence: An E-Mail Interview with Raymond Federman," *Atlantic Critical Review* 2.4 (October–December 2003), 169.
4. Eva Figes, *Little Eden: A Child at War* (New York: Persea Books, 1978), 131.
5. See note 1.
6. Patra, "Writing the Silence," 169. For discussions of Federman's work, see *Contemporary Literary Criticism*, vol. 47 (Detroit: Gale Research, 1988), 118–33.
7. Figes, *Little Eden,* 19.
8. Joyce Carol Oates, "Monet, Summer, 1900," review of *Light,* by Eva Figes, *New York Times Book Review,* October 16, 1983, 11.
9. Anthony Thwaite, "Wandering Women," review of *Nelly's Version,* by Eva Figes, *Observer,* July 17, 1977, 29.

10. Peter Ackroyd, "Salad Days," review of *Days,* by Eva Figes, *Spectator,* January 12, 1974, 43.

11. Timothy Mo, "Sick Fantasy," review of *Days,* by Eva Figes, *New Statesman,* January 18, 1974, 88.

12. Alan Sillitoe, "For the Journey," review of *The Seven Ages,* by Eva Figes, *New Statesman,* September 25, 1987, 31.

13. Sue Vice, *Holocaust Fiction* (London: Routledge, 2000), 161.

14. Eva Figes, *Patriarchal Attitudes: Women in Society* (London: Faber and Faber, 1970). *Patriarchal Attitudes,* although not technically innovative in any way, is, thematically at least, quite uncompromising in its feminism—uncompromising enough to produce cautious demurrals on the part of even strong-minded women reviewers like Claire Tomalin and Patricia Beer. It is a savage polemic against historical and current (in the 1960s) intellectual formulations and institutional arrangements that devalue and oppress women. It points out patriarchy's intellectually fragile and hysterical foundations, and the long-enduring opposition of many women to its restrictions and cruelties. In terms of this essay, it is striking to note the complete absence of a specific Jewish thematic in it. Jewish topics are present, but only as they illustrate a widespread oppression of women. For complex responses to *Patriarchal Attitudes,* see Patricia Beer, "Man-Made," *The Listener,* July 23, 1970, 122–23; and Claire Tomalin, "What Does a Woman Want?" *New Statesman,* June 26, 1970, 917.

15. Eric Korn, "Facing Backwards," *Times Literary Supplement,* July 22, 1977, 885; Tom Paulin, "Captain Fist," *New Statesman,* July 22, 1977, 123; Lorna Sage, "Monstrous Intimacies," *Observer,* January 13, 1974, 25.

16. Eva Figes, *Equinox* (London: Secker and Warburg, 1966), 35. Further references to this edition will appear in the text.

17. Eva Figes, "The Long Passage to Little England," *Observer,* June 11, 1978, quoted in Peter Conradi, "Eva Figes," in *British Novelists Since 1960,* ed. Jay L. Halio, *Dictionary of Literary Biography,* vol. 14 (Detroit: Gale, 1983), 299.

18. Patra, "Writing the Silence," 175.

19. Figes, *Equinox,* 29.

20. Eva Figes, *Konek Landing* (1969; repr. London: Panther, 1972), 22.

21. There are clearly echoes of Kafka's fiction here (as well as, perhaps, the dramas of Harold Pinter). Figes has acknowledged the influence of Kafka's work on her writing; see Manuel Almagro and Carolina Sánchez-Palencia, "Eva Figes: An Interview," *Atlantis* 22.1 (June 2000), 184–85.

22. In recent novels, the Anglo-Jewish writers Norman Lebrecht and David Baddiel also refer to doubts cast by contemporaries on accounts of atrocities committed against European Jews in the 1930s and 1940s. See Lebrecht's *The Song of Names* (London: Review/Headline, 2002), 121, and Baddiel's *The Secret Purposes* (London: Abacus, 2004), 71.

23. Eva Figes, *Ghosts* (London: Flamingo, 1989), 28. Further references to this edition will appear in the text.

24. Eva Figes, *Days* (London: Faber and Faber, 1974), 11. Further references to this edition appear in the text.

25. Ackroyd, "Salad Days," 43.

26. The protagonist-narrator's name in Nelly Dean. This may be a reference to one of the narrators of Emily Brontë's *Wuthering Heights,* a text that is, finally and complexly, a celebration of heterosexual passion. However, much more likely is the reference to the traditional song "There's an Old Mill by the Stream, Nelly Deane," a sentimental glorification of married love. In either case, the protagonist's name is deeply ironic.

27. Eva Figes, *Nelly's Version* (1977; repr. London: Flamingo, 1988), 10. Further references to this edition will appear in the text.

28. Figes, *Patriarchal Attitudes,* 15.

29. Jenny Diski, "Temporal Pain and Paradoxes," review of *Ghosts,* by Eva Figes, *New Statesman,* May 13, 1988, 32.

30. Peter Ackroyd, "All About Eva," review of *Nelly's Version,* by Eva Figes, *Spectator,* July 30, 1977, 22–23.

31. Eva Figes, *Light* (1983; repr. London: Flamingo, 1990), 8.

32. Ellen G. Friedman and Miriam Fuchs, "Contexts and Continuities: An Introduction to Women's Experimental Fiction in English," in *Breaking the Sequence: Women's Experimental Fiction,* ed. Ellen G. Friedman and Miriam Fuchs (Princeton, NJ: Princeton University Press, 1989), 33.

33. Ruth Pavey, "Ungrateful Daughters," review of *The Tree of Knowledge,* by Eva Figes, *Observer,* September 23, 1990, 56.

34. Robert Buckeye, "Eva Figes, *The Seven Ages,*" *Review of Contemporary Fiction* 9.1 (Spring 1989), 257.

35. Phoebe-Lou Adams, "Brief Reviews," *Atlantic Monthly* (February 1987), 94.

36. This remark is printed on the back cover of Eva Figes, *The Seven Ages* (1986; repr. London: Flamingo, 1987).

37. Angelina Goreau, "The Midwives' Tales," *New York Times Book Review,* February 22, 1987, 7.

38. Eva Figes, *The Seven Ages,* 39–40.

39. Barbara Misztal, "The Sacralization of Memory," *European Journal of Social Theory* 7.1 (2004), 68.

40. Ibid., 78.

41. Martha Tuck Rozett, "Constructing the World: How Postmodern Historical Fiction Reimagines the Past," *Clio* 26.2 (Winter 1996), 6. In an interview published in 2000, Figes contends that history "because of women, has to be re-angled" (Almagro and Sánchez-Palencia, "Eva Figes: An Interview," 180).

42. Figes, *The Tree of Knowledge* (1990; repr. London: Minerva, 1991), 2.

43. Figes, *The Seven Ages,* 2.

7

OTHERNESS AND TRANSCENDENCE

The Poetry of Ruth Fainlight and Elaine Feinstein

PETER LAWSON

In this essay I want to consider the poetry of Ruth Fainlight (1931–) and Elaine Feinstein (1930–), with some reference to their novels, short stories, biographies, and autobiographical writings. Further, I want to examine the work of both poets within an Anglo-Jewish minority context. To date, no book-length study has appeared on either writer. Where critical attention has focused on them, the emphasis has tended to be on their significance as translators,[1] feminists,[2] and poets with a close connection to American rather than English poetry. For example, the editor of *The Oxford Book of English Verse* (1999), Christopher Ricks, chooses to include two of Feinstein's free translations from the Russian of Marina Tsvetayeva while ignoring her original work.[3] Stressing the non-Englishness of Feinstein's poetry, Deborah Mitchell notes the defining influence of "the American moderns" on her verse methods.[4] Similarly removing Fainlight from her English context, *The Oxford Companion to English Literature* (2000) defines her as an American merely "resident in England" rather than as an Anglo-Jewish poet.[5] This is despite the fact that Fainlight is a British citizen who has lived and written mainly in England since 1946.

By contrast with such critical approaches, I want to place the poetry of Fainlight and Feinstein in its Anglo-Jewish cultural context. I suggest that Fainlight seeks a transcendence of Jewish otherness in art, whereas Feinstein constructs such otherness as a form of romanticized exile. Feinstein's imaginary exile implies transcendence of the limitations imposed on Anglo-Jewish culture.

In what follows I argue that Fainlight and Feinstein express concern with allegiances to ancestry and cultural inheritance. While Fainlight ambivalently perceives Jewish history as both a burden and a cherished constituent of a hybrid global culture, Feinstein strongly affiliates herself with the continuity of Jewish culture and its exilically imagined displacements. Fainlight and Feinstein resemble one another in expressing a cultural "inbetweenness." I contend that both deploy their "doubleness" as minority Jewish and majority English poets to explore the hybridity of Anglo-Jewishness. This is not to overlook the significance of the Holocaust for both poets, but rather to suggest that the lessons they draw from the Shoah concern continuity in Anglo-Jewish culture.

Ruth Fainlight

> But I am released by language,
> I escape through speech:
> Which has no dimensions,
> Demands no local habitation
> Or allegiance, which sets me free
> From whomsoever's definition:
> Jew, poet, woman.

Ruth Fainlight, "Definition," 1976[6]

If we want a neat summary of Fainlight's concerns, we could do worse than look at her collection *Another Full Moon* (1976). What this volume makes clear is that Fainlight's consciousness of herself is a result of sociocultural interpellation ("whomsoever's definition"), as well as historical and geographical contingencies. The poem's "I" insists on being read as a lyrical construction of self. "Definition" is a meditation on what it means to learn one's place:

> Who told me my place?
> It takes generations
> To breed such a true believer—
> I am of the race
> Of dutiful captives; it needed
> Centuries, millennia, to produce
> Someone who instinctively knew
> The only movement possible
> Was up or down (1–9)

Jewishness envisaged as servitude ("the race / Of dutiful captives") is key to this pondering on alienation in the world. "The only movement possible / Was up or down" for the speaker who apprehends that there has never been "space for me on the earth's surface" (14). In a later version, renamed "Vertical" in her *Selected Poems* (1995), Fainlight cuts the reference to "race."[7] Although the word "Jew" remains in the final line of "Vertical" ("Jew. Woman. Poet." instead of "Jew, poet, woman"), it is no longer juxtaposed with meek submissiveness. Instead, its meaning is recast in terms of deterritorialization, as suggested by the new title. In this latter version, Jews, women, and poets almost indistinguishably share freedom from entrapment in "horizontal" geography and a "local habitation" inhospitable to them (lines 9 and 15). Consistent with Fainlight's project over four decades of writing poetry, "Vertical" makes further moves toward eliding the outsider situations of the speaker as a Jew, woman, and poet.

Of course, Fainlight does have local geographical allegiances. "My Position in the History of the Twentieth Century," also in *Another Full Moon,* addresses the centrality of place in the speaker's life:

> Lucky to live where it has not been dangerous
> To be easily identified—(no need
> For a yellow star). My good fortune took me far
> From the holocaust.[8]

In an interview with Lidia Vianu, Fainlight expounds on this sentiment: "I am fortunate enough not to have had direct experience of the Holocaust, nor did my immediate family. But of course, being Jewish, it affected me profoundly."[9] Growing up as a Jew in Britain and America during the 1930s and 1940s, Fainlight was made aware of her Jewishness. After five years in New York between 1931 and 1936, her parents brought Ruth to England. Of her evacuation during the London Blitz to a Welsh village, Fainlight writes: "In that village I first became conscious of myself as an alien and a Jew."[10] Returning to America with her mother and brother, while Ruth's Anglo-Jewish father served in the Royal Air Force, she lived with her aunt in Virginia. By now, the United States was at war with the Axis powers.

Antisemitism was in the air. Writing of this period, the American Jewish feminist critic and activist Carolyn G. Heilbrun has commented on "the adamant anti-Semitism all around me as I grew up."[11] In Fainlight's childhood milieu, Aunt Ann insisted that "no one must know she was a Jew."[12] At the very least the European persecution and killing of Jews affected Ruth's upbringing indirectly. Thus "My Position in the History of the Twentieth Century" focuses on geography and history, rather than psychology and inheritance, to explain personal feelings: "And what seemed most private and unique in me / I find dependent on my place and time" (35–36). Further, the Holocaust may be the source of Fainlight's early poems about suicidal survivors. As "My Position in the History of the Twentieth Century" reveals, the speaker empathizes with those "stripped down / To hopelessness, labelled, numbered or docketed" (26–27).

I want to argue that such an emphasis on "my place and time" counters the poet's multiple experiences of displacement and otherness. Unlike Elaine Feinstein, Fainlight does not exoticize otherness as a desirable means of transcending the tensions of Anglo-Jewish culture. On the contrary, she envisages exotic dreams as an imaginative trap; for example, in her poem "Cages" (1966):

> Dawn wind and rising sun get trapped by the trees
> Stain my eastward windows into Moorish lamps
> Cages of light fretted like stilled twigs
> That flicker again as the candle flame stirs.[13]

Here, Eastern exoticism combines with the "flame" of Holocaust fire and the "stain" of racial impurity to evoke a medley of contemporary versions of Jewish identity. However, this post-Holocaust scenario of exoticized Jewishness is also dismissed as a dead-end: "trapped," in "cages."

The "stain" of inheritance appears again in "Hymn" (1966), where the speaker addresses her mother, the matriarch through whom Jewish lineage traditionally passes:

> If I can hymn you well enough,
> You'll know your stain has taken:
> The dye has permeated me,
> I'm marked by absolute necessity
> Fit for the sacrifice, the transmutation.[14]

Jewish inheritance seems to suggest a social stigma and the genetic fate, "marked by absolute necessity," of martyrdom ("sacrifice," perhaps with a double entendre on "dye"). Hope appears to lie in "transmutation," some sort of escape from her Jewish family and female role within it. The poem's title, "Hymn," hints at a religious context to this conflict. The language of "transmutation" expands this religious association by suggesting, paradoxically, Christian transubstantiation or resurrection following "the sacrifice."

"Ego-Death" (1966) concerns escape through suicide. Fainlight's friend and fellow expatriate American poet, Sylvia Plath, had committed suicide in 1962[15]; another meditation on suicide, "Autumn Stirring" (1966), may well have been written with Plath in mind.[16] Suicide in "Ego-Death," however, is associated with the Judaic dietary laws of *kashrut,* whereby kosher meat must be cleansed of blood:

> Perhaps I'll bleed to death.
> Appropriate,
> If I still seek a role.
> Then I will be
> As clean as any animal
> My family eats. [17]

The poem appears to position the speaker as a victim of her Jewish "family." Indeed, "family" is linked with an "I" that the speaker can escape only through suicide. Without such family, the speaker would apparently be free to relax, from an "ego" that "stiffens," into "flaccid" "drift."[18] However, freedom from family leaves the speaker with nothing but victimhood: the passive "role" of meat without identity.

In Fainlight's yearning for a place of calm, she frequently comes close to a masochistic abandonment of self. The poems in *Sibyls and Others* (1980), for example, teem with self-destructive references to the "perfect sacrifice" ("The Cimmerian Sibyl"), "the glee of surrender to nullity" ("Introspection of a Sibyl"), the "hoping for catastrophe" ("Danger Areas"), and the "relics of a martyrdom—some tortured part" ("Meat").[19] Some of Fainlight's short stories are sexually masochistic. In "My Little Sister" (1994), Mary confesses: "Sometimes I could sense, with a resigned, almost exalted prescience, when he was going to hurt me; accepted it as part of his strangeness, a sign of his love."[20] Both the female figures in this text subject themselves to sadistic men. Libidinous pleasure and pain are inextricably connected, too, in the short story "Pleasure," which features, with slight variations, in both of Fainlight's collections of fiction, *Daylife & Nightlife* (1971) and *Dr Clock's Last Case* (1994).[21] Indeed, from the beginning of her writing career, Fainlight has been fascinated by abjection. *To See the Matter Clearly* (1968) includes "Solo Scrabble," a poem that playfully distils attraction toward the "abject" down to a postmodern word game:

> Ecstatic or abject, (twenty six points)
> Belief in my potentialities
> Oscillates like needles on electric magnets.[22]

Despite the humor, the choices remain stark. Is the speaker to find a place of rest in ecstasy or abjection? If calm exists in neither state, then how is she to survive the sense of painful agitation between the two? "Definition" (1976) describes

> Someone who instinctively knew
> The only movement possible
> Was up or down:
> Spurting ascent to heaven's
> Pleasures and mysteries, or else:
> Madness, disgrace, chaotic
> Infernal glee.
> No space for me on the earth's surface. (7–14)

For this poem's "Jew, poet, woman" there is no "horizontal" way forward, only an oscillation between "heaven's" ecstasies and hell's "disgrace." I suggest that Fainlight locates metaphorical homes in her oeuvre precisely where the "ecstatic" and "abject" appear to achieve equilibrium. Fainlight, I argue, finds calm in the religious (abject) sacrifice of the artist's (ecstatic) vocation.

In the introduction to her verse in *The Bloodaxe Book of Contemporary Women Poets: Eleven British Writers* (1985), Fainlight explicitly associates suffering and excitement with the process of creating poetry. "Being a poet," she explains, "can be a cause of suffering, yet it brings the greatest excitement and pleasure I know." She continues by discussing the poet's vocation as subjection to a metaphorical god of aesthetics:

> But as Baudelaire wrote in his study of Poe, the poet cannot freely determine his condition—Providence has "prepared him for it from the cradle," "dedicated him to the altar," "consecrated him, so to speak." The poet's only freedom is "transforming this curse into a blessing . . . for poetry is liberation within this destiny, and the being who avoids this one avenue of escape is simply crushed; there will be no other way out." Perhaps the flaying of Marsyas by Apollo, leader of the Muses and inspirer of sibyls and poets (from whom not even the Muse of Poetry can grant protection) is a metaphor for the special suffering of the poet, who in spite of the most glorious effort can never hope to win his or her challenge to the god.[23] (ellipsis in original)

In this view, poetry is a pagan religion with its own "god," "altar," and "consecrated" "condition." Chosen from the "cradle" for a life of "special suffering," poets are imagined classically ("Muses") rather than Judaically. Possibly, Judaism is displaced by "the Muse of Poetry" in Fainlight's formulation. Like a religion, poetry is presented as offering the "one avenue of escape" from being "simply crushed." Fainlight concludes her introduction with an extremely violent image of torture: "the flaying of Marsyas by Apollo." Whether this is related to Jewish martyrdom is a moot point; Fainlight's introduction does not make the connection explicit. What is clear is the inextricability of binary opposites—and indeed paradoxes—in the posited condition of the poet, a condition that is simultaneously cursed/blessed, tortured/inspirational, painful/glorious, defeated/victorious, chosen/liberated. In poetry, it appears, the Jewish woman's choice is no longer between the irreconcilable "up or down" ("Definition"), "Ecstatic or abject" ("Solo Scrabble"), since both are essential to the religion of aesthetics.

Indeed, Fainlight's references to Charles Baudelaire and Edgar Allan Poe are no coincidence. Her Virginian upbringing may go some way to explaining Fainlight's penchant for Poe. In an autobiographical essay, she writes of being "enthralled by the sonorous vocabulary and elaborate rhyme schemes of Edgar Allan Poe."[24] Further, several of Fainlight's gothic short stories, such as "Soir de Fête" and "Mid-Term," suggest Poe as a Southern source of inspiration.[25] Moreover, what principally links Baudelaire and Poe in Fainlight's critical appreciation is their emphasis on a perfected artistic space. Both offer Fainlight an imaginary home in the transcendent art object.

"With David in the Nimrud Galleries" (1980)[26] exemplifies the manner in which abjection and pleasure can coexist in art that is imagined as a transcendent home. Significantly, the poem concerns a visit to an art gallery by mother and son. A public art space serves as a surrogate home, as in Fainlight's "My Grandparents" (1973), which opens: "Museums serve as my grandparents' house."[27] In the Nimrud Galleries, we are informed that Fainlight's son David immediately "noted how delicately the shallow streams / of blood from the arrow-wounds had been graved down the lions' / sides." The speaker continues:

> This precise observation confirmed my pleasure, and his.
> I wondered about the craftsmen who did these carvings.
> The columns of captives are endless: how they bind
> the composition together. Such strong horizontals:
> women, children. One too small to walk
> into slavery straddles his father's shoulders.
> On another tablet a group of prisoners have
> abased themselves.[28]

References to "slavery" and "abased" people echo those in "Definition," and again may suggest the Holocaust as well as more ancient Jewish history. Further, they imply that art is unique in rendering abjection and suffering beautiful, and therefore bearable. Jews and non-Jews are included in Fainlight's understanding of this history: "a wordy / confusion of Bible tales and Mongol invasions, / time's desolations." The poem concludes by evoking "the precious detritus of Nimrud,"[29] an oxymoron worthy of Walter Benjamin's "Theses on the Philosophy of History" (1940). Much as Benjamin posited that "there is no document of civilization that is not at the same time a document of barbarism,"[30] so Fainlight suggests that the "detritus" of a barbaric emperor is also "precious" as part of the art that constitutes a hybrid, confused global civilization. If Jewish suffering is a concern at all in this poem, it is implicitly universalized by setting it within a global history of enslavement.

From her earliest writings, Fainlight has pronounced her faith in art as a place of transcendent calm that offers the consolations of a (non-Judaic) religion. In "Paradise" (1968), for example, she contemplates the artistic endeavor of depicting heaven, rather than belief in such a place, as her source of hope:

> Against death-fear I can oppose
> Only a steel engraving I remember,
> Some lost craftsman's detailed labour,
> Lines and dots and miniscule cross-hatching[31]

Anxiety ("death-fear") is abated in the "detailed labour" of the work of art, its "[l]ines and dots and miniscule cross-hatching." Art offers its own "safe harbour," which is the closest Fainlight imagines herself coming to "paradise" (lines 14 and 13). The poet's regular allusions to paintings may be related to her training as a visual artist at Birmingham and Brighton Colleges of Art and Crafts in the 1950s.[32] When Fainlight imagines a place where tensions can exist in harmony, she often does so through the metaphor of color. In "Green" (1973), for example, she states:

> Between blue and yellow
> Green fuses into unity.
> It signifies untried,
> Is hope's pure colour—[33]

Such a synthesizing through color might reflect Fainlight's position as a Jew seeking a universalist language through which to blend differences. As an Anglo-American Jewish woman, Fainlight may well empathize with a

synthesizing green that is "[b]etween blue and yellow." If "blue" bears connotations of the WASP with her blue-blooded ancestry, so "yellow" is redolent of the "yellow star" of David badge that Jews across Nazi-occupied
Europe were compelled to wear between 1941 and 1945.[34] Fainlight is "[b]
etween" both. The color green can, at least metaphorically, succeed in blend-
ing the two together.

Occupying an in-between space, the color green also resembles the posi-
tion of the half-wild, half-tame cat in Fainlight's "Animal Tamer" (1980).[35] As
Bryan Cheyette has remarked, almost a century earlier the Victorian Anglo-
Jewish poet Amy Levy deployed a similar literary trope of inbetweenness in
her poem "Captivity" (1889). Cheyette astutely discerns Levy's sense of "semi-
acculturation," of being "neither 'wild' nor 'tame,' neither Jewish nor English."[36]
Fainlight's narrator, I suggest, sees her identity in a similar light. The speaker in
"Animal Tamer" addresses her partner, and describes his "taming the wild black
cat / that appeared last week at the bottom of the garden."[37] As he systematically
earns the cat's trust, the man both domesticates and traps her:

> Today, for the very first time, you turned and stared
> at those yellow, survivor's eyes, and the cat stared back
> a moment before she swerved and ran to safety.
> But then she stopped, and doubled round and half
> gave in, and soon, as I know well, you'll have
> that cat, body pressed down on the earth and fur
> electrified, stretching her limbs for mercy. (18–24)

Domestication is associated here with submission, sexual exploitation, and
torture. Indeed, the "tamer" suggests a Nazi tricking a Jew into reluctant
trust before the kill. Equally, the cat evokes a Jewish survivor ("survivor's
eyes") habituated to being attacked before its eventual "flight and escape" (17).
This "black" and "wild" creature is tamed with white "milk," suggestive of the
cat's status between black and white, as well as between wild and tame. The
cat's movement between opposite tones and colors hints at the discourse of
the Jews' racial indeterminacy, between wild black and tamed white.[38] Like a
woman, a poet, and a Jew, this cat is "half" way to being a survivor, "half" way
to becoming a victim. From these masochistic and survivalist perspectives,
Jews, women, and poets occupy analogous positions.

In a more recent collection, *Burning Wire* (2002), Fainlight humorously
conveys a sense of remaining "the alien" in England. Attempts to assert
belonging prove laughable in "The English Country Cottage":

> A Jewish poet in an English village:
> incongruous and inappropriate
> as a Hindu in an igloo, a Dayak in
> Chicago, a giraffe at the South Pole. (1–4)[39]

Despite the speaker's assays at passing ("mimicking the locals dutifully"), she discerns that imitation cannot "camouflage / the alien" in their eyes (39, 40–41). Sardonically, she reflects that since "Oliver Cromwell" readmitted them, Jews have been granted no more than "the privilege to be legally present in England" (11). Thus Jews continue to occupy the situation of guests. They are neither unwelcome enemies nor welcoming hosts. In theory, the speaker suggests, the Jews' "privilege" of staying is revocable (14).

Several other poems evoke the uncertain status of home for Jews in England. "House-Guest" (1980), for example, is a meditation on mistakenly imagining that one is unequivocally accepted in the home of others and discovering that, in fact, she is dependent on the goodwill of "hosts."[40] The speaker in "other peoples'" houses feels "exposed" to their scrutiny ("an intercepted / glance exchanged between our hosts") and consequently insecure. "Words and friendship" lose their ability to reassure. As outsiders, the house-guests ("we") only presume liberal "familiarity" with their "human" acquaintances (respectively, lines 1, 8, 16–17, 11, 12, 18, 11). In reality, they are not fully accepted. Consequently, the guests begin to doubt their own humanity, which seems real only in the suffering of their bodies:

> Then that skin crackles and splits, the blood beads out
> on its shiny rawness, and we clutch at the nearest cloth
> to wrap around the wound, even though it may be
> an ancient silken robe, their most precious heirloom. (19–22)

Such imagery of burning flesh evokes the victims of the Holocaust. Whether or not the speaker is experiencing Judeophobia as such, the poem suggests that the Jewish "[g]uest" in England is made to feel other: an outsider to the hosts' "precious heirloom[s]."

By contrast, "At Home at Last" (1976) considers the stultifying security that domestic space may impose:

> I force my way through muffling veils of lethargy,
> Eyes itching and swollen, throat stale, as if I had
> Been drugged;

and:

> One afternoon they'll find me, empty, vacant,
> Like a snake's shed skin or a papery chrysalis
> Husk: with muscles flaccid, heart still beating
> And eyes wide open.[41]

The speaker's passive impotence suggests that she has not chosen her life but, like a biblical Jew, has rather been chosen for an unspecified role. Such stanzas evoke the dehumanized *Muselmann* of Holocaust memoirs, many of which were available in English translation by the mid-1970s. Though resting at "home," the speaker feels like a stranger:

> I hear familiar voices. But it's all strange. Why
> Did I wake here? I could surface somewhere else
> As easily [. . .] (12–14)

Through these oblique references to exclusion and persecution, I want to suggest, Fainlight offers an Anglo-Jewish poetry of otherness. Yet "At Home at Last" concludes by evoking a mixture of death, religion, mysticism, and art ("I'll be reborn into / Eternity," "escape," "at last perfected and complete" [21–23, 25]) which together might offer a deterritorialized and transcendent "home." "Definition" (in the same collection) similarly invokes the transcendent "ascent to heaven's / Pleasures" of the Jew, poet, and woman beyond "delusive" security in England.[42]

Elaine Feinstein

In the preface to her *Collected Poems and Translations,* Elaine Feinstein remarks on the factors that made her feel like an outsider: "Born in Liverpool into a family of Jewish immigrants from Odessa, and moreover a woman, it is hardly surprising that three privileged years at Newnham College, Cambridge were not enough to eradicate my sense of being at the periphery."[43] Like Ruth Fainlight, moreover, Elaine Feinstein writes with a pronounced awareness of the Shoah. In an autobiographical essay, Feinstein remarks: "[Adolescent] security was exploded once and for all, at the war's end, when I read what exactly had been done to so many children as young as I was, in the hell of Hitler's camps. You could say that in that year [1945] I became Jewish."[44] Here, I want to discuss her lyrical poems of transcendence against the background of the Holocaust.[45]

  Like Fainlight, Feinstein writes for a general, rather than Jewish, readership. Her participation, alongside Fainlight, in *The Bloodaxe Book of*

Contemporary Women Poets (1985) and *The Hutchinson Book of Post-War British Poets* (1989) indicates that she is being read within feminist and British contexts. However, Feinstein differs from Fainlight in lyrically celebrating an otherness that she associates both with Jewishness and femaleness.

Feinstein is undaunted by Theodor Adorno's anti-transcendent, post-Holocaust admonition that "to write lyric poetry after Auschwitz is barbaric."[46] Indeed, her poems are replete with phrases such as "elation" ("New Year '66" [1966]), "exultation the / street sings" ("Votary" [1971]), and "the sunlight is euphoric" ("Picnic" [1997]).[47] Yet the shadow of the Holocaust may not be far from such expressions of euphoria. As Feinstein notes in "Lisson Grove" (1997):

> At your bedside, I feel like someone
> who has escaped too lightly
> from the great hell of the camps,
>
> except that I don't altogether escape.[48]

"Song of Power" (1966) goes further, since it juxtaposes the "fire" of the camp crematoria with an assertion of strength to protect the next generation against Jew- and other- "baiting."[49] Thus the references to "escape," "rescue," and "release" in Feinstein's poetry can be seen as more than simply expressions of lyrical transcendence.[50] When Feinstein extols "golden hours" in a "supernatural city,"[51] she is doing so, I suggest, in counterpoint to "the great hell of the camps." When she writes of "flying" or "rising" to some sort of lyrical paradise, she is also counterbalancing "Jewish" memories of "the hell of Hitler's camps."[52]

For example, "To Cross" (1971) juxtaposes an idyllic English awakening with the flight of wartime fugitives:

> Nobler, they wrote on the
> run in holes lonely
> unloved
>   what respite
> to have an August morning green at five
> young men lying in their clothes between
> blankets ash about them
> their unfrightened faces.
> Now in this bare room
> I speak with love only

> of those who keep their way in
> a mad calm bearing uncertainly
> the trap in which they are taken[53]

Although the speaker is not herself "on the / run," she identifies with those who were to the degree that she compares her own peace now with theirs as "respite." The "young men" around her are part of the "green" pastoral assembly. However, the relaxation suggested by cigarette "ash about them" and "unfrightened faces" carries a counter-image of crematoria "ash" and hence, possibly Jewish, frightened "faces." What the speaker recalls in the midst of this transcendent space—"this bare room" like a *tabula rasa*, speaking "with love only"—is "the trap" of a hellish world. Further, she relates empathetically to this "trap," as her switch to the present tense in describing fugitives who "are taken" implies. Indeed, the poem suggests that the speaker may also be one "of those who keep their way in / a mad calm." Although she feels "respite" for the moment, she is aware of the discrepancy between recent "mad" European persecution and England's apparently "calm" safe haven. Feinstein's "mad calm," I suggest, resembles the tension between violence and aesthetics in Fainlight's work, and highlights the dynamic unease of Anglo-Jewish women poets since the Holocaust.

Feinstein may not be fleeing political persecution in England, but she is very well aware of "the mist of invisible / English power" ("Exile" [1971]).[54] "Out" (1971), for instance, expresses a wish to get beyond the subtle, pervasive force of the dominant culture:

> The diesel stops. It is morning. Grey sky
> is falling into the mud. At the waterside
> two builders' cranes are sitting like birds
>
> and the yellow gorse pushes up
> like camel-thorn between oil-drums and old cars.
> Who shall I take for my holy poet
>
> to lead me out of this plain? I want an
> innocent spirit of invention   a Buster Keaton
> to sail unnaturally overhead by simple leverage and
>
> fire the machinery. Then we should all spring out of our
> heads, dazzled with hope, even the white-faced ticket
> collector dozing over his fag, at such an intervention

> suddenly in this stopped engine, we should
> see the white gulls rising out of the rain over
> the fen   and know our own freedom.[55]

Clearly, the speaker wants to rise "up" and "out" of this English landscape; to escape it and "sail unnaturally overhead." All around her is English deliquescence ("Grey sky / is falling into the mud"), and the only human represented, "the white-faced / ticket collector," is inert. "Out" contrasts England with imagined dynamism and energy. Indeed, Feinstein may be invoking a Jewish and female transcendence of English male inertia. She pleads for a "holy poet / to lead me out of this plain." The prayer echoes those of the Israelites following Moses through the Sinai desert to the Promised Land.[56] Here Feinstein finds biblical inspiration for a poetry that can transfigure England into an "innocent" Eden.

Whereas Fainlight writes without idealizing the America where she was born and raised, Feinstein looks to America as an immigrant culture in order to transcend England's literary traditions. As a metonym for American immigrant culture, "Buster Keaton" suggests the new, artificial, and transcendent "intervention" of immigrant imagination in England. "Keaton" also represents an exemplary Yiddish dreamer, or "*luftmensch*": "someone who walked and lived on air, with only his wits to help him survive."[57] In this sense, "Keaton" signifies Jewish imagination, sailing with Chagall-like otherness over England.

As a type of Jew, Keaton stands, or rather floats, in contrast to the "white-faced ticket / collector." He rises up, the "ticket / collector" sinks down. Further, Keaton's levitation "overhead" resembles the movement "up" of the "yellow gorse." Feinstein is perhaps associating "Keaton" with the color yellow in contradistinction to the "white-faced" Englishman. Yellow has a long history of publicly marking Jews as pariahs; moreover, the Nazis reintroduced a compulsory yellow badge for European Jews. When viewed in this historical context, it may be significant that the color yellow proliferates throughout Feinstein's poetry; for example in "Mother Love" (1966), where "shit slides out / yellow"; and in "Urban Lyric" (1990), which frames a "face yellow in its frizz of hair."[58] Again, the extended poem "Gold" (2000), ostensibly narrated by Mozart's Jewish librettist, Lorenzo da Ponte, describes in its opening stanza "a yellow flare in the mirror."[59]

Yellow is often transformed to gold in Feinstein's writing, as though lyrical transfiguration were a type of aesthetic alchemy; for example, in her novel *Children of the Rose* (1975): "In February the weather changed. . . . Yellow light everywhere. Even the grey walls of Lalka's town garden turned yellow. The twigs of the bare trees had an aureole of sunlight like golden smoke in their branches . . . Katie had found a new man. She was walking in the garden of Eden. Everything was changed for her; she was every dead thing in which love wrought new alchemy."[60] "Yellow" is the color of "sunlight," which transforms the "grey." It also resembles the color of gold, which "alchemy" derives from base everyday metals. Possibly, Feinstein's strategy here is to transmute the shame and victimhood of both the medieval Jewish badge and the Nazi *Jude* patch into a text of value and beauty. In the same novel, Lalka visits the Jewish cemetery in Krakow: "The Shammus [synagogue caretaker] was determined to finish his task. He showed them the wall, in which the names of the thousands who had been murdered by the Nazis had been etched. It was all that remained of them now, that golden etching."[61] From Holocaust fire, something alchemically precious remains: a "golden etching." Feinstein's own writing may be an attempt to similarly transcend and transform the hell of the Shoah and its yellow *Jude* badges into the "golden etching" of her words. Moreover, "golden" relates to the imaginative transformation of England. For example, "Renaissance Feb. 7" (1971) begins:

> In the true weather of their art
> these silver streets bustle, skin lit towers:
> we have broken some magic barrier into
> the daylight of the Duc de Berry's golden hours
> and now in a supernatural city what is
> possible changes[62]

The poem's reference to the "golden hours," or illuminated manuscripts,[63] of a French Renaissance aristocrat suggests imaginative transformation of restrictive circumstances. Indeed, "we" have risen above local constrictions on several levels by breaking through "some magic barrier": barriers of time, place, and social status. Consequently, "possible changes" are intimated as much for the speaker on the "streets" as for the "streets," through the "art" of the poem. In being a manuscript that transfigures the quotidian, the poem itself resembles the *duc's* "golden hours."

By contrast, the "yellow and bitter" Jew in "The Old Tailor" (1986)[64] has failed to transform his situation. Yet his wife, who may also be Jewish, remains courageous in the face of his "miserable" existence. She is described in language reminiscent of the cheery, English war veteran. In the face of her husband's bellicose "sneers," this "plucky wife smiled through." The old tailor's wife transcends her husband's failure by coming "through" it.[65]

Repeatedly, then, Feinstein categorizes Jews as "yellow" rather than white. For Jacqueline Rose, this "inbetween" category is that of women too: "Like being a Jew, being a woman can also be described as a state of non- or partial participation in the available or dominant cultures." Here and elsewhere, Feinstein deploys such overlapping discourses of semitic and sexual otherness precisely to distinguish a *female* Jew's imaginative transcendence from a male Jew's "certainty of failure."[66]

Since women are accorded a central role within Jewish life as mothers, it may not be surprising that Feinstein identifies maternal love as her strongest emotion. "My strongest impulse is maternal," she claims.[67] Titles such as "Mother Love," "At Seven a Son" (1966), and "Prayer for My Son" (2000) further attest to the importance of motherhood and family within Feinstein's oeuvre.[68] In an interview, Feinstein declares: "Family is very important. The family has kept me going, really."[69] Thus, while identifying her position within English literature and society as peripheral—as a woman, a Jew, and a northerner[70]—Feinstein finds an empowering Ashkenazic centrality within her family as a mother. This is a long way from Fainlight's victimized and survivalist perspectives on motherhood and domesticity, for example in "Ego-Death," "At Home at Last," and "Animal Tamer."

Domestic security, however, subjects Feinstein's speakers to emotional pressure of great intensity. Since family in this sociocultural context may well be the primary locus for emotional expression, it can also become a place identified with claustrophobia. In Feinstein's novel *The Survivors* (1982), Benjy Katz finds such an intense Anglo-Jewish family atmosphere claustrophobic. Driving around with a friend, he feels "[d]elighted to be out of the small, tight world of the house and synagogue which clenched round his own family so protectively. Out."[71] The repetition of "out" calls to mind Feinstein's poem of that name. It suggests the wish to escape a constraining Jewish family home ("the small, tight world of the house"), as "Out" invokes transcendence of England's restrictions beyond that home. Like the persona of that poem, Benjy desires a transcendent "freedom."[72] He yearns for a life beyond Jewishness, as the persona of "Out" aspires to escape Englishness. Both Benjy and the speaker of "Out" seek a centered "I," one that is not centered, however, within Jewish or English traditions perceived as similarly narrow. Feinstein depicts such an "I" as exilic, and her poetry as correspondingly produced on the peripheries of both Jewish and English traditions.

Indeed, Feinstein has written several poems with the title and theme of "Exile"[73] and declared to an interviewer: "I always felt myself to be an exile."[74] In a similar vein, the poet's biographies narrate peripheral or exilic lives: Bessie Smith, "uprooted and Empress of her own domain"; the Russian poet and "natural outsider" Marina Tsvetayeva, "more of a guest than a host" beyond her native Russia; D. H. Lawrence living "outside the Christian traditions" in New Mexico; Pushkin, the "African" "outsider," banished from St. Petersburg to the provinces; and Ted Hughes, a working-class northerner who, like Feinstein, went to Cambridge University in the 1950s and felt excluded from "the English literary centre."[75] In Feinstein's choice of biographical subjects, affiliations with those in exile from dominant cultures are clearly evident.

Feinstein also writes of Jewish women in England. "Amy Levy" (1997),[76] for instance, recounts a dream of the Victorian Anglo-Jewish poet. The parallels between Levy and Feinstein extend beyond race, gender, and poetic vocation. Levy, after all, was the first Jewish woman to be admitted to Newnham College, Cambridge, which Feinstein attended some seventy years later:

> Precocious, gifted girl, my nineteenth-century
> voice of Xanthippe, I dreamed of you last night,
> walking by the willows behind the Wren,
> and singing to me of Cambridge and unhappiness.
> "Listen, I am the first of my kind and
> not without friends or recognition,
> but my name belongs with my family
> in Bayswater, where the ghosts
>
> of wealthy Sephardim line the walls,
> and there I am alien because I sing.
> Here, it is my name that makes me strange.
> A hundred years on, is it still the same?"

Rhetorically, Feinstein suggests that, "[a] hundred years on," the situation of Anglo-Jewish women poets is "still the same." Like Levy, Feinstein must transcend Jewish "family" claustrophobia to express her lyrically individualistic "I." Her poetic vocation also conflicts with a culture that primarily venerates "wealthy," rather than intellectual, Jews. Further, the poetic "I" remains "alien" in the context of traditional Jewish roles allotted to women. Beyond her family, within an insular English literature and society, the contemporary Jewish woman poet occupies a similar in-between situation: "my name . . . makes me strange." Indeed, "Amy Levy" invokes an Anglo-Jewish textual tradition of the "alien" that has much in common with the exilic scenarios of Feinstein's other poems. To this extent, Levy's displacement provides Feinstein with a usable tradition of exile in England: in the tension between living "Here" and being culturally "strange."

Conclusion

Like Ruth Fainlight, Elaine Feinstein negotiates her inbetweenness as an Anglo-Jewish woman poet by imagining alternative cultural spaces. For both poets, Jewishness and femaleness represent different but overlapping forms of otherness that demand articulation. Poetry offers Fainlight a saving aesthetic state where otherness within the dominant male culture can be provisionally transcended. By contrast, Feinstein's lyrical poetry flees the "mad calm" of Anglo-Jewish culture to offer readers transcendence through a celebratory Jewish and female otherness.

Notes

1. Ruth Fainlight and Elaine Feinstein are both translators: Fainlight of Portuguese verse by Sophia de Mello Breyner, Feinstein of Russian poetry by Marina Tsvetayeva and others. See, for example, Sophia de Mello Breyner, *Navegações,* trans. Ruth Fainlight (Lisbon: Casa da Moeda, 1983), and Elaine Feinstein, *Collected Poems and Translations* (Manchester: Carcanet, 2002).

2. See Virginia Blain, Patricia Clements, and Isabel Grundy, eds., *The Feminist Companion to Literature in English: Women Writers from the Middle Ages to the Present* (London: B. T. Batsford, 1990), 351, where Fainlight's "feminist iconography" is stressed, while her Jewishness is reduced to religion (and placed in parentheses): "(RF's religion is Jewish)." Both Fainlight and Feinstein feature in *The Bloodaxe Book of Contemporary Women Poets: Eleven British Writers,* ed. Jeni Couzyn (Newcastle upon Tyne: Bloodaxe, 1985), 112–43.

3. Christopher Ricks, ed., *The Oxford Book of English Verse* (Oxford: Oxford University Press, 1999), 652–53, includes Feinstein's free translations of Tsvetayeva's poems "Insomnia (3)" and "An Attempt at Jealousy."

4. Deborah Mitchell, "Modes of Realism: Roy Fisher and Elaine Feinstein," in *British Poetry Since 1970: A Critical Survey,* ed. Peter Jones and Michael Schmidt (Manchester: Carcanet, 1980), 130 and 125–30.

5. See Margaret Drabble, ed., *The Oxford Companion to English Literature* (Oxford: Oxford University Press, 2000), 345. The entry on Fainlight begins: "poet and translator, born in New York, but for many years resident in England."

6. Ruth Fainlight, "Definition," in *Another Full Moon* (London: Hutchinson, 1976), lines 19–25. Subsequent line citations of this poem appear in parentheses in the text.

7. Ruth Fainlight, "Vertical," in *Selected Poems* (London: Sinclair-Stevenson, 1995), 45.

8. Ruth Fainlight, "My Position in the History of the Twentieth Century," in *Another Full Moon,* 54–55, lines 11–14. Subsequent line citations of this poem appear in parentheses in the text.

9. Lidia Vianu, "Desperado Literature: Interview with Ruth Fainlight" (2001): www.lidi-avianu.scriptmania.com/ruth_fainlight.htm.

10. "Ruth (Esther) Fainlight," in *Contemporary Authors Online*: gdc.gale.com/gale-literature-collections/contemporary-authors (accessed February 28, 2014).

11. Carolyn G. Heilbrun, *Reinventing Womanhood* (London: Victor Gollancz, 1979), 20.

12. "Ruth (Esther) Fainlight," in *Contemporary Authors Online*.

13. Ruth Fainlight, "Cages," in *Cages* (London: Macmillan, 1966), 6, lines 1–4.

14. Ruth Fainlight, "Hymn," in *Cages*, 2, lines 4–8.

15. For further discussion of Fainlight's relationship with Plath, see Ruth Fainlight, "Jane and Sylvia," *Crossroads: Journal of the Poetry Society of America* 61 (Spring 2004), 8–19.

16. See "Autumn Stirring," in *Cages*, 7: "Those who kill themselves are angels. / They last longest, / Have found the way of power, / Despising all oblivion."

17. Ruth Fainlight, "Ego-Death," in *Cages*, 41, lines 7–12.

18. Ibid., lines 5, 15, and 23.

19. Ruth Fainlight, *Sibyls and Others* (London: Hutchinson, 1980), 29–30, 46–48, 53, and 130–31.

20. Ruth Fainlight, *Dr Clock's Last Case and Other Stories* (London: Virago, 1994), 154 and 153–61.

21. See Ruth Fainlight, "Pleasure," in *Daylife & Nightlife* (London: André Deutsch, 1971), 101–9; and idem, *Dr Clock's Last Case and Other Stories*, 65–71.

22. Ruth Fainlight, "Solo Scrabble," in *To See the Matter Clearly* (London: Macmillan, 1968), 37, lines 1–3.

23. Ruth Fainlight in *The Bloodaxe Book of Contemporary Women Poets*, ed. Couzyn, 128–43 (132).

24. "Ruth (Esther) Fainlight," in *Contemporary Authors Online*.

25. Ruth Fainlight, *Dr Clock's Last Case and Other Stories*, 55–63, 85–96.

26. Ruth Fainlight, "With David in the Nimrud Galleries," in *Sibyls and Others*, 66–67.

27. Ruth Fainlight, *The Region's Violence* (London: Hutchinson, 1973), 30.

28. Fainlight, "With David in the Nimrud Galleries," in *Sibyls and Others*, 66, lines 12–14 and 17–24.

29. Ibid., 67, lines 42–44 and 48.

30. Walter Benjamin, "Theses on the Philosophy of History," in *Illuminations*, ed. Hannah Arendt (London: Fontana, 1982), 258 and 255–66.

31. Ruth Fainlight, "Paradise," in *To See the Matter Clearly*, 62, lines 1–4. Subsequent line citations of this poem appear in parentheses in the text.

32. "Ruth (Esther) Fainlight," in *Contemporary Authors*.

33. Ruth Fainlight, "Green," in *The Region's Violence*, 72, lines 10–13.

34. See Ruth Fainlight, "My Position in the History of the Twentieth Century," 54–55.

35. Ruth Fainlight, "Animal Tamer," in *Sibyls and Others*, 89.

36. See Bryan Cheyette, ed., *Contemporary Jewish Writing in Britain and Ireland: An Anthology* (London: Peter Halban, 1988), xxi–xxii..

37. Fainlight, "Animal Tamer," in *Sibyls and Others*, 89, lines 2–3. Subsequent line citations of this poem appear in parentheses in the text.

38. See Bryan Cheyette, "Neither Black nor White: The Figure of 'the Jew' in Imperial British Literature," in *The Jew in the Text*, ed. Linda Nochlin and Tamar Garb (London: Thames and Hudson, 1995), 31–41.

39. Ruth Fainlight, *Burning Wire* (Newcastle upon Tyne: Bloodaxe, 2002), 32–33. Further references will appear in the text.

40. Ruth Fainlight, "House-Guest," in *Sibyls and Others*, 119, line 17. Subsequent line citations of this poem appear in parentheses in the text.

41. Ruth Fainlight, "At Home At Last," in *Another Full Moon*, 47, lines 6–8 and 16–19. Subsequent line citations of this poem appear in parentheses in the text.

42. Ruth Fainlight, "Definition," in *Another Full Moon*, 7, lines 10–11 and 15.

43. Elaine Feinstein, "Preface," in *Collected Poems and Translations*, xiii.

44. "Elaine Feinstein," in *Contemporary Authors Autobiography Series*, vol. 1 (Detroit: Gale, 1984), 219 and 215–24.

45. For a discussion of Feinstein's fiction in the context of the Holocaust, see Phyllis Lassner, "Elaine Feinstein's Holocaust Imagination," in *Anglo-Jewish Women Writing the Holocaust: Displaced Witnesses* (Basingstoke: Palgrave Macmillan, 2008), 129–55.

46. See Theodor Adorno, "Commitment," in *Aesthetics and Politics*, ed. Rodney Livingstone, Perry Anderson, and Francis Mulhern (London: New Left Books, 1977), 177–95.

47. Elaine Feinstein, *Selected Poems* (Manchester: Carcanet, 1994), 4, 51; idem, *Daylight* (Manchester: Carcanet, 1997), 26.

48. Elaine Feinstein, *Daylight*, 21, lines 6–10.

49. Feinstein, *Selected Poems*, 21, lines 27 and 1, respectively. During an interview with Bryan Cheyette on November 11, 2001, at the New End Theatre, London, Feinstein acknowledged that "fire" referred to the camp crematoria, since the poem was written in the wake of the Eichmann trial.

50. See "Separations" (1997), "Respite" (2000), "New Year '66" (1966), respectively, in Feinstein, *Daylight*, 22; *Gold* (Manchester: Carcanet, 2000), 35, and *Selected Poems*, 4.

51. See "Renaissance Feb. 7" (1966), in Feinstein, *Selected Poems*, 66, lines 4–5.

52. See "Aubade for a Scientist" (1966) and "At Seven a Son" (1966), in Feinstein, *Selected Poems*, 8, 10. See also "Elaine Feinstein," in *Contemporary Authors Autobiography Series*, 219.

53. Feinstein, "To Cross," in *Selected Poems*, 47.

54. Feinstein, "Exile," in *Some Unease and Angels* (London: Hutchinson, 1977), 21, lines 17–18.

55. Feinstein, "Out," in *Selected Poems*, 27.

56. Feinstein evokes the desert in several other poems. See, for example, "The Celebrants VI" (1973), where she describes "my desert / grandmother" who came from "nomads, wilderness people"; "June" (1977), which features an "old cactus / yellowing" by which "we remember the desert"; and "New Songs for Dido and Aeneas 9" (1986), with its "cactus and desert grass." See also "Aviation" (1990): "I have a monster in my head, yellow / and surly as a camel": Feinstein, *Selected Poems*, 70, 98, 123, and 145. Similarly, "Regret" (1986) depicts a biblical leader guiding his "children" up to a "mountain ledge," while admonishing them to "forget" what "still lies below." In this poem, the speaker to whom Feinstein refers is Lot leaving Sodom and Gomorrah. "And here among these salty pillars / the unforgiving stand," s/he says: "Forget the smoking city": Feinstein, *Selected Poems*, 109, lines 1, 6, 9, 2, 4–5, 9.

57. Elaine Feinstein, *Dark Inheritance* (2000; repr. London: Women's Press, 2001), 15.

58. Feinstein, *Selected Poems*, 14, lines 16–17; 133, line 3.

59. Feinstein, "Gold," in *Gold*, 9, line 3.

60. Elaine Feinstein, *Children of the Rose* (1975; repr. Harmondsworth: Penguin, 1976), 77.

61. Ibid., 125.

62. Feinstein, *Selected Poems*, 66, lines 1–6.

63. The Duc de Berry (1340–1416) invested fortunes in his treasures—paintings, tapestries, jewelry, and illuminated manuscripts (including the world-famous *Très riches heures du duc de Berry*).

64. Feinstein, *Selected Poems*, 112, line 1.

65. Ibid., 112, lines 11, 9, and 8, respectively. See also Feinstein, "Photographs" (1990), in *Selected Poems*, 139, lines 17–18: "What you / think of as disadvantages will bring you through."

66. See Jacqueline Rose, "Dorothy Richardson and the Jew," in *Between "Race" and Culture: Representations of "the Jew" in English and American Literature*, ed. Bryan Cheyette (Stanford: Stanford University Press, 1996), 125 and 114–28. See also Feinstein, "The Old Tailor," in *Selected Poems*, 112.

67. See A. S. Byatt, "Writers in Conversation: Elaine Feinstein," video recording (London: ICA Video, 1987).

68. Feinstein, *Selected Poems*, 10, 14; and idem, *Gold*, 36.

69. Peter Lawson, "Way Out in the Centre: In Conversation with Elaine Feinstein," *Jewish Quarterly* (Spring 2001), 66.

70. Ibid., 67, and 65–69.

71. Elaine Feinstein, *The Survivors* (1982; repr. New York: Penguin, 1991), 64.

72. See Feinstein, "Out" (1971), in *Selected Poems*, 27.

73. See, for example, Feinstein, "Exile" (1971), in *Selected Poems*, 38; idem, "Exile" (1997), in *Daylight*, 34; and idem, "Exile" (2000), in *Gold*, 39.

74. Byatt, "Writers in Conversation: Elaine Feinstein."

75. See Elaine Feinstein, *Bessie Smith* (Harmondsworth: Viking, 1985), 13; idem, *A Captive Lion—The Life of Marina Tsvetayeva* (London: Hutchinson, 1987), 35, 180; idem, *Lawrence's Women: The Intimate Life of D. H. Lawrence* (London: HarperCollins, 1993), 148; idem, *Pushkin* (1998; repr. London: Phoenix, 1999), 12, 164; and idem, *Ted Hughes: The Life of a Poet* (London: Weidenfeld & Nicolson, 2001), 24.

76. Feinstein, "Amy Levy," in *Daylight*, 57.

8

THE TRAUMA OF ASSIMILATION

Anita Brookner as Jewish Novelist

LOUISE SYLVESTER

Anita Brookner (b. 1928) has been described as a novelist in the English tradition, and her fiction has attracted comparisons with that of Jane Austen and Barbara Pym.[1] In the first full-length study of Brookner's novels, however, John Skinner questions these alignments. Skinner looks closely at the relationship of Brookner's fiction to its French models and influences, in particular Balzac's *Eugénie Grandet* and Brookner's *A Start in Life,* and Constant's *Adolphe* and Brookner's *Providence* (in which the heroine is required to teach Constant's novel). He also questions "attempts to endow Brookner with the same quintessentially English insider status as Pym," citing the Central European origins of Brookner's family as evidence against this.[2] It is clear, then, that Skinner is alive to a quality in Brookner's work that is European rather than English. He also indicates a willingness to read the novels in the light of Brookner's life, stating that the autobiographical is a dimension of her fiction that cannot be ignored. Indeed, the family resemblances that he finds among all Brookner's protagonists validate what he terms a "psycho-biographical" approach to her work.[3] Equally, Skinner is manifestly familiar with the extensive interviews that Brookner has given. It is remarkable then, in the light of his rejection of Brookner as a parochial English novelist, and his interest in the autobiographical aspects of her fiction, that Skinner evinces an extreme reluctance to take on Brookner's self-identification as a Jew. It should perhaps be added that Skinner is not alone in this: the Jews in Brookner's novels, both disguised and overt, have received almost no critical attention. My argument in this essay is that assimilation, and modern attitudes toward it, lie at the root of this silence.

Brookner's background, though not unusual, demands attention to its particularities. Her father was born in Poland, her mother in England, but Brookner describes them both as Polish Jews.[4] Brookner herself was born and grew up in London, and her origins are thus typical of those of much of Anglo-Jewry. This background brings with it religious and cultural impera- tives directed toward preserving difference and separation: consequently, Anglo-Jews turn to the inner self, the immediate family, and the Jewish com- munity. In one of her interviews, Brookner observes that she was brought up to look after her parents: "My family were Polish Jews and we lived with my grandmother, with uncles and aunts and cousins all around, and I thought everybody lived like that [. . .] I felt that I had to protect them. Indeed that is what they expected."[5] In the twentieth century this mode of being carried with it the risk of opprobrium from the majority culture: as seen, for example, in the discourse surrounding the Aliens Act of 1905, which was aimed pri- marily at Jews and responded to propaganda that accused them of clannish- ness.[6] Anglo-Jewish identity, usually incorporating a European background, also carried a strong sense of existing on the margins of a dominant English culture; Anglo-Jews also looked out, therefore, toward the opportunities pre- sented by the outside world as well as its prejudices.[7] These two viewpoints played off against each other, producing an acute sensitivity to the conno- tations of the label "Anglo-Jew." The resulting conflict had its beginnings in childhood, as Anglo-Jewish children absorbed the message that they were supposed to achieve acceptance and success in the outside world, but on the other hand they mustn't stray too far from the confines of the family: they must keep close, and not marry out.[8]

Examining the reporting of antisemitism by the *Jewish Chronicle* since the late nineteenth century, David Cesarani quotes an editorial from June 1893 titled, "Some Jewish Defects," warning readers against the obtrusion of Jewish luxury, such as the wearing of diamonds on inappropriate occasions and in abnormal profusion, and that "loud" clothes and talk attract more attention than they deserve, reflecting unfavorably on the Jewish character and Jewish interests.[9] Cesarani traces this attitude throughout the twentieth century, finding an analysis of antisemitism that blames the victims for its occurrence. This theme recurs, more or less overtly; for example, in 1917 the violence of the anti-Jewish riots in Leeds is ascribed by the *Jewish Chronicle* to the aloofness of a rapidly expanded and highly visible Jewish population that aroused economic jealousies.[10] The British Union of Fascists' East End campaign in 1935–36, and the eruption of widespread political antisemitism, triggered an editorial in 1937 claiming that it was necessary to stamp out "the materialism which is rampant among some of our people" and "the vice of vulgar display."[11]

In the nineteenth century, the newspaper places the greatest blame for these social solecisms on immigrants from Eastern Europe, reflecting the fears of middle-class Anglo-Jews that derive from their understanding of the ideology that led to their emancipation. As Cesarani argues, the prevailing belief was that the Jews had merited civic equality by virtue of their contribution to English society and concordance with English mores, so any deviation from accepted ways, or any charge of "parasitism," could jeopardize their civil status.[12] This is one explanation for the inexorable attraction of assimilation: the suppression of ethnicity in favor of merging with the host culture is the price that must be paid by those in the minority in order to obtain equal rights of citizenship. The possibilities presented by assimilation, as strategies both to gain acceptance and to prevent antisemitism, continued to be debated until the later part of the twentieth century within Anglo-Jewry. Thus, in response to events in the Third Reich, the *Jewish Chronicle*'s editorials urged Jews to conform to the expectations of a society that was ambivalent toward Jewish difference; though one of its leader writers argued that religion and tradition inevitably set Jews apart from their fellow citizens, and it was therefore futile to strive for the total acceptance that Victorian Jews had thought was possible.[13]

Brookner's own response to her Anglo-Jewish background is suggestive. One interviewer observes that the foreignness of her heroines is emphasized by the contrast between them and the solidly English Protestant men to whom they are attracted. Tellingly, Brookner responds that it is more that the contrast is between those who are damaged and those who are undamaged. She draws Englishness and Christianity together, arguing that they are indissolubly linked within the mainstream of British culture.[14] More than that, though, Brookner has said that she feels herself to be a displaced person: despite having been born in England, she has never really felt at home. In another interview she responds in the affirmative to the question of whether she was "entirely brought up in England with a regular schooling," but follows up this answer with a delineation of her feelings of alienation: "I've never been at home here. I took on protective colouring at a very early age, but it didn't stick."[15] This admission runs counter to the general view of assimilation, which holds that it is a process that takes only a couple of generations to complete. In the novel *Now,* by the French-born writer Gabriel Josipovici, one of the characters announces to his daughter that he is not English:

— I'm not English

— What are you?

— I don't know. Not English.

— Am I English?

— A bit more than me.

— And my children? Will they be English?

— A little more each time.[16]

For a number of reasons, however, this model is insufficiently nuanced: assimilation may be a project always and already doomed to failure. Writing of assimilation, in particular Anglicization, Homi Bhabha speaks of the "*double* vision of racial discourse which constructs a subject of difference that is almost the same, but not quite [. . .] in which to be Anglicized is *emphatically* not to be English."[17] More and more, we understand that holding more than one identity in juxtaposition is not necessarily a process of shedding one and securing another. It is complicated, however, because of the power differential between the mainsprings of those identities. The roots of the minority culture may go back further in time, but this, of course, brings it into conflict with the mainstream, dominant culture, which comes to represent the present, and therefore the future. Marilyn Demarest Button adopts this understanding of the temporal positioning of dominant and minority cultures, one in the past and one in the present; she suggests that one of Brookner's characters conveys a sense of "belonging to two cultures—that of a European past and an English present" and discusses "the psychological cost of trying to blend two cultures—European and English, the past and the present."[18] Button makes no mention of Judaism in her essay, but the point is made very clearly by Brookner in her answer to Haffenden's question, "*Do you have a particular grouse against Christianity? Yes.* I have many grounds for complaint. I wish I could accept the whole thing—it would make one terribly cheerful, and give one a stake in the country, as it were—but I can't."[19]

A Failed Attempt at Assimilation: *Providence*

In a study that] *Providence* (1982) with Cynthia Ozick's story "Virility," Cheryl Alexander Malcolm argues that Brookner's novel reveals what is often over-looked: that the condition of being assimilated is not static but, rather, is often fluctuating and precarious.[20] In Malcolm's assessment, the single ambition of Brookner's protagonist, Kitty Maule, is to be assimilated. It is interesting, in the light of this assessment, to discover how far notions of Kitty's difference are explicit in Brookner's descriptions of her. In the first sentence we are told that "Kitty Maule was difficult to place."[21] Kitty herself seems to embody an ambivalence about this; we are almost immediately offered a sense of the way that she thinks that others should see her: "Yet Kitty felt herself to be English; hence her explanation, 'My father was in the army.' And indeed *no one had ever faulted her on the grounds of Englishness.* Yet she felt a part of her to be shrewd and watchful, mistrusting others, paying less attention to their words than to the words they were not saying" (5–6, my italics). The description, expressed as it is in the third person, appears contradictory: if Kitty truly felt herself to be English, why would she expect to be "faulted [. . .] on the grounds of Englishness"? Moreover, we discover that she simplifies descriptions of her family background, considering it too colorful, too much in need of expla-nation and information about "alien professions, habits, customs that most people could not be expected to understand and which were to her as native as the colour of her own hair" (5). She foregrounds her father, who was in the army and died before she was born, instead of her dead mother and her liv-ing grandparents, who are French. This evidence, offered in the guise of free indirect thought attributable to Kitty, is contradicted in the narrator's report of a conversation between Kitty's colleague Pauline and Pauline's mother on the subject of Kitty:

> "She has such a pretty voice," said Mrs Bentley. "Such very precise English. You rarely hear such good enunciation these days. It comes from her being a foreigner, of course."

> "Oh, really, Mother. She was born in London. Although I agree that she gives the impression of someone not quite at home here. Trying to learn the rules as it were." (150)

Kitty's careful enunciation, slightly too-noticeable clothes, and near-silence on the subject of her home life indicate an ethnicity that is amenable to being hidden, but which, it is feared, may reveal itself. We might expect that a character who is leading "a virtual double life" would be disguised a little better and, most especially, would repress the knowledge of her own difference.[22] Instead, what we seem to see in *Providence* is the protagonist seeking simultaneously to hide and to display this difference. It is immediately noticeable how close Brookner's portrayal of Kitty is to her depiction of herself in the interviews quoted.

The plot of *Providence,* and its denouement, are revealing about Brookner's attitude toward the idea of assimilation. Kitty falls in love with Maurice Bishop, a "romantic and devout Christian" (18). For Malcolm, the words, "I want a future away from this place. I want Maurice" (60), are "not so much the plaintive cry of a lonely woman as the sentiments of a pragmatist who sees the only escape from a marginalized existence is to marry an insider."[23] In her article on cultural experiences and identity in Brookner's early novels, Gisèle Marie Baxter suggests that Maurice Bishop and Richard Hirst (the love-object in *A Start in Life*) "stand for socially integrated, traditional values represented by a religious faith which reflects the security of their position."[24] It is clear, however, that it is not simply religious faith that secures Maurice Bishop's identity but rather the fact that he is a Christian: his faith is that of the mainstream of English culture and society. Malcolm believes that Brookner's female protagonists, Kitty Maule in particular, are "most aggressive in their pursuit of a firm place of belonging in English society."[25] While this reading is possible, it is interesting to note that Brookner generally denies her heroines this outcome. Consequently, Kitty's love for Maurice Bishop is thwarted from its fulfilment by the concealed intervention of one of her students, Jane Fairchild, with Maurice's engagement to Jane forming the final set-piece of the novel.

It is not only twists of the plot that announce these denials: Brookner's heroines often decide at the last minute that marriage, and its concomitant social position, is not what they want. Most famously, Edith Hope drives round the park instead of attending her own wedding, precipitating an enforced stay at the Hotel du Lac; here she refuses another offer of marriage, one which she is expected to accept on the same pragmatic grounds as those outlined by Malcolm.[26] For Baxter, Brookner's heroines have "a strong sense of personal identity which prevents them from entirely abandoning their moral codes. Their choices of cultural experience are not a simple desire to 'pass.'"[27] Baxter appears to have picked up both on Brookner's sense of the importance of Christianity to the dominant culture and on the way in which Kitty (and others) are presented as being outside this dominant culture. In fact, I would argue that the heroines' moral codes, alluded to by Baxter, are their inherited Jewish identities. In this view, it is their Jewishness that Brookner's heroines cannot quite renounce. In this respect, the Jewish historical experience represents a particular problem, to which Brookner alludes in her interview with John Haffenden when she states: "You can never betray the people who are dead, so you go on being a public Jew."[28]

Immigrants and Their Children:
Family and Friends and The Next Big Thing

As with Brookner's earlier novels, there is no overt reference to Jews in *Family and Friends* (1985).[29] Nevertheless, critics have felt confident in asserting that it portrays a Jewish family. D. J. Enright, for example, describes the characters as "members of a wealthy European and (very faintly) Jewish family living in England."[30] Others go further, suggesting that the family portrayed in the novel is Brookner's "own family seen through art."[31] For those who can hear them, the echoes of Jewish customs are quite strong: they include mourning rituals, such as the covering of mirrors and rending of garments, and constant references to "the old country" and to the custodianship of its traditions. The eldest son's fiancée is marked out in this way: Sofka, the matriarch, feels resentment toward her even though "the woman has unconsciously conformed to Sofka's family tradition." Other echoes of the Jewish experience are not heard by all of the novel's readers: some critics deplore the exclusion of the wider world, and World War II, from *Family and Friends*. A slightly different reaction is found in Enright's review of the novel, which observes that it is "a relief to discover a novel with Jewish characters but no Holocaust."[32] Arguably, however, the war is alluded to in the urgency with which Betty (Sofka's daughter) and Max (who is Hungarian) leave Paris for America. It is glimpsed, too, in the anxious question Sofka asks her friend Irma Beck when the latter knocks at her door selling lace: "At last, and fearfully, Sofka enquires, 'Your children?' For the first time the woman relaxes, and smiles. 'Safe,' she says. 'Here'" (99). The motifs of hurried departure and fear for relatives remaining

behind, and of having to earn money in ways that are alien to one's upbringing and expectations, may be seen as tropes for the émigré experience of Jews
before and during the war.

In her later work Brookner becomes more open about the Jewish background of her characters and its implications. In *The Next Big Thing* (2002), a
number of elements only suggested in the earlier fiction are brought to the
surface.[33] The protagonist, Julius Herz, is a clearly a Jew: "his mother had
never forgiven her sister for marrying out, though by no means observant
in her own right" (2). His family members are refugees from Germany, and
Brookner is at her most explicit about the effects of this start in life: these
include the mental illness suffered by Herz's brother Freddy, a former musical
prodigy, the intense loneliness of the whole family, and an ongoing sense of
exile and rupture from the life that should have been theirs. The book shows
us Herz's belated understanding of the inability of parents who have suffered
in this way to accept the notion that the young might be entitled to freedom
from the burden of the family. Herz, for example, silently takes on the task of
visiting his brother in residential care: "Julius accepted that his parents were
unequal to the task he shouldered every week. Those parents (and Freddy
too knew this) were too fearful of confronting the shipwreck of their hopes,
and lived an obstinate illusion of normality in absolute denial of the facts of
the case. It was a tactic which had ensured their survival, and one on which
they fiercely relied. The burden was shifted to their younger son, who became
guardian to all three of them, unaware of his own entitlements" (20).

In this novel Brookner alludes to Herz's grandparents, who are bound by
all the prohibitions of Judaism. These duties are not transferred down the
generations, however. Indeed, Herz's aunt is forgiven her intermarriage, since
it is her Protestant husband who guarantees the family safe passage out of
Berlin. It is thus not a betrayal of faith that is feared and forbidden; rather,
it is the possibility of happiness, the forgetfulness of origins, that is not
allowed. This shows itself in a mass of tiny details. Each week, for example,
Herz must walk his mother's only friend to the bus stop and wait with her
until her bus arrives: "even on radiant summer evenings, when young men
of his age were preparing to enjoy themselves, he was imprisoned by Bijou
Frank's little hand on his arm, and her slow steps" (13–14). The opposition of
the terms "enjoy" and "imprisoned" seems designed to underline the point.
Brookner thus dramatizes the cycles of suffering and response observed in
Howard Cooper and Paul Morrison's study of Jewish families in late twentieth-century Britain; they note that the overenmeshment of Jewish families

can mean that parents, while consciously wishing for their children's success and independence, may unconsciously fear or resent or envy it too.[34] This dual message of push (toward security and achievement in the outside world) and pull (stay close, stay Jewish) is seen in all its loving destructiveness in *The Next Big Thing*, and the novel's plot delineates the corresponding impossibility of fulfilment for dutiful sons and daughters forever indebted to the desperate unhappiness of their parents. Only once is the nature of the family, and the demands it has made on Herz, considered explicitly in the consciousness of one of the characters. As the family confronts a move to another, smaller flat, Herz's father voices, in an inner monologue, his secret wish to be a bachelor again: "The task of making his beloved wife happy was beyond him, as it was beyond everyone now. He dreaded the day when his unhappiness would break cover, was grateful to Julius—not his best-loved son—for his tact, realized sorrowfully that Julius had been sacrificed, by virtue of a family bound together by grief and with no prospect of rehabilitation" (30).

The Legacy of the Holocaust: *Latecomers*

In their study of British Jewish identity, Cooper and Morrison trace the difficulties experienced in postwar Anglo-Jewish families back to the wartime emigrations from Europe, to the flights from persecution or the fear of it, the arrival in an alien place with a new language and culture, and the struggle to survive materially and spiritually. Cooper and Morrison observe that painful separations were part of the process, and Brookner's novels of parents and their adult children dramatize this legacy.[35] In *Latecomers* (1988), Brookner charts the history of two middle-aged business partners of German origin, Hartmann and Fibich. They share a first name, and their lives are intertwined from the moment they meet at boarding school in England. The most important motif of their relationship, and the subject of the novel, is their respective attitudes to the past and the ways they cope with it, which differ profoundly. Hartmann sees himself as fully assimilated—to achieve this state he has struck a bargain with the fates involving an effort "to screen out the undesirable, the inadvertent," and so he carefully polices his memories: "He remembered his father, in a magnificently odorous and gleaming emporium, pointing with his cane to a pineapple, a box of peaches, and asking for them to be taken out to the car. Or himself, when tiny, walking with his nurse in the Englische Garten. Or first love, at the age of ten, and a game of hide-and-seek with the beloved at Nymphenburg, beside the long paths rustling with fallen leaves and the commotion of birds."[36]

Just as Kitty Maule "felt herself to be English" and yet is concerned not to be faulted on the grounds of Englishness, so, in the continuation of this description, we may note again the paradoxical element that enters Brookner's work when the subject matter touches on her own ethnic origins. Hartmann, we learn, is troubled by his inability to recall an event that he did not see—perhaps, the narrative suggests, does not even know about: "He did not remember, because he had never witnessed the event, his elegant parents, dressed for some *fête-champêtre*, being hoisted, slightly puzzled, on to farm carts, but behaving with good grace, thinking this part of the entertainment. They were driven off, never to be seen again, but how could he know that? How could one remember absence? Was it not one's duty to fill the void, when there were so many agreeable ways of doing so?" (7–8). He worries, however, about whether he should try to remember his parents' disappearance from his life, as well as about how he could do so without breaking down altogether. This is never alluded to again in the novel: Hartmann's strategy for surviving in his new environment demands that he remain focused solely on the here and now. Only occasionally does he recall his early years in England when, sent away to school, he knows himself to be "Doubly, even trebly an outsider" (10).

In contrast, Fibich, Hartmann's partner, is introduced by Brookner with the words "Fibich remembered" (33). What Fibich remembers, however, are only fragments of a life that he seems never to have owned. He fears the future, has nightmares about it, and envies Hartmann's "easy acceptance of the world as it was, not reaching back towards a past which he had never properly possessed" (34). Fibich, it seems, cannot take possession of his present, and his life in England, because he feels he has never been given the opportunity to own his past. He "had left home at the age of seven," the narrative voice comments, "and therefore could hardly hope to recapture his lost life" (34). As with Herz, Fibich's past, his start in life, has robbed him of the possibility of fully owning his own life. What the two men share is an exaggerated love for their children, and a fearfulness for those children's future that is typical of survivors, even European Jews who found safety in Britain or America. This fearfulness is connected to the conflict between aspiring to insider status and the need to hold on to that which places the foreign-born or descendant of foreign-born Jews at the margins of society. It is as if Hartmann fears that remembering his foreign origins will undermine his attempts at assimilation into Englishness: that assimilation on which, as we have noted, the prevention of antisemitism is believed to depend. He fears too, however, that not remembering is a dereliction of an important duty.

In her book *The War After: Living with the Holocaust*, Anne Karpf, the British-born daughter of survivors of Auschwitz, observes that her parents could not bear to allow their children to go out without thick coats on: "I never really understood what lay behind their obsession with trussing me in wool—one which seemed to go beyond normal, even normal Jewish, parental concern [. . .] it dawned on me that cold was not just a meteorological fact but also a psychic state. My parents experienced the post-war world as cold, both in their bodies and minds. Cold for them was life outside the home, cold represented what awaited you when you went out."[37] When Fibich, who cannot remember anything before his arrival in England, reveals that he wants to go back to Berlin, Hartmann appears shocked; perhaps most of all by the notion of going back, especially since neither of them seems clear what it is they are looking back at:

". . . Are you mad?"

"I feel," said Fibich with difficulty, "like a survivor. As if I arrived where I am by accident. After a shipwreck, or some sort of disaster that blacked out my memory. As if I will never catch up until I find out what went before."

Hartmann sighed. "You are not a survivor. You are a latecomer, like me. Like Yvette, for that matter. You had a bad start. Why go back to the beginning? One thing is certain: you can't start again."

"Do you never look back?" asked Fibich.

"Not if I can help it," said Hartmann. (141)

While this moment may seem to capture the strategy of avoidance that it describes, I would argue that Brookner is here counting the cost of assimilation, a cost that includes the willed annihilation of memory. While Fibich cannot look back, his memory seems to have been wiped clean of all trace of his earlier life; Hartmann, not so fortunate, indicates the threat posed to the present by the intrusion, even in thought, of the past. Although it is not explicitly alluded to again in the novel, the reader must be aware of what it is that both Hartmann and Fibich, in their different ways, have excluded from their lives. This price is one that Brookner is ambivalent about paying.

The echoes in her novels may be faint, but the message of the interviews is unequivocal: as a Jew, denial of one's origins constitutes a betrayal of the dead. It may also, however, be the only possible strategy for survival.

Foreign vs. Assimilated: *A Family Romance*

For his anthology of contemporary Jewish writing in Britain, Bryan Cheyette selected an extract from *Latecomers,* although he notes that it is in Brookner's later novel, *A Family Romance* (1993), that she includes openly Jewish characters.[38] Perhaps Cheyette's choice was guided by the overt presence in *Latecomers* of the tragic theme of the Holocaust and its attendant losses, which English readers would be likely to associate with Jewish literature. It seems to me that it is in *A Family Romance* that the problem of assimilation is raised from subtext to text, although this is not an aspect of the book that has attracted the attention of scholars of Brookner's work.

The novel is narrated by Jane who, with her mother, Henrietta, and her father, Paul, is part of a quiet and peaceful English family. Jane notes, "I grew up English and unafraid," as though fear is a concomitant of not being properly English.[39] *A Family Romance* tells the story of the narrator's life-long involvement with Marie-Jeanne Schiff, known as Dolly, who is her aunt by marriage. As I have argued elsewhere, Dolly is troped as Jewish in a number of ways.[40] She is an emigrant: We are told that she was born in Paris in 1922, her father having had the sense to leave Germany, and she is presented as a reflex of her Viennese-born Jewish mother-in-law, Toni Ferber. The novel's portrait of Englishness and its antithesis operates by splitting the figure of the mother into a good (usually dead) mother and an evil stepmother typical of fairy tales. This configuration allows the child to feel anger at the bad "stepmother" without endangering the goodwill of the true mother, who is viewed as a different person.[41] In Brookner's novel, Jane's mother, Henrietta, is Jewish, while her aunt (by marriage) Dolly, technically, is not (only her father is Jewish). However, Henrietta, beloved by her husband and by Jane, is given all the attributes of non-Jewish Englishness, while Dolly, the "misfit," bears all the difficulties associated with foreignness (1). In an early description of Dolly, for example, Jane observes that "she had a squat European figure, with shortish legs and a full bosom" (14); Henrietta, on the other hand, is "thin, pale, shy, self-effacing" (34).[42] Henrietta tells her husband "I like a very quiet kind of life" (26), whereas Dolly is depicted as "a vivid woman, with a questing, ardent expression, as if she could not bear to be wasting time" (14).

As noted earlier, Kitty Maule's secret identity is visible in her clothes: made by her French grandmother, and clearly too stylish for one on her restricted income, they give away the information Kitty has repressed about her foreign background. Clothes offer a code to be deciphered in *A Family Romance*, too: Dolly's apparel is constantly remarked upon, disapprovingly, by Jane from the first meeting when she registers the presence of her aunt as "a stranger in a black and white dress which I thought was too tight" (3).[43] Dolly's clothes signify her sexuality, as well as her unfailing and blatant awareness of money, the latter being yet another trait that marks her out as un-English.

As an exploration of the dilemmas and costs of assimilation, *A Family Romance* is, I think, Brookner's most daring novel. To Jane, through whose eyes we view all the events and characters, Dolly is an entirely unsympathetic character, mainly because she is the antithesis of Jane's mother, but also because she poses a threat to the Englishness that Jane sees as her rightful inheritance: "I knew then, as I was to relearn later, that Dolly signified a sad estrangement from everything which I assumed to be rightfully mine: my family, my friends, my school, my peaceful English life" (5). As Jane matures, her observations of Dolly begin to be contextualized against a view that Dolly might have taken of herself. In a manner typical of Brookner's protagonists, Jane represents herself as knowing more than she does, and therefore of being able to offer judgments about others:

> It was entirely to her credit that she refused to make a fairy story of her life, that she accepted each successive phase of it without question, that she adapted to each new set of circumstances with such remarkable facility that one tended to forget her previous incarnation. She now believed herself to be living the life of an average English-woman, although in fact her life was far from typical. Her accent was English, her good sense was English, her endurance was English. Yet she had a look of readiness, of adroitness, that was not English, and which led back to her early need to make her way in the world. Above all it was easy to discern from Dolly's now evasive, now conspiratorial gaze that she was a woman of passion. (122–23)

Each of these statements that express a belief that Dolly holds about herself—that she is living the life of an average Englishwoman, for example—is undercut by Jane's superior knowledge both about Englishness and about

Dolly herself. These contradictions register the strong sense of Jane's disapproval of Dolly that pervades the novel.

The qualities that mark Dolly out as un-English, for Jane, are her cleverness and her passion, and it is passion, wholly absent from Jane's life, through which Dolly meets her downfall. Dolly hooks up with a younger and somewhat vulgar businessman named Harry, with whom she falls in love. Jane feels herself to be humiliated by this affair and ignores her aunt for several years, while Dolly invests all her money in Harry's business, following which he leaves her. On the visit to Dolly when Jane learns about this outcome, she immediately notices that Dolly has changed: "She had lost weight; her figure had fallen and flattened" (205). Walking Jane to the station, Dolly puts on "an ordinary cloth coat in a rather sour ginger colour, in any event unbecoming, and a world removed from the fur coat scented with Joy which dated from my childhood and which had been remodelled at great expense several times since then" (205). Gradually, the transformation is completed, and Jane tells us that Dolly's handmade silk dresses have now been replaced by discreet viscose dresses from John Lewis (217). Having bought Dolly a flat in a block inhabited by elderly English women, Jane now loves her—this new, thin Dolly who dresses in English chain-store clothes, and who lives alone, surrounded by quiet English neighbors. To become lovable to Jane, Dolly must perfect her assimilation to Englishness; crucially, perhaps, to a somewhat déclassé mode of Englishness.

A sentimental reading of the émigré Dolly is not entirely available to us. To Jane's family, "however silent we remained on the matter, we—my mother, my father, and myself—considered her excessive, and that she was thus destined to remain something of a stranger among us" (176). As we have seen, however, Dolly considers herself as fully assimilated to an English way of life. She does not appear to be marked by the ambivalence about origins and the desire for acceptance that we saw, finally, in Kitty Maule. Nevertheless, Dolly clings to the passion that marks her as foreign. When Jane asks her about Harry, Dolly answers: "I'm talking about something you wouldn't understand, Jane: love, attraction, sex if that's what you want to call it" (200). Throughout the novel, viewed through the eyes of Jane and of her father, Dolly deserves only disapproval. The changed Dolly is the one whom Jane comes to love; and yet, Jane cannot help musing: "She may get tired of this; perhaps she will. Perhaps she will at last be ready for stronger sensations than these so English friends can provide; perhaps she will long for an evening visitor. That visitor will be missing, and his absence will be her one source of pain, and the one element connecting her to the person she once was" (216–17).

It was Dolly herself who wistfully suggested to Jane that she would love to live in the block of flats and to know these women as friends and neighbors; nevertheless, Jane imagines for her a renewed sexuality, apparently in order to determine that it remain unfulfilled. Brookner thus leaves a number of questions unresolved: as readers, we must decide if Dolly is incapable of becoming fully assimilated, or if Jane simply cannot see her in any other way than as the passionate, opportunistic, clever, émigré. If Jane comes to love her in her final incarnation, why does she need Dolly still to embody these elements of difference and otherness? Brookner's conclusion in *A Family Romance* runs counter to that offered throughout the novel by her narrator, and the implications of that conclusion carry a degree of pain in their final embrace of otherness and un-Englishness.

Conclusion

In an article on British Jewish literature, Bryan Cheyette poses the question: "What is it about English culture that saps the confidence of writers who happen also to be Jews?" He goes on to assert that "Jewish writers in Britain have been made to feel distinctly uncomfortable with their Jewishness," noting that Brookner, for example, writes out virtually any reference to her Jewishness.[44] In a later discussion, Cheyette offers a partial answer to his own question, arguing that "British-Jewish writing articulates a specific set of identities that are framed by the dominant culture of unremitting assimilation."[45] It is against this background, a personal context that is recognized by Brookner herself in her interviews, that we must understand the dilemmas associated with assimilation as a strong thread running through Brookner's fiction. Although the drive to assimilation has been observed as a theme, in particular by Malcolm, critics have not been able to confront the unresolved, irresolvable nature of the problem in Brookner's writing.

It is interesting to remember the comparisons of Brookner with Barbara Pym, comparisons that are rooted in an impulse to read the life in the work, but ultimately in an insufficiently nuanced way: gender and marital status are presumably the points of similarity recognized here. As her interviews indicate, Brookner associates Jewishness with various kinds of trauma, and it is perhaps this, most of all, that has led critics to look the other way. What they have evaded, then, is the discomfiting rupture that in Brookner's work accompanies the attempt to live inside English culture as the child of foreigners: to attempt both to blend in and to preserve the inherited culture, each aim impossible in its own way, and each seemingly irreconcilable with the other.

For Brookner's parents, as for successive waves of immigrants from other ethnic groups, to become English in acceptable ways involves ambivalence and loss. Their daughter's assimilation was not a goal pursued wholeheartedly by her parents, who wished that their daughter could have learned Hebrew and studied Judaism but decided that she was too frail to do so.[46] Through Jane, the narrator of A Family Romance, Brookner characterizes the ambivalence, even disgust, felt by the assimilated Jew confronting her foreign-born relatives. We should be aware, too, of the discomfiture and disapproval of English critics, such as D. J. Enright's relief at the absence of the Holocaust from Family and Friends noted earlier. In his review of A Family Romance, Frank Kermode exhibits a heightened awareness of the dilemma when he notes that "[s]ome would say that the portrait of Dolly is a little overdone."[47] Despite the general reception of Brookner as an English novelist, her work increasingly indicates that she is all too aware of the betrayal entailed in the denial of one's origins, the risk that these will, in any case, reveal themselves, and the horror of never feeling at home in the country of one's birth.

Notes

1. See John Updike, review of *Latecomers*, *New Yorker* (May 1, 1989), 111–13. See John Skinner, *The Fictions of Anita Brookner: Illusions of Romance* (London: Methuen, 1992), 3–6, for similar comparisons by reviewers.

2. See, in particular, the first chapter of *The Fictions of Anita Brookner*, which is entitled "The French Connection."

3. Skinner, *The Fictions of Anita Brookner*, 12, 141.

4. Interview with John Haffenden, *Literary Review* (September 1984), 57–75 (60).

5. Shusha Guppy, "The Art of Fiction XCVIII: Anita Brookner," *Paris Review* 29 (1987), 146–69 (149).

6. David Cesarani, "Dual Heritage or Duel of Heritages? Englishness and Jewishness in the Heritage Industry," in *The Jewish Heritage in British History: Englishness and Jewishness*, ed. Tony Kushner (London: Frank Cass, 1992), 29–41 (34).

7. These opportunities and prejudices often shadow each other, of course. David Cesarani notes that when it was suggested that Jews were disproportionately numbered among doctors, lawyers, and accountants, the *Jewish Chronicle*, Anglo-Jewry's main newspaper, seriously considered whether it might be a good thing if Jews were to ration their representation in the professions. He reports that in June 1939 the paper joined with B'nai B'rith in the establishment of a career guidance service. See David Cesarani, "Reporting Antisemitism: The Jewish Chronicle, 1879–1979," in *Cultures of Ambivalence and Contempt: Studies in Jewish–Non-Jewish Relations*, ed. Siân Jones, Tony Kushner, and Sarah Pearce (London: Vallentine Mitchell, 1998), 247–82 (268).

8. Howard Cooper and Paul Morrison, *A Sense of Belonging: Dilemmas of British Jewish Identity* (London: Weidenfeld & Nicolson, in association with Channel 4, 1991), 18.

9. Cesarani, "Reporting Antisemitism," 254–55.

10. Ibid., 260.

11. Ibid., 267–68.

12. Ibid., 255.

13. Ibid., 265.

14. Guppy, "The Art of Fiction XCVIII," 150.

15. Haffenden interview, *Literary Review*, 61.

16. Gabriel Josipovici, *Now* (Manchester: Carcanet Press, 1998), 138–39. Josipovici was born in Nice in 1940, but after the war he returned with his mother, the daughter of a Russian Jewish doctor, to her family in Cairo, where the writer received his early education. It may be noted that this hybrid identity does not prevent Josipovici's inclusion in an anthology of British Jewish writing: Bryan Cheyette, ed., *Contemporary Jewish Writing in Britain and Ireland: An Anthology* (London: Peter Halban, 1998).

17. Homi Bhabha, "Of Mimicry and Men: The Ambivalence of Colonial Discourse," *October* 28 (1984), repr. in *The Location of Culture* (London: Routledge, 1994), 87; emphasis added. See also Sander Gilman, *Jewish Self-Hatred: Anti-Semitism and the Hidden Language of the Jews* (Baltimore, MD: Johns Hopkins University Press, 1986).

18. Marilyn Demarest Button, "A Losing Tradition: The Exotic Female of Brookner's Early Fiction," in *The Foreign Woman in British Literature: Exotics, Aliens, and Outsiders*, ed. Marilyn Demarest Button and Toni Reed (Westport, CT: Greenwood Press, 1999), 171–81.

19. Haffenden interview, *Literary Review*, 67.

20. Cheryl Alexander Malcolm, "Compromise and Cultural Identity: British and American Perspectives in Anita Brookner's *Providence* and Cynthia Ozick's 'Virility,'" *English Studies* 78 (1997), 459–71 (459).

21. *Providence* (1982; repr. London: Penguin, 1991); page references appear in parentheses in the text.

22. This phrase appears on pages 459 and 466 of Malcolm's "Compromise and Cultural Identity."

23. Malcolm, "Compromise and Cultural Identity," 467.

24. Gisèle Marie Baxter, "Clothes, Men and Books: Cultural Experiences and Identity in the Early Novels of Anita Brookner," *English* 42 (1993), 125–39 (129).

25. Malcolm, "Compromise and Cultural Identity," 370.

26. *Hotel du Lac* (London: Jonathan Cape, 1984).

27. Baxter, "Clothes, Men and Books," 131.

28. Haffenden interview, *Literary Review*, 67.

29. *Family and Friends* (1985; repr. London: Grafton Books, 1986), 72. Further page references appear in parentheses in the text. As with so many of Brookner's novels, it is almost impossible to state with any certainty when the scene is set. *Family and Friends* begins with the narrator looking at Sofka, the matriarch of the family, in what may be a wedding photograph, and near the end we learn what has become of her family since her death. This death does not seem to be long ago, but the timing of the action of the book is, perhaps deliberately, obscured by Brookner, who often imparts a sense of the historical to her novels as if aware, in advance, of their afterlife. An example of this is her comment in *A Family Romance* that Dolly is envied for having a live-in maid, "rare at that date." *A Family Romance* (1993; repr. London: Penguin, 1994), 85. Further page references appear in parentheses in the text.

30. D. J. Enright, "Depositions," *New York Review of Books,* December 5, 1985, 35–37 (37).

31. Olga Kenyon, *Women Novelists Today: A Survey of English Writing in the Seventies and Eighties* (Brighton: Harvester, 1988), 157.

32. Enright, "Depositions," 37.

33. *The Next Big Thing* (2002; repr. London: Penguin, 2003). Further page references appear in parentheses in the text.

34. Cooper and Morrison, *A Sense of Belonging,* 20.

35. Cooper and Morrison, *A Sense of Belonging,* 16–17.

36. *Latecomers* (1988; repr. London: Grafton Books, 1989), 7. Further page references appear in parentheses in the text.

37. Anne Karpf, *The War After: Living with the Holocaust* (London: Heinemann, 1996), 4.

38. Cheyette, ed., *Contemporary Jewish Writing in Britain and Ireland,* xli.

39. *A Family Romance,* 74.

40. Louise Sylvester, "Troping the Other: Anita Brookner's Jews," *English* 50 (2001), 47–58.

41. See Bruno Bettelheim, *The Uses of Enchantment: The Meaning and Importance of Fairy Tales* (London: Peregrine Books, 1978), 68–69.

42. The implications of this comparison are made explicit in Brookner's later novel, *Visitors,* in which the protagonist, Dorothea May, reflects on the difference between her appearance and that of her in-laws: "with her thin frame and her meek but decided presence she had represented a majority to which they could never belong." *Visitors* (1996; repr. London: Penguin, 1997), 202.

43. Skinner writes: "One is also aware, in retrospect, of how another of Brookner's major sources of metonymic detail from *A Start in Life*—clothes—joins food in the drive towards full metaphoric status." Skinner, *The Fictions of Anita Brookner,* 15. See also Baxter's statement that "Brookner explores her protagonists' dislocation and reveals their self-definition and capacity for delusion chiefly through three cultural phenomena: apparel and physical presentation, relationships with men, and texts used as guides, or; clothes, men and books." Baxter, "Clothes, Men and Books," 126.

44. Bryan Cheyette, "Moroseness and Englishness: The Rise of British-Jewish Literature," *Jewish Quarterly* 42 (Spring 1995), 22–26 (22).

45. Cheyette, ed., *Contemporary Jewish Writing in Britain and Ireland,* xv–xvi.

46. See Brookner's interview with Shusha Guppy: "*Were you brought up Jewish?* Yes, very much so." Guppy, "The Art of Fiction XCVIII," 149.

47. Frank Kermode, "Small but Perfectly Formed," *Spectator,* June 19, 1993, 29–30 (30).

9

DRAMATIZING BRITAIN'S HOLOCAUST MEMORY

PHYLLIS LASSNER

Why is the Holocaust still being written? While survivors are responding to the pressures of time, and the second generation grapples with its legacy, the Holocaust has also gripped the imaginations of those with no personal connection to its events. If, as many argue, representing the Holocaust is always problematic, why do young writers continue to struggle with this impossible mission?[1] While the suffering continues to be documented, debates resound about proliferating Holocaust memorials and writing, and concerns are expressed about manipulating the memory of the Holocaust for the purpose of assuaging national pride or guilt. In Britain the memory of the Holocaust is anything but absent from historiography and museum displays, yet British Holocaust literature has received little critical attention. In this essay I will be discussing the haunted and compelling Holocaust plays of two Anglo-Jewish women writers: *Kindertransport* (1993) by Diane Samuels (b. 1960) and *Holocaust Trilogy* (1990) by Julia Pascal (b. 1949), texts that open up the question of responsibility for the destruction of European Jewry.

Theresa, the first play in Pascal's *Trilogy*, was inspired by a belated World War II news break. Brought up with the myth that the British would never have collaborated if the Nazis had invaded, Britons were shocked to learn the truth about the Nazi occupation of the Channel Islands.[2] In 1989, a year before the fiftieth anniversary of the German invasion, the *Observer* revealed that it was a British official who handed over three Jewish women to the Gestapo, but that he "forcibly kept" one of them "on the island even *before* the Nazis arrived . . . Theresa Steiner was murdered in Auschwitz in 1942" (4; italics Pascal's). While the history of the Nazi occupation of the Channel Islands has been well documented, the story of the Jews was not part of the narrative. Researching the play in Guernsey, Pascal discovered that "this police inspector" was not the only guilty party "but the whole of the island government, with one exception" (4–5).[3] Pascal's play has been banned in Guernsey ever since, although a radio version made its way there.[4]

These media events challenged the story of Britain's stalwart resistance to Nazi conquest as well as its claims to indomitable democratic instincts. Working as testimony, Pascal's play replicates dialogue from her Guernsey interviews. One of Theresa's friends described her as "very pretty except for her big Jewish nose." Pascal notes: "This was 1990: anti-Semitism certainly has not disappeared from the island" (5). The fact that Pascal considers this remark antisemitic is interesting because it points to the liminal position of the Jew. In this case Theresa is not even permitted the status of worthy refugee but instead suspect on the grounds of racialized difference and strangeness. As I will argue in this essay, Pascal and Samuels insist that, instead of reifying the Holocaust as the horrific past or solely a German crime, it must be recognized as integral to the racism that upheld any imperial domination.[5]

Diane Samuels's *Kindertransport* is based on a story that contrasts dramatically with that of *Theresa*, and supports Britain's sense of its humane democratic soul. In 1938–39, with help from Jewish and Quaker organizations, the British government rescued about 7,400 Jewish and non-Aryan children from Germany and its environs.[6] As it was commemorated in sixtieth-anniversary exhibitions, this rescue represents an uplifting memory of Britain's moral rectitude in the face of European capitulations.[7] The idea of a singularly humanitarian Britain has been especially important to the nation and empire's sense of itself, as evident in the words of Commander Oliver Locker-Lampson, MP, who introduced a bill on July 26, 1933, that would create citizenship opportunities in Palestine "for Jews deprived of citizenship elsewhere," reminding the House that "it is un-English, it is caddish to bully a minority" and suggesting that the British Empire should "stand by Jewry in its trouble."[8] Claiming the higher moral ground has remained important in Britain as it tried to reconstitute its national pride after the empire ended and world power fell to the United States. And now, with the devolution of Great Britain, and as the nation suffers the prolonged birth pangs of fully recognizing and integrating its multicultural populations, Pascal and Samuels insist that it must reconsider its national identity in relation to the Holocaust, Jewish culture, and an evolving Jewish identity.

Samuels's play concerns three mother-daughter relationships. It charts the movement of the child protagonist, Eva, from the anxious foreshadowings of the Holocaust in Germany to the plucky quotidian of middle-class English life. Nine-year-old Eva Schlesinger is sent by her parents to the relative safety of Manchester from Germany, where a legalized antisemitism foreclosed the Jews' ability to live an ordinary life anywhere. Unlike 80 percent of the children who actually were part of the *Kindertransport* who never saw their parents again, Eva (now Evelyn) meets her mother after the war, replaying the trauma of separation to show the prolonged effects of the racism that underwrote both the Holocaust and British imperial ideology. Based on research, Eva's adoptive mother, Lil, resembles many kindly British women who took in Jewish children, but in Samuels's portrait Lil also participates in the trauma of separation and the implicit pressure to suppress Jewish identity.[9] Samuels notes that the fiftieth anniversary of the *Kindertransport* inspired "many people who . . . remained silent about it all their lives . . . to identify themselves, finally facing . . . a watershed moment . . . when many of them turned their backs on family, religion, and country for a chance to live. It was as if a dark national secret had come to light."[10] Both plays explore how the story of Britain and its stoic heroism are glossed by a relationship between the rescue and integration of its Jewish refugees and the denial or erasure of Jewish identity.

These plays challenge those wartime myths of British identity as it was solidified in the rhetoric of the British Empire standing alone against the Axis imperial alliance while the home front muddled through with patient good humor and traditional allegiances to liberty, the law, and the community.[11] Even if British antisemitism prevailed, the expulsion of the Jews in the Middle Ages and the Aliens Act of the early twentieth century seemed to be redeemed by the rescue of Jewish refugees from Hitler's Europe. There was no Dreyfus case in Britain, as there had been in Continental Europe, and neither antisemitic outbreaks in South Wales in 1911 nor in the East End in the 1930s resembled the pogroms of Eastern Europe. By 1940 the government had imprisoned Oswald Mosley, leader of the British Union of Fascists.[12] And yet despite this evidence, the story of Jewish rescue is strained by the responses of British officials and the Jewish community. Colonial injunctions prevented endangered Jews from entering Palestine and other colonies, and domestic restrictions kept most parents from joining their children in Britain. Anxieties about their own position produced Anglo-Jewry's ambivalence toward those refugees. Even as refugees adapted, the Jewish community complied with official expectations that they remake themselves in a British image by revising their European Jewish identities and styles of being.

This revision would not prove to be easy. Like the secrets shaping the two plays, a hidden message was woven into Britain's welcome mat; no matter how well they might adapt, Jews and their cultural and religious differences were not part of its design. Absence became silence; none of the welcoming documents ever alluded to Jewish identity or culture. How this absence served a vulnerable British national pride can be inferred by viewing the silence as representing a complex British ambivalence about supporting refugee immigration. After all, a European Jewish presence might threaten the myth of a homogeneous nation that included the imperial imperative of keeping its Others in their places. In contrast, Britain's pride in its distance from Continental Europe included the defense, under political and military siege, of its liberal principles.[13] From 1933 onward, rather than follow the xenophobia of fascist Europe, Britain encouraged Jewish immigrants to acculturate. Yet immigrants were also repeatedly warned about the terms and limits of acceptance.

Anglo-Jewry's responses to refugees were driven by ambivalence among the communal leadership and a fear of antisemitism. Despite cooperation between Jewish and Christian communities, apprehension about reigniting antisemitism through activism prevailed in the Jewish community.[14] This anxiety is apparent in the defensively cautious instructions they issued for Jewish immigrants. Anticipating the government's lack of support, the Jewish community played down the extent of Jewish victimization by the Reich. Instead, the community offset the refugees' cultural differences or economic privation by promoting only those who were "young, self-supporting, skilled, and assimilated."[15] Anglo-Jewish defensiveness is only too apparent in a booklet issued by the German Jewish Aid Committee and Jewish Board of Deputies: *While You Are in England: Helpful Information and Guidance for Every Refugee.* For example, the first word in the title, "While," assumes a temporary stay. Moreover, as the following proviso indicates, the agency's urge to be "helpful" is matched by broader impulses to keep the refugees in their designated place as forever alienated but grateful: "Do not criticize any government regulations, nor the way things are done over here. Do not speak of 'how much better this or that is done in Germany.' It may be true in some matters, but it weighs as nothing against the sympathy and freedom and liberty of England which are now given to you. Never forget that point."[16]

Even if refugees followed these instructions to the letter, they would be confounded by the imperfect fit of Anglo-Jewry and British cultural styles and values. Unlike most Britons who, despite differences, felt unified in their resolve against a common enemy, Jews had to devote "scarce resources and time to combating antisemitism in Britain during the war" while worrying about refugees, those left behind, and their own fate if Germany invaded.[17] Nonetheless, the government decreed that child refugees should be treated to the political and cultural benefits of a humane society. British schools and homes would educate and acculturate them. The system would embrace them. At the same time, however, instead of being integrated into the heroic battle of the British Empire against the Reich, adult refugees were mistrusted as itinerants for lacking national loyalty and for imposing on national security and economic opportunity. A 1940 survey revealed that of "all comments concerning oppressed people, 47% were directed towards the Jews, yet only 18% felt Jews were deserving sympathy."[18] Having escaped their toxic fate as despised objects of the Reich's imperial designs, refugees were now mistrusted objects of British benevolence. Instructed "to keep a low profile, so as to avoid the impression of a substantial and menacing Jewish body within England,"[19] the refugees occupied a precariously liminal space in Britain, recognized as different enough not to fit any British cultural category.[20] As Victor Seidler notes, Jewish refugees from Nazi persecution "could not feel so confident in the hopes and aspirations of a liberal culture, for they had experienced the revoking of their rights in Germany and Austria, which had supposedly cherished the ideals of an Enlightenment modernity." But they clung to the "feeling that they could give to their children the precious gift of 'becoming English'. . . for to be English was to be 'safe.'" In gratitude, these refugees pressured their children "to become invisible," to express their Jewish cultural and religious identities only privately.[21] As the character Judith, in Pascal's third play of her trilogy, *The Dybbuk*, wails, "Keep your head down. Be British, be cool, be part of the crowd."[22] This edict conformed to a marginal British identity and imperial outlook accepted by an insecure Anglo-Jewish community. In exchange for their growing economic stability, the Jews helped maintain Britain's cultural hegemony by adopting what modes of British social culture were made available to them.

For those Jewish refugees who stayed on after the war, acculturating to British society would mean submerging their own history and culture. *Kindertransport* refugee Hans Schneider testifies: "A past in a different country is a burden on a teenager attempting to make a new life . . . and . . . (I am tempted to say 'requires') memory loss of one's previous life. Silence, unless with others similarly placed, is needed by a young outsider for fitting into a [homogeneous] society—a silence which becomes deeply ingrained."²³ Samuels translates this dilemma by asking, How can we narrate a past that is being repressed or even resisted? Using drama—that is, showing rather than telling—she stages the repercussions of British and Jewish post-Holocaust memory and silence on three generations. Evelyn's daughter Faith disinters traces of her mother's buried European Jewish identity, and the playwright gives them a living presence by dramatizing them as an ongoing identity crisis for Britain and its Jews. That this crisis is relevant to British subjectivity today is shown as Eva, the anxious Jewish refugee, shares the stage with her adult, nervously assimilated British self, Evelyn. Even twenty years later, Evelyn is so haunted by her oppressive past that it seems as though victory over Nazi domination has been costly not only to Britain but to the Jews whose security is won at the expense of open Jewish expression. We see this living legacy in Evelyn's emotional paralysis, which is acted and projected everywhere on stage. The hidden objects and persistent stage presence of Eva and her mother tell us that the Jewish past presses urgently on the reserved Evelyn, on us, and on Britain's memory of its heroic imperial power.

Evelyn's effort to feel safe in her constructed English identity suppresses but expresses the trauma of escaping the Holocaust and of embracing Englishness. Choosing to be adopted by her English foster mother marks a definitive step in acquiring an English middle-class identity and denying her Jewish foreignness. Most definitively, she breaks the chain of Jewish tradition by rejecting her Jewish birth mother. But despite Evelyn's altered identity papers and her baptism, her Jewish identity and exile are staged as inextricable reminders of her intractable vulnerability. We see this in Evelyn's chain smoking; even her clipped English speech and compulsive housecleaning register as tics, disclosing her obsessive efforts to erase the past and perfect the self whose credulity she doubts. This play questions the postmodern idea that the self may be no more real than a convincing performance through the anxiety performed by Evelyn's gentile identity. Nowhere is this challenge more apparent than in performance, where the real presence of an actress impersonating the fictional character of Evelyn, who is passing as a gentile, suggests not fluidity but the unalterable ontology of Jewishness. Regardless of how integrated Evelyn may be, moreover, her desperate mimicry of Britishness marks her as a colonized subject.

Samuels also encourages the audience's doubts and anxieties about Anglo-Jewish assimilation, linking modern, tolerant Britain with Germany's past and present. Gently prodding Eva to leave Germany, her mother, Helga, says of England: "They don't mind Jews there. It's like it was here when I was younger" (9). Like a palimpsest of Holocaust memory, in this juxtaposition, the lukewarm "don't mind" suggests that an omnipresent antisemitism lurks within the performance of tolerance. Instead of a successful escape, Eva/Evelyn enacts her own erasure. Yielding to the pressures to assimilate, she buries the few traces of her Jewish identity in a box in her attic. If Eva/Evelyn's act also recalls Nazi imprisonment and mass graves, it evokes an even more distant British past—the medieval expulsion of the Jews. But Eva/Evelyn stops short of performing a symbolic act of destruction. As though suspended in resistance, the Jewish past of persistent persecution may be buried alive, torn up, and discarded, but not so completely that the possibility of recuperation in Britain is foreclosed. In fact, these questions hang in the air of the stage, as though part of the set design.

The play's design divides the stage between scenes from Evelyn's past as Eva and her present, as though performing and challenging her dual identities. The role-playing of the actors calls attention to the cultural and psychological role-playing of Evelyn herself. The more convincing the actress, the more we are able to apprehend Evelyn performing herself as an assimilated British woman. At the opposite end of the stage is Eva, a performance that serves as an unsettling projection of the childhood self contained within her, a split that exposes the perils of performing an assimilated self. If we feel defensively estranged as a way of warding off the combined anxieties of Eva and Evelyn, and because we may or may not wish Evelyn to embrace her Jewish self, we also cannot feel "secure as to who the character really is."[24]

Instead of representing the possibility of a total schism, characters from the past and present intertwine, as we hear when Eva or Helga seems to respond to something Evelyn or her daughter Faith says or when act 2 begins with Evelyn sitting in the attic surrounded by Helga and Eva. These designs convey not only the tensions of the plot but also Evelyn's own repressions. As scenes from past and present cut each other off, they suggest a persistent disorder that arises from Evelyn's frantic measures to maintain a clearly defined but amnesiac identity. The result is a complex destabilization: of Evelyn's character, of a redemptive myth of British stability and safety, and of the narrative of a regenerative Jewish family life and culture. This destabilization reaches a climax halfway through the play when Helga, having survived the war, comes to England to claim her daughter. Her efforts to reunite and restore the family are futile, however, in the face of Eva/Evelyn's rejection. But if Helga is made to disappear by this rejection, she is also present in the play's continued rehearsal of the traumatic separation of mother and child, including Eva's despair at leaving Lil for safety. In tandem with the play's shifting chronologies, such repetitions suggest that Evelyn's plot "is a traumatized text whose narrative voice starts, affirms, lurches, breaks off," but whether it "laments" remains an open question for Evelyn and for the audience.[25] Samuels formulates this question as follows: "What is the cost of survival? What future grows out of a traumatized past?" (vii). The "cost" of Evelyn's suppressions and of absorbing and normalizing the Holocaust is apparent later in Faith's bursts of anger at being disinherited from her own mother's past. Constantly jarring our senses and consciousness, like short-circuited and jump-started memories of trauma, scenes from the past ignite the story of Evelyn's struggle in the present, suggesting that Holocaust trauma cannot be laid to rest or worked through.

In *Kindertransport,* the traumatic Jewish past is a very dangerous foreign country. It threatens not only the characters in the European past but also those in the safety of England. Combining archetypal childhood fears and the specific threat of the Third Reich is the character of the Ratcatcher, who originates in a German children's book titled *Der Rattenfanger,* the prototype for *The Pied Piper of Hamelin*.[26] Embodying a threat that extends from his origins in medieval folklore through his rendering as a symbol of Nazism, he is never defeated. The Ratcatcher hovers over the entire play, the action, dialogue, props, and spaces on which characters move, and in several manifestations. For ordinary times, this story can be read as an allegory of growing up, of the terror and thrill of separation, individuation, and facing the unknown. Samuels ascribes the story's global popularity to "the universal dilemma and contradiction" of "separation" when parents want to save their children from danger and children "would say, no."[27] But the play's historical frame incorporates the temptations of a different context, in which the child is rescued from one danger only to be delivered into a problematic safety. Nowhere is this parallel more apparent than when Evelyn accuses Lil of being a "Child-stealer" (62). Too close for comfort to the Ratcatcher, this slur indicts the woman whose very acts of rescue and mothering have encouraged the Jewish child to betray her past. Eva succumbs to the temptation to assuage the painful memory of loss with the solace of forgetting. But instead of comfort, forgetting assumes an ominous cast, as the persistently shadowing presence of the Ratcatcher suggests. When Eva buries her own origins, her Jewish character disappears, like those children who follow the Pied Piper, but here, into the gentile Evelyn. The Ratcatcher inspires a fantasy enacting the threat of Nazi violence and a replay of fears about promises of protection. Every warning and promise is overshadowed by our knowledge and Evelyn's suspicion that Eva's fears have materialized, not in having experienced the Holocaust but in the cost of her escape and rescue. As in the children's tale, the piper will be paid. Unlike the Jewish mother or Jewish identity, the Ratcatcher cannot be denied or forgotten because he is present in the consciousness of Evelyn as a hypnotizing, shadowy stalker from whom neither acculturation nor passing provides escape.

Despite the safety and stability of postwar England, the play's attic setting is haunted by peril, not only by the Ratcatcher but by the story of Anne Frank. If the Franks' annex home turned into a dead end, the attic storeroom in *Kindertransport* represents a displacement so radical that it questions Evelyn's frantic efforts to make a home anywhere. Even at the end, when Faith and Evelyn reconcile, the play undercuts the promise of continuity with its final stage direction: "The shadow of the RATCATCHER covers the stage" (88). Like the restored sections of Anne Frank's *Diary*, this ending subverts any uplifting message that would comfort us.

Yet Eva's traumatic past survives not only as Evelyn's buried memory and defensive habits but as a legacy of Jewish culture that her daughter will claim. As Samuels's "Author's Note" tells us, "Past and present are wound around each other throughout the play. They are not distinct but inextricably connected. The re-running of what happened many years ago is not there to explain how things are now, but is a part of the inner life of the present" (n.p.). This is a Jewish past that, despite its fragmentary presence in this play, is a dynamic if ephemeral force, one that must be reckoned with. Insistently, even as it is presented as attenuated and estranged, the memory of the Holocaust is an obstacle that prevents the characters from developing unless it is integrated into the present. The very nature and legitimacy of Evelyn's Englishness remain untenable without its Jewish component, without the integration of the Jewish Eva into the British woman. As Evelyn's daughter Faith insists, her own character development is stalled unless her identity, and by extension, the genealogy of contemporary Britishness, is traced to its involvement with the Jewish past and its relationship to Jewish refugees. This quest for knowledge represents a possible revision of the tale of the Ratcatcher: a movement away from the fantasy represented by Evelyn's willed amnesia and toward honesty about the past.

Like *Kindertransport*, Julia Pascal's play *Theresa* begins in 1938, at the moment of *Kristallnacht* in Vienna, where the "sweetness" of "The Blue Danube Waltz" and of Black Forest cake marks the end of nostalgia for one empire (the Austro-Hungarian) and the fear of another's aggression (18). With no props or set, Theresa dominates the stage, at first as she dances her jagged history and then as she describes the crystal-glassed café that she cannot afford to enter. But since the play is also about the Jews' efforts to find safety in Britain, its repeated references to "highly polished glass" prod us to view this scene as a window into Britain's responses (16). Eschewing the ambiguity and irresolution that shape Samuels's play, Pascal's verdict about Britain's role in the Jews' deportation from the Channel Islands is bitterly certain. Guernsey may be geographically and even culturally separate from mainland Britain, but the islanders' behavior under Nazi occupation reflects and expresses attitudes that are too close to Continental Europe's for Britain's comfort. However humane the *Kindertransport* proved Britain to be, *Theresa* provokes an unsettling if unanswerable question, one that now haunts the story of British resistance. How would mainland Britain have responded to Nazi occupation? Would its self-image as humanitarian nation and benign and liberating empire prevail? Like *Kindertransport*'s shadows of the past, those emanations in the staging of *Theresa* predict a dark future. Indeed, much of the time the actors are surrounded by darkness or shadow, with spotlights or torches highlighting Theresa's isolation from or captivity by those on whom she depends for safety. Pascal's stage direction to have the same actors play various British, Jewish, and German roles produces the effect of transfusing Nazi malevolence into British officials and civilians.

The play's unequivocal indictment of British collaboration throws into question the position of the Jews in Britain. Pascal draws on the historical record to present Theresa as a professor of music who, as a refugee, is forced into domestic service. Regardless of whether a refugee music teacher could actually have found employment in Britain, Pascal links this treatment of Theresa to her dismissal from the Vienna Conservatory and the Nazi designation of Jewish culture as "degenerate" (20). Pascal, moreover extends the link to contemporary Britain, which is, she argues,

> still uneasy with the notion of producing a rich body of explicitly British-Jewish work. [The] climate in Britain . . . rightly encourages black, Asian and Chinese arts, but does not give Jewish theatre the same funding possibilities. . . . The very act of making Jewish theatre is a way of reconstructing what existed before Hitler. The Holocaust did not just destroy Jews, but also left a huge hole in Jewish—and indeed European—culture.[28]

Theresa critically reconstructs the destruction of European Jewish culture on British soil. In the original productions, Theresa was played by Ruth Posner, a survivor of the Warsaw Ghetto who passed as a Polish Catholic, and who Pascal felt "would not have to act the part of a refugee."[29] The play also featured Thomas Kampe, the son of a German soldier, who filled all the male roles, including that of Theresa's son, Josef; a German refugee in London; the British police inspector, William Sculpher; and a Gestapo officer. Where Samuels creates two characters, Evelyn and Eva, to show the process of a single woman's psychological and cultural rupture, *Theresa* splits the performances of its actors to show the political pressures that blur the distinctions between German and Guernsey characters. In a scene depicting "The Occupation of France," Kampe morphs from a child merrily singing "Frère Jacques" into a victim of Nazi brutality as his song drifts into the German version, "Bruder Jakob." The actress who plays a Guernsey woman seduced by a German soldier's promise of a silk blouse also plays the nurse who betrays Theresa. Pascal's direction notes that this double performance "suggests she's the same character" (48). Collaboration leads not only to personal and political betrayal, but to a British island sacrificing its image of resistance to becoming the agent of the Reich.

The play's international and multilingual character links not only "the occupation of sleepwalking France" and that of the Channel Islands, but how the fate of European Jews and their culture was betrayed by the slippage of British authority into Nazi collaboration (5). In one scene, where Kampe turns round and round, transforming repeatedly from British policeman to Gestapo officer by simply changing his hat, we feel that if he could move fast enough, one figure would simply merge into the other. In contrast, Pascal's portraits of Theresa and Lydia, her domestic employer, closely mirror each other. In one ironic juxtaposition Lydia reads her own outsider status in Theresa's story. Despite Lydia's secure position as an upper-class British citizen, she has been displaced by social codes that isolate her emotionally and socially. If Lydia can tell her story only to Theresa, it is because the Jew's undisguised expression of profound anxiety is, like Lydia's, beyond the pale of polite restraint, that hallmark of British civil society. For Lydia, the other side of Britain's intrepid and stoic isolation is a culture of rigid rules and froideur.

Both the performance and written text of the play show us this doubleness. In the opening scene, Theresa's English monologue is accompanied by a chorus of voices reciting her words in German, and when she reverts to her childhood Polish, the chorus speaks in English. In performance these languages and voices are spoken simultaneously, while in the text they are printed as twin columns, a way of approximating simultaneity but remaining necessarily separate. Though we can't possibly read the dual-language presentation in concert, as our eyes dart from one column to another, or even if we read or view one at a time, we too perform an interweaving that dramatizes the voices as more dissonant than harmonious. Unlike the performance, where the effect is both dissonant and harmonious, reading creates a critical gloss on the play's intended synchronicity. For whether we read or merely look at the languages we might not know, in combination the different languages effect a disconcerting stammer, suggesting Vivian Patraka's "theatre of disturbance."[30] The interjection of German and Polish alongside the English reminds us that Theresa cannot escape her foreignness, either to pass or assimilate. All her performances are doomed to failure. The concurrence of the voices means that they cannot hear, address, or understand each other, and the lingering effect is a fusion that both validates and erases them. In the context of the play's historical narrative, the merging also reminds us that all of Theresa's voices are erased by a trajectory of Germany's invasion and occupation, from Austria and Poland and on to Guernsey.

While performing this historical fusion and erasure, the voices' simultaneous translation conveys Theresa's emotional and political isolation. Though her performance suggests a ghostly presence, her irretrievability, the echoing versions of her story in her different languages leave traces no matter where she goes. In this reading, the double columns inscribe an imperative to retell Theresa's story until it is heard. But given her forced exile from Poland to Vienna and then to England, Guernsey, and Auschwitz, given the cruel indifference and betrayal that await her, despite the fact that they accompany her, the echoing voices are ultimately cut off. When Theresa is rejected by potential British employers, by the British policeman, and by the Gestapo officer, her responses have no meaning. "Subject closed," she is told on two different occasions (26, 35). The repetition emphasizes the doubleness of Theresa's erasure: her murder and the deletion of her story. The word "subject" reminds us that Theresa will be denied the protection awarded to British subjects and that her betrayal will be denied by Guernsey's official narrative.

Unlike Brecht's theater of alienation, which emotionally distances audiences in order to activate their political consciousness, Pascal's *Theresa* invokes the audience as a political act. And not a comforting one. When this play is produced, typically in a small theater, the enclosed space that enwraps players and audience creates an intensely claustrophobic atmosphere. At the time of the play's 1995 revival, Pascal reported that it "is often too much to bear. 'People who lived it have walked out because they couldn't take it.'"³¹ *Theresa* is hard to take. Its expressionist style screams at us, impelling us to watch Theresa's increasing entrapment, challenging us not to desert Theresa one more time. The play's style is confrontational: very often, when the sympathetic characters, Theresa, Lydia, and Josef, narrate their troubled lives, they face the audience no matter whom they address. In other cases, the play's "elements of absurdism" highlight the distance between characters and audience and remind us that whatever our responses, they are futile (32).

There is neither restoration nor redress for the multiple betrayals of the endangered Jews in this play, only the replay of trauma. Dramatized by its circular structure, the play's depiction of trauma begins with Theresa narrating her position as outcast in Nazi-occupied Vienna and ends with the escalating sound of a train drowning out her voice and transporting her back to Europe to a final destruction. When we first see Theresa, she is peering into a Viennese café, the symbol of civilized culture and enlightened equality. By the scene's end, the glassed-in café reflects and confronts us with the shockwaves of *Kristallnacht*. From this beginning, enlightenment has already turned rotten, as elderly Jewish workers are beaten and defiled in the street by Hitler's henchmen while inside the crystal-clear glass "the well-dressed men and women in the café continue sipping their chocolate and ordering another cake" (19). Our own position is to confront the indifference that marks complicity with the Reich's persecution.

The play's many short scenes, shifting from one catastrophic setting to another, depict the political chronology of Theresa's story, which is also reflected in its expressionistic style. Shifts between dance, song, and dialogue in different languages destabilize the audience, beginning with the play's prologue, where Theresa begins to dance gracefully to "The Blue Danube Waltz." As her movements fragment over several minutes, they are "expressed jaggedly against the sweetness of the Strauss" (15). Pascal's stage directions choreograph the dance as a microcosm of the play's ineluctable political and historical trajectory: "Memories of a first ball in Vienna. Being in a concentration camp and observing horror. Reaching out to fellow camp inmates: it is a foretaste of the play itself. It also suggests the end of an empire" (15). The juxtaposition of a Viennese ball and a concentration camp, of the froth of one empire and the foulness of another, challenges any claim that any imperialism can be benign. Note that Pascal does not name the empire that needs to end. Instead, her generic empire connotes a legion of contenders. The Jew is trapped not only in the middle of imperial succession—from the Austro-Hungarian to the Third Reich—but in the war between the British Empire and Nazi Germany.

Both Pascal's and Samuels's plays are about forgetting and denial, about how the narratives of World War II have been transformed, remembered, erased. They are also acts of remembrance, albeit fraught with the pitfalls of Holocaust representation, as Abigail Morris notes: "This means there is a danger that we will imprison ourselves in a relentless, unconstructive pattern of repetition [. . .] without gaining either insight or relief. [But] we need to remember, to remind others to grieve and try and make sense of all those deaths. On the other hand, we have to face the possibility that some of these feelings may never be resolved."[32] Another danger of the "endless repetition" of Holocaust images is that it will produce indifference. However, Marianne Hirsch argues that rather than anesthetize us, such repetition "connects the second generation to the first, *producing* rather than *screening* the effect of trauma that was lived so much more directly *as compulsive repetition* by survivors and contemporary witnesses."[33]

The combination of *Theresa*'s dead end and *Kindertransport*'s unresolved ending inscribes a rite of passage for contemporary witnesses. When Faith discovers her mother's Haggadah and insists on taking it with her, we are reminded of the recitation of the Haggadah at Passover, when participants are enjoined to confront both the tragedies and achievements of Jewish history by remembering and identifying with the Jews' ancient bondage and their escape. Placing Jewish memory and culture in the hands of the second generation, *Kindertransport* suggests that Evelyn's radical forgetting is not the end of the Holocaust story or the Jewish saga in Britain. In *Theresa*, the only antidote to denial and forgetting is the unsettling and haunting knowledge acquired by the audience. But instead of comforting us with this shared remembrance, both plays confront audiences with the necessary failure of Holocaust stories to offer comfort. Neither play performs a memorial service. Instead of eulogies that offer the solace of closure, they ask us to bear the painful, unrelieved burden of our acquired knowledge beyond the theater.

Notes

1. Most Holocaust critics begin their work by interpreting Adorno's warning about art after Auschwitz. Berel Lang argues that "imaginative writing about the Holocaust . . . typically, eschews standard literary devices . . . in favor of historical ones—purporting to present factual narratives which are not factual at all, splicing actual juridical testimony into fictional frames, appealing to historical genres like the diary or letter or memoir but as imagined rather than historical." See "Second-Sight: Shimon Attie's

Recollection," in *Image and Remembrance: Representation and the Holocaust*, ed. Shelley Hornstein and Florence Jacobowitz (Bloomington: Indiana University Press, 2003), 24. Michael Rothberg argues that "the desire for realism and referentiality is one of the defining features" of Holocaust study. See *Traumatic Realism: The Demands of Holocaust Representation* (Minneapolis: University of Minnesota Press, 2000), 99. For Janet Wolff, "realist work . . . that presents a literal, illusionistic representation—performs a premature movement of closure, enticing the viewer to accept the belief that he or she has now seen the object (. . . the Holocaust itself). This seduction . . . forecloses . . . the recognition that this is in the end only a story . . . a combination of false coherence or closure and refusal of dialogue between work and viewer." See "The Iconic and the Allusive: The Case for Beauty in Post-Holocaust Art," in *Image and Remembrance*, ed. Hornstein and Jacobowitz, 158–59. Marianne Hirsch and Susan Suleiman note the "tension between referentiality and aestheticism" in "Holocaust Representation, Material Memory: Holocaust Testimony in Post-Holocaust Art," in *Image and Remembrance*, ed. Hornstein and Jacobowitz, 90. In the United States, we have seen controversial art exhibits and read fictions that many feel exploit the Holocaust to questionable ends. In addition to Judy Chicago's Holocaust Project, the New York Jewish Museum's "Images of Evil" exhibit inspired not only debate but protests by survivors.

2. Julia Pascal, *Theresa*, in *The Holocaust Trilogy* (London: Oberon Books, 2000). Further references to this edition will appear in the text.

3. As advised by Channel Island authorities during the time of the invasion, most Jews left, and Jewish businesses were sold. In March 1941 the remaining five Jews on Guernsey and twelve on Jersey—mostly single women who were Austrian and German Jewish refugees—had their identity cards conspicuously marked with a red "J." Madeleine Bunting, *The Model Occupation: The Channel Islands Under German Rule, 1940–1945* (London: HarperCollins, 1995), 106. Along with Theresa, the fates of two other refugees, Auguste Spitz and Marianne Grunfeld, remained uninvestigated for forty years. Theresa's brother Karl, her only relative to survive, learned her fate in 1993, when the Guernsey Occupation archives were opened. He was welcomed by people willing to share their memories of Theresa and their guilt about not hiding her. Other islanders claimed "that no one had had any idea of what was happening to the Jews in Europe. . . . The truth is that no official in either Guernsey or Jersey considered the welfare of a handful of Jews sufficiently important to jeopardize good relations with the Germans" (Bunting, *The Model Occupation*, 113). After three years on Guernsey working as a nurse, Theresa Steiner was twenty-six when she was deported to Drancy, and on July 20, 1942, she and Auguste Spitz joined 824 people who were sent to their deaths in Auschwitz three days later (ibid., 110). Although he is very critical of Bunting's research and provides a more complex portrait of island collaboration, Paul Sanders does not disagree with Bunting's notes about the fate of European Jews on the islands. He concludes that "[t]he story of the island Jews is of such great interest because it documents the classic case of one battle among a number of battles the authorities did not elect to fight." *The British Channel Islands under German Occupation, 1940–1945* (Jersey: Jersey Heritage Trust, 2005), 136. Sanders also points out that Guernsey went further in its collaboration with the occupation than its sister island, Jersey (80).

4. The press and Pascal were told that the play was rejected because of its "distasteful" language, which in the play could refer only to the "shit and piss" thrown at Jews being

forced to scrub the streets of Vienna. Pascal was also told that the theater, "a converted church, was not equipped to stage the play." Alan Montague, "Guernsey Says No to Holocaust Play," *Jewish Chronicle,* December 14, 1990, 1. A recent ITV British TV miniseries, *Island at War,* depicts an English Jewish woman, but she is subjected to an age-old plot of rape by an unequivocally evil Nazi.

5. Todd Endelman notes that Britain's imperial power is seen in histories of the Jews as pivotal, including its influence in the Middle East and the Suez Canal, as well as its role in Palestine. *The Jews of Britain 1656 to 2000* (Berkeley: University of California Press, 2002), 3.

6. This figure represents only 10 percent of Jewish children who remained in Germany by 1939. Priority was given to orphans, children from single-parent homes, those whose parents were in concentration camps, and boys targeted for incarceration. Each child was permitted one suitcase and ten Reichsmarks. As depicted in Samuels's play, valuables could be confiscated by guards who had learned to look for jewelry sewn into clothing or tacked into the soles and heels of shoes.

7. Records show that resistance to rescue missions occurred in North America as well, for after debates in Congress and in state legislatures, after complaints that refugee children would take Americans' jobs, the United States decided against rescue. For all its empty vastness, Canada took in 5,000 Jews. Tony Kushner notes that in 1938–39, "more than 40 per cent of the Jews who escaped the Nazis found refuge in Britain," albeit on temporary visas. See Kushner, *The Holocaust and the Liberal Imagination* (London: Blackwell, 1994), 51. See also David Cesarani's introduction to *Into the Arms of Strangers: Stories of the Kindertransport,* ed. Mark J. Harris and Deborah Oppenheimer (London: Bloomsbury, 2000). British immigration policies regarding Jews through the end of the war are discussed by Bernard Wasserstein, *Britain and the Jews of Europe, 1939–1945* (Oxford: Clarendon Press, 2001), and Louise London, *Whitehall and the Jews, 1933–1948* (Cambridge: Cambridge University Press, 2000).

8. Quoted in A. J. Sherman, *Island Refuge: Britain and Refugees from the Third Reich, 1933– 1939* (London: Frank Cass, 1994), 39. Although the Nationality of Jews Bill was read in Parliament, it was neither printed nor given a second hearing. See also Pamela Shatzkes, *Holocaust and Rescue: Impotent or Indifferent? Anglo-Jewry, 1938–1945* (Basingstoke: Palgrave, 2002).

9. Many children were taken to Jewish hostels, but though Jewish organizations tried to place others in compatible homes, the experience was mixed, from outright abuse to acceptance and even love. One transportee reports, "On the day I arrived they gave me a hot drink and an hour later I did the ironing for the whole family. . . . What frightened me most was the thought that I would be giving strangers absolute power over me." *The Last Goodbye: The Rescue of Children from Nazi Europe* (London: Jewish Museum, 2004). 54.

10. Quoted in Rob Pratt, "Future Past," www.metroactive.com/papers/cruz/09.08.99/ taylor-9936.html.

11. Despite differences between "populist and nonpopulist" perspectives on attitudes of different classes and regions of Britain, British rhetoric of World War II (reinforced by American journalists in London) is upheld by the fact that "the British people did endure the Blitz without cracking." Paul Smith, "Review of Angus Calder's *The Myth of the Blitz,*" *Times Literary Supplement,* September 13, 1991, 28.

12. Colin Holmes shows that in Britain, "anti-semitism never secured a major policy foot-hold," and "the forces of a stable social-political system could be deployed against those who threatened to make anti-semitism a major issue." See *Anti-Semitism in British Society, 1876–1939* (London: Edward Arnold, 1979), 226. According to Tony Kushner, "political antisemitism" was considered "a threat to law and order." See "The Paradox of Prejudice: The Impact of Organized Antisemitism in Britain During an Anti-Nazi War," in *Traditions of Intolerance: Historical Perspectives on Fascism and Race Discourse in Britain*, ed. Tony Kushner and Kenneth Lunn (Manchester: Manchester University Press, 1989), 85.

13. Tony Kushner, *The Persistence of Prejudice: Antisemitism in British Society During the Second World War* (Manchester: Manchester University Press, 1989), 93. Kushner also reminds us that, despite this difference, tolerance remained an obstacle to attacking the freedom of Jews to practice their religion. See Kushner's *The Holocaust and the Liberal Imagination* for a trenchant analysis of relationships among liberal ideology, immigration policies, and concerns about British national identity.

14. Holmes and Richard Bolchover agree that, despite British differences, "a tradition of anti-semitism in Britain" was not "insignificant"; to dismiss it would be "a cruel deception" (Holmes, *Anti-Semitism in British Society,* 234). See Richard Bolchover, *British Jewry and the Holocaust* (Cambridge: Cambridge University Press, 1993), 49. Endelman emphasizes how the Jews' anxieties and antisemitic experiences made community politics in the interwar and wartime periods "fractious and ferocious, perhaps more so than at any earlier time." Endelman, *Jews of Britain,* 204.

15. Bolchover, *British Jewry and the Holocaust,* 49.

16. The German Jewish Aid Committee, *While You Are in England: Helpful Information and Guidance for Every Refugee* (London: Woburn House), 12.

17. Kushner, *Holocaust and the Liberal Imagination,* 131.

18. Kushner, *Persistence of Prejudice,* 117.

19. By June 11, 1940, with the fall of Dunkirk, military pressure succeeded in galvanizing public fears, and 27,000 enemy aliens were interned, with more than 7,000 sent overseas. See Kushner, *Persistence of Prejudice,* 145.

20. Bolchover, *British Jewry and the Holocaust,* 50.

21. Victor Seidler, *Shadows of the Shoah* (Oxford: Berg, 2000), 4.

22. Julia Pascal, *The Dybbuk,* in *The Holocaust Trilogy,* 106.

23. Review, *Into the Arms of Strangers: Stories of the Kindertransport, Shofar* 20.4 (Summer 2002), 116. Jewish indifference and the resultant placement of one third of the children in Christian homes probably led to the "high rate of radical assimilation among German Jews in Britain after the war" (Endelman, *Jews of Britain,* 215). Diane Samuels testifies, "When I go into an English context I feel like a foreigner because the vocabulary of my world and culture are very different to the English one." Sonja Lyndon, "Speaking Out: An Exchange between Four Women in Theatre," *Jewish Quarterly* (Autumn 1994), 19–25.

24. Richard Hornby delineates various strands of voluntary and involuntary role-playing that have stimulated my analysis (Richard Hornby, *Drama, Metadrama, and Perception* [Lewisburg, PA: Bucknell University Press, 1986], 74). His example of involuntary role-playing as influenced by the realpolitik of Nazi Germany and the Soviet Union shows how characters are "manipulated by an unseen, mysterious, powerful authority" (ibid.,

82). In *Kindertransport*, authority is associated with the threats not only of Nazism but of a dominant British culture.

25. Carol Zemel, *"Z'chor!* Roman Vishniac's Photo-Eulogy of East European Jews," in *Shaping Losses: Cultural Memory and the Holocaust,* ed. Julia Epstein and Lori H. Lefkovitz (Urbana: University of Illinois Press, 2001), 79.

26. The story, based on an unspecified catastrophe in the town of Hameln, Germany, is traced to June 26, 1284. A rhyme inscribed on the *Rattenfangerhaus,* built in 1602–3 in Hameln, has been translated as follows: "In the year 1284, on John's and Paul's day was the 26th of June / By a piper, dressed in all kinds of colours, / 130 children born in Hamelin were deduced and lost at the 'calvarie' [place of execution]." In 1816 Jacob and Wilhelm Grimm reworked the story from eleven sources, but its most famous version is Robert Browning's 1842 poem, *The Pied Piper of Hamelin.* Some critics speculate that the fable originally represented the recruitment of settlers for new colonies in Eastern Europe, while others find evidence for references to a plague or a children's crusade. Peter Arnds, "Innocence Abducted: Youth, War, and the Wolf in Literary Adaptations of the Pied Piper Legend from Robert Browning to Michel Tournier," *Jeunesse: Young People, Texts, Culture* 4.1 (Summer 2012), 61–84.

27. *"Kindertransport* Writer Diane Samuels Q & A Exclusive," Octagon Theatre, Bolton, www.octagonbolton.co.uk/kindertransportAdded Extra.htm (last accessed November 30, 2004; link no longer accessible).

28. "Drama Out of a Crisis," *Jewish Chronicle,* October 12, 2001, 33.

29. Neil Roland, "Guernsey's Nazi Collaboration," *Manchester Jewish Gazette,* March 6, 1992, n.p.

30. Vivian Patraka, *Spectacular Suffering: Theatre, Fascism, and the Holocaust* (Bloomington: Indiana University Press, 1999), 44. Patraka describes Holocaust plays that "ask audiences to become implicated in fascist ideology and its operations, to be caught by surprise in something we might want to condemn but do not want to understand quite that well." Susanne Greenhalgh draws attention to the play's "multilingualism" as an "aural memoryscape" that marks "an unstable, and destabilizing, terrain for identity in the post-Holocaust world." Greenhalgh, "'A Space for Me': Jewishness, Memory, and Identity in Julia Pascal's *Holocaust Trilogy,"* in *Jewish Women's Writing of the 1990s and Beyond in Great Britain and the United States,* ed. Ulrike Behlau and Bernhard Reitz (Trier: Wissenschaftlicher Verlag, 2004), 33.

31. Lena Corner, "Truthsayer," *Big Issue,* November 13, 1995, n.p.

32. Abigail Morris, "Beware the Treadmill," *Jewish Quarterly* (Winter 1994–95), 4.

33. Marianne Hirsch, "Surviving Images," in *Visual Culture and the Holocaust,* ed. Barbie Zelizer (New Brunswick, NJ: Rutgers University Press, 2001), 218 (Hirsch's italics).

10

JEWISH MOTHERS AND JEWISH MEMORY IN CONTEMPORARY MEMOIRS

DAVID BRAUNER

It is my fate now . . . to scramble among the ruins of my mother's memory in search of my past, of who all of us are. To have grown up as a Jewish daughter into an insistence of [*sic*] the importance of memory, knowing that without it, we are animals.

Linda Grant, Remind Me Who I Am, Again, 1998[1]

My need to know what had happened to my maternal grandfather and his wife was matched by my mother's need not to know, so she took refuge in silence and, occasionally, improbable lies.

Eva Figes, Journey to Nowhere, 2009[2]

There are infinite ways of telling the truth, including fiction, and infinite ways of evading the truth, including non-fiction.

Jenny Diski, Skating to Antarctica, 1997[3]

Eva Figes (1932–2012), Jenny Diski (b. 1947), and Linda Grant (b. 1951) have much in common: all are Anglo-Jewish authors with significant bodies of fiction, who are nonetheless better known for their nonfiction. Diski has published a collection of stories and ten novels, most of which have been well received, but she is best known for her regular contributions to the *London*

Review of Books; her travel books, *Skating to Antarctica* (1997) and *Stranger on a Train: Daydreaming and Smoking Around America with Interruptions* (2002; the recipient of both the Thomas Cook Travel Book Award and the J.R. Ackerley Prize for Autobiography); and her recent work of popular history, *The Sixties* (2010). Linda Grant's first novel, *The Cast Iron Shore* (1996), was nominated for the Guardian Fiction Prize and won the David Higham Award; her second, *When I Lived in Modern Times* (2000), won the Orange Prize for fiction; and her fourth, *The Clothes on Their Backs* (2008), was short-listed for the Man Booker Prize, but she is arguably best known for her journalism, particularly her features and blogs on fashion, and for her book on the subject, *The Thoughtful Dresser* (2009). Finally, Eva Figes published fourteen works of fiction but is still most frequently referred to as the author of the influential feminist book *Patriarchal Attitudes* (1970).[4]

They have all also published nonfiction books that defy easy generic classification. Diski's *Skating to Antarctica* and *Stranger on a Train* are part travelogues, part memoirs, part philosophical essays. Grant's *Remind Me Who I Am, Again* (1998) is similarly hybridic, mingling family history with childhood memories and discursive reflections on subjects such as aging and grieving. Figes published *Little Eden: A Child at War* (1978), which interweaves a social history of Cirencester with a memoir of her experience as a child evacuee there; *Tales of Innocence and Experience: An Exploration* (2003), a series of meditations on fairy tales and the nature of childhood, and an account of how her relationship with her granddaughter led her to a reevaluation of her own childhood, family history, and the Holocaust; and *Journey to Nowhere: One Woman Looks for the Promised Land* (2008), which is part biography, part autobiography, and part political polemic. These books are also all inquiries into the nature of Jewish memory and Jewish motherhood; portraits of Jewish mothers whose withdrawal, voluntary and involuntary, from their family history functions as a metaphor for Jewish identity in the post-Holocaust era.

An immigrant, the daughter of an immigrant, and the granddaughter of an immigrant, respectively, neither Figes nor Diski nor Grant have any religious affiliation to Judaism, yet all three grew up with an acute awareness of their ethnicity, and of the particular difficulties it posed in assimilating into English society. Grant observes that it was "hard to tell" what class her parents belonged to, since they were "neither part of the great proletariat . . . nor of a peasantry" (34). "What their class really was," she concludes, "was Immigrant [sic]" (35). Similarly, Figes points out that the spinster sisters who ran the school in Cirencester that she and her brother attended as wartime evacuees, although they notionally catered only for the children of officers, were "happy to accept us as pupils since, as refugees from Nazi Germany, we could not be categorized socially in the normal way."[5] Diski, too, notes that "being Jewish" meant that she could never "quite fit myself into the English class system," since her family "weren't middle class, not exactly working class" but, as the children of immigrants, "*different*" (105; italics in original). For Diski this difference is constantly reinforced, both from within and from without: "The Jewishness of our neighbours and ourselves was plain during my childhood. There was almost nothing in the way of religious practice . . . . But our Jewishness was constantly reiterated . . . by my parents in their everyday conversation. . . . It was also evident from the outside world. At school the other kids told me I was not English, but Jewish. Killing Christ was still something— just a few years after the Second World War—I was held responsible for in the playground" (104–5).

Whereas Figes—growing up in a German Jewish family that felt itself to be "constantly on probation" and which responded by "trying to hide" and "become English"—is made aware of her Jewishness for the first time when her best friend at boarding school tells her that she "was a Jew and Jews did not believe in God" (*Little Eden*) and is told by another schoolmate that "Germany had done a good thing in getting rid of the Jews" (*Tales*), Diski, growing up as a secular English Jew in the postwar era, finds herself in a more ambiguous position.[6] Diski's family and their Jewish neighbors identify themselves as Jewish in spite of their lack of religious conviction, whereas the antisemitism of Diski's schoolmates is based both on ancient religious prejudices (the label of "Christ-killer") and on the more recent pseudo-science that categorized Jews as a separate race and that manifested itself in the genocide of World War II, to which Diski alludes (hence their belief that Diski could not be both English and Jewish).

Like Diski, Grant testifies both to the tenacity of English antisemitism in the postwar period (she reproduces a letter received by her father in 1948 in response to his application for naturalization as a British citizen, warning him to "Get out!!! Otherwise your address will be entered on our list for destroying" [49]) and to her family's sense of its Jewish heritage: "In her kitchen my mother cooked recipes . . . that her own mother had brought with her from Kiev, and the dishes that came to the table were our link to the vanished communities of earlier times; they traced the wanderings of the Jewish people across the earth" (77). That the collective memory of what is of course a matrilineal religion is transmitted through the female line (Grant's mother reproducing her own mother's recipes) seems to reinforce the popular image of the mother as both nurturer and repository of family history. Indeed, the last three decades have seen a significant body of writing, both academic and popular, emphasizing the importance of the mother-daughter bond for the successful development and mature realization of the female subject.[7] Diski, Grant, and Figes all seem to owe their vocation as writers to their mothers, but not in the sense of having been inspired by their example or enabled by their self-sacrifices. On the contrary, the mothers in these texts empower their daughters only in the negative sense that they force them to become emotionally autonomous and intellectually self-sufficient at an early age.

Figes's mother may seem rather marginal to *Tales of Innocence and Experience* and *Journey to Nowhere*—books that focus on other kinds of maternal bonds and maternal figures (the relationship between Figes and her granddaughter in the former, the wartime and postwar experiences of Figes's mother's housemaid, Edith, in the latter)—but she turns out to be a central figure in both narratives. Toward the end of *Tales,* Figes pithily summarizes the end of the intimacy between herself and her mother—"I lost my mother, she her child" (170); at the start of *Journey to Nowhere,* she laments the changes that led to this breakdown in relations, observing that, by the end of the war, "my mother was no longer the kind, gentle woman of my early childhood, but a difficult, embittered one" (11). Figes returns repeatedly to the subject of the deterioration and ultimate disintegration of the relationship between her and her mother; both books, while explicitly addressing larger issues, such as the nature of childhood and the origins of the state of Israel, are about Figes's alienation from her mother.

Both *Remind Me Who I Am, Again* and *Skating to Antarctica* are avowedly about the authors' mothers—Grant announces that her book is "an account of how two grown-up daughters [Grant and her sister Michelle] watched their mother decline into dementia, watched her memory disappear" (30); and Diski confirms that she had always envisaged *Skating to Antarctica* as "a book in part about my mother" (95), notwithstanding its ostensible subject (an account of the author's voyage to the Southern polar regions) and the fact that, as Heidi MacPherson puts it, the passages about her mother seem to be written "almost unwillingly."[8] Yet, paradoxically, the mothers themselves figure more as absences than presences. Partly this is to do with the particular circumstances in which the books are written: Diski's mother storms out of her life when the author is still a teenager and never returns; Grant's mother, suffering from a debilitating disease—multi-infarct dementia—that erodes her memory incrementally through a succession of tiny strokes, gradually ceases to become recognizable as herself, prompting Grant finally to ask: "Who was she? The mother who had once bought our school uniforms and sewed our Locke's name-tapes into the collars was gone. How were we related to her, as she would one day ask me herself?" (199).

Metaphorically, however, these mothers were not there—that is, not present *as mothers*—long before illness and estrangement took them away. In spite of the elegiac note that Grant strikes by invoking an image of parental care (the mother buying clothes for her children and sewing their names into them so that they will not be lost), it is quite clear that Rose Grant was not the conventionally maternal type. Typically, Grant represents Rose's mothering as perfunctory at best, negligent at worst: she is "more intent on coffee mornings than reading a child a book" (213). Just as Diski's mother seems to embrace the role only insofar as it provides her with reflected glory ("I was the best medium for her display" [13]) or vicarious fulfilment of her own ambitions ("I would be the youngest champion ice skater ever, and she would be the mother of the champion. It would mean fame, money, travel and a good marriage, and she would accompany me on the route to all these good things" [20]), so Rose Grant "wanted what went with motherhood, the prestige, but none of the work" (82). Whereas Diski claims to be "unable to be angry at my mother's inadequacy" (111), Grant admits that she "didn't forgive . . . ha[s] not forgiven now . . . my mother's ongoing demeanor of couldn't-be-bothered-with-that-nonsense [that] summed up her mothering" (80). Her resentment at Rose's failure to be the mother whom she wanted and needed is reciprocated by her mother's disappointment in her ("in [her] eyes I was a failed daughter" [166]), which is in turn mirrored in her judgment of herself as an "inadequate, undutiful daughter" (166).

In all three cases, the mothers not only abdicate their responsibilities as mothers but invert the conventional maternal dynamic, so that their daughters are expected to mother them. In *Tales*, Figes recalls how her father, whenever he came home on weekend leave from the army, would instruct her to "look after my mother" and how she would "feel responsible" for her, "take care" of her, try to "pre-empt her wishes" (170). "I had been taught," she observes, "that it was her feelings which mattered, mine were irrelevant" (170). In spite of Figes's best efforts to protect her mother's feelings and to bear the burden of the housework, she finds herself, as she puts it in *Journey*, "blamed . . . for . . . not helping out enough, not cleaning enough floors, not washing more dishes" (45).

When, in the advanced stages of her illness, Linda Grant's mother, Rose, begins to mistake her daughters for her sisters or nieces, Grant comments that "she has now repudiated the idea of herself as a mother," but in fact the implication of Grant's account is that she had always resisted the idea of herself as a mother, preferring to remain "not a wife nor a mother but a daughter" (234, 82). Just as Diski's mother "responded to pressing emotional needs as an infant responds to its physical wants—instantly, thoughtlessly" (*Skating*, 107), and Figes's mother "behaved throughout the war as though Hitler had been invented specifically to make her life unpleasant, always moaning on about something" (*Journey*, 47), so Grant's mother continues to behave like "the spoilt youngest child" even after she herself has had children (82). Whereas Figes, as a child, has little choice but to try to look after a mother who cannot or will not look after her, Grant and her sister, as adults, are unwilling to offer Rose the mothering that she failed to give them: "looking after her ourselves" was "unimaginable," since "[t]he intimacy simply wasn't there to begin with" (187). Because "her mothering sometimes felt like a vacuum," it is perhaps hardly surprising that when Grant poses to herself the question, "do I love my mother?," instead of answering it she admits to "collud[ing] in the public convention that children love their parents," while at the same time affirming, somewhat equivocally, that "I care what happens to her" (82, 265).

This question of the relationship between filial feeling and maternal feeling is one that Diski and Figes discuss repeatedly. Whereas Grant suffers from her mother's neglect, Diski and Figes, as victims of emotional and physical abuse, have stronger reasons for not conforming to the commonplace expectation that everyone must love her/his mother. Figes writes, in *Journey*, of her mother's "violent temper, the physical and verbal abuse I was regularly subjected to" and of the "explosions of emotional and physical abuse" which erupted periodically during her father's absence in wartime (60, 51). On one occasion, she recalls that she had "pleaded to a friendly neighbour for help, telling her that my mother 'had gone mad', and been laughed at for my pains" (*Journey*, 51). Although "[t]he crockery stopped flying" after the war, when her father gives her "protection," issuing a "shocked rebuke to my mother when she smacked my face in public," between 1939 and 1945, Figes writes, "my mother and I had our own private war" (*Journey*, 45). Feeling relentlessly, "unjustly persecuted" by a mother whose "main objective was not to leave me in peace at any price," Figes concedes that she "ended up hating her" (*Little Eden*, 129–30), although she does also attempt to extenuate her mother's behavior somewhat, acknowledging that she "was coping alone with stresses which my generation has not had to face" and even expressing some empathy for her predicament: "as a mother myself, coping alone, I know how easily unhappiness and anxiety . . . can build up inside . . . and unwittingly cause an outburst quite dispropor-tionate to the offence" (*Little Eden*, 129–30). In stark contrast, Diski expresses neither condemnation nor exoneration of her mother's offenses.

Readers of Diski's partly autobiographical novel *Like Mother* (1988), in which the protagonist, Frances, is sexually abused by her alcoholic, mentally unstable mother, Ivy, will have recognized many of the details of the mother-daughter relationship described in *Skating to Antarctica* and will have been unsurprised by the revelation that both her mother and father had incestu-ous relations with her.[9] For those readers unfamiliar with her earlier work, however, Diski's narrative treatment of her mother up until this point in *Skat-ing* might seem to confirm her mother's view that her daughter was "quite heartless about her" (42). Indeed, Diski's decision to withhold the informa-tion about her mother's sexual abuse of her until almost halfway through the book, and even then to treat it in a muted, elliptical way, almost as though it were the least of her mother's failings, is part of a consistent pattern of under-statement, a determined effort to resist melodrama. Careful not to give this aspect of her relationship with her mother undue prominence, Diski refuses to represent herself as a victim, to invite sympathy or pity from her reader. On the contrary, she unsettles her readers, challenging complacent assumptions about the intimacy of the mother-daughter bond, by discussing her mother in an objective, clinically detached manner.

At the beginning of *Stranger on a Train*, Diski refers in passing to her "dis-tressed and distressing mother," but for most of *Skating* she carefully eschews such emotive language, preferring to treat her mother—and her relationship to her—in quasi-scientific terms.[10] This rhetorical strategy is clear from the outset: the title[11] of the first section of the book is "Schrödinger's Mother," an allusion to the famous thought-experiment expounded by the physicist wherein he imagines confining a cat to a box in circumstances that will in due course produce a scenario in which the animal will, in strictly scientific terms, be simultaneously alive and dead (that is to say, both possibilities will be equally likely and will coexist until empirical observation can verify one or the other). Explaining her own reluctance to discover whether her mother is still alive or not, Diski adapts the experiment and invites her readers to

> [i]magine a box, inside which is a flask of hydrochloric acid, some radioactive material, a Geiger counter—and my mother. The

apparatus is wired up so that if the radioactive material decays, the Geiger counter will be triggered and will set off a device to shatter the flask and thereby kill my mother. We set the experiment up, shut the lid of the box, and wait until there is a precise fifty-fifty chance that the radioactive decay has occurred. What is the state of my mother before we open the lid to look?

Common sense says that my mother is alive or dead, but according to quantum theory events such as the radioactive decay of an atom . . . become real only when they are observed. The case is not decided until someone opens the lid and looks. (*Skating*, 23)

Diski's detached tone here—her casual discussion of her mother being subjected (albeit only hypothetically) to a kind of torture followed by death—is calculated to provoke. She is daring her readers to condemn her as an unfeeling, "bad" daughter.

Whereas Grant confesses to harboring resentment at her mother's poor mothering, and Figes to "hating" her mother, Diski professes neither love nor hate for her mother, but complete indifference: "Thinking about her as my mother, I can only manage a shrug, a sense of random misfortune that I was in the charge of a woman with the emotional capacity of a small child" (*Skating*, 108). Her mother's erratic, "inexplicable" (106) behavior, so Diski claims, left "[n]o room for anger, but no room for affection either" (107). Told repeatedly by her mother that "everyone need[s] their mother," Diski responds by asserting emphatically that "I cannot recall a moment in my life when I have wished she was there" (108). Reflecting on her childhood, Diski professes to feel no sense of injustice, on the basis that "human child-rearing arrangements are a crap shoot. You might as well be enraged at the ice for being too fragile to hold your weight" (107–8). To feel aggrieved, Diski's objectifying language implies, would be irrational: rather than seeing herself as the victim of a peculiarly disturbed individual, Diski prefers to contextualize her experience of mothering in anthropological terms, to see it as the result of the arbitrariness of "human child-rearing arrangements."

In doing so, she knows full well that she is likely to be accused of being "in denial" about her own feelings toward her mother. At one point Diski reflects with dry irony that "[e]veryone now knows that mothers are an essential item of equipment in any psyche, and that though relations with mothers may be difficult or even dreadful, attachment to them is mandatory. They also know, as a corollary, that a denial of attachment is a failure to confront the reality of mother-attachment" (21).[12] Later in the narrative, when Diski's own daughter, Chloe, unearths evidence of her grandmother's probable death, Diski asks herself, "What did I feel? Nothing," and then reflects that "popular psychology told me there must be some feeling attached to the positive news of the death of my mother . . . I told myself that I really ought to try harder" (144, 83).[13] Diski's tone here is partly self-satirical, but her contempt for "popular psychology" is sincere (earlier in the book she complains that "[t]here seems to be no limit to [its] reach and power" [21]) and helps to account for her uncompromisingly dispassionate representation of her mother, and of her relationship with her.

Her impatience with the skepticism of others concerning her (lack of) feelings toward her mother—when people "asked me if I wasn't disturbed by the riddle of my mother's absence, they meant didn't I feel guilty about not knowing or caring. And I didn't" (31)—is a recurring theme in the book, and expresses itself at times in a defensive stance toward the implied reader: "I last saw my mother on 22 April 1966. You may find my certainty of the date significant, but I remember it because I know the last time I saw her was two days after my father died. The date in my memory is the date of his death" (24). Whereas Figes writes, with candid resentment, that she cannot ever "recall getting a good-night kiss" from her mother (*Journey*, 38), Diski observes that "[t]he one truly generous act of my mother's that I could put my finger on [was] her leaving me alone," and insists that "I had never thought about the fact of my mother—*my* mother—as my gestation site," self-consciously puncturing what she sees as the prevailing romantic and sentimental myths about mother-daughter relationships (28, 81).[14]

Writing about *Skating to Antarctica*, Paola Splendore, in her essay "Bad Daughters and Unmotherly Mothers: The New Family Plot in the Contemporary English Novel," at first acknowledges that "[t]he text contains neither an emotional redress nor the desire for rehabilitation," but later concludes that "[m]uch is forgiven in the end and one has the feeling that the confrontation with the maternal ghost was necessary for the daughter['s] acceptance of [her] own identity. The mother . . . appears rehabilitated, in spite of [her] severe shortcomings and failures."[15] Later in the essay, Splendore writes, this time referring to *Like Mother,* that "on the one hand the novel appears to brutally debunk the rhetoric of maternal love. . . . On the other hand, by allowing her daughter to be born, Frances appears to want to redeem the creative function of motherhood."[16] Splendore may be right to see a certain ambivalence in

Diski's novel toward the idea of motherhood (though the fact that Frances's daughter is born with no brain and named "Nony" must qualify any redemptive reading), but there is surely no softening of Diski's attitude toward her own mother at the end of *Skating.*

When she receives final confirmation of her mother's death, Diski is alarmed not by the fact that she is deceased but rather by the years of continued life that her mother had led after their final estrangement: "only since 1988 had I been really orphaned, truly safe" (*Skating,* 243). Again, Diski deliberately inverts conventional social values, presenting her orphanhood as a desirable state that offered security, rather than a loss that leaves her vulnerable. Although she concedes—tentatively—to her daughter that she is glad to have learned the truth about her mother's death (Chloe says, "Good to know about your mother at last, eh?" and Diski replies, "Mmm. Yes, I think it is"), she does so not in a conciliatory spirit but because she feels her decision not to seek a reconciliation with her mother while she was still alive has been vindicated. When she first begins to read the result of Chloe's investigation into her mother's last years, she experiences a "sharp moment of anxiety that everything I recalled . . . might have been imagined, fantasized, fictioned," but is relieved to discover confirmation of her mother's erratic, aggressive behavior, "preferr[ing] my mother's continued unhappiness to finding myself to have been deluded all these years" (250).

If Diski is determined to avoid replicating the conventional pieties about mother-daughter relationships, *Skating* nonetheless tends to reinforce the notion that, as Adalgisa Giorgio puts it, "the mother-daughter dyad is still the dominant structuring principle of female identity in Western cultures."[17] Grant's representation of her relationship with her mother makes this point even more clearly. In the introduction to her book, *Writing Mothers, Writing Daughters: Tracing the Maternal in Stories by American-Jewish Women,* Janet Handler Burstein argues that mother-daughter relationships are peculiarly vexed because of "the particular tangle created . . . by the inability to see one's mother as separate from oneself," and goes on to claim that "the labor of both dismantling and reconstructing the mother's image and story . . . is vital to the daughter who would know and speak herself as subject."[18] Growing up, Grant "wanted more than anything else not to be like my mother" (*Remind Me,* 38), but of course this desire to break free of her mother's influence paradoxically reinforces it, since her self-definition is still entirely governed (albeit negatively) by her mother's personality: she does not know who she wants to be, only who she does not want to be.

When her mother begins to lose her memory, Grant clearly feels that her own identity, as much as her mother's, is in peril: "Without memory we don't exist. When a member of the family starts to lose their memory . . . It's almost a challenge to your own existence" (268). So for Grant the question posed by her mother's dementia is fundamentally ontological: "it isn't just about what she can or can't remember for I have to ask myself, which bit was the illness and which her own real personality? . . . And my own self . . . was it partly formed out of the slow composition of blood that . . . clumped itself into clots which made their silent way into her head?" (104). The image that Grant uses here—of her "own self" coagulating from the residue of her mother's thickening blood—reflects not simply her imaginative identification with her mother's illness but her deep-seated anxiety that it might also afflict her, that it might be a hereditary condition. Grant alludes repeatedly to her fear that she, too, will fall victim to the dementia that has claimed her mother ("Until I die or senile dementia gets me first, as I am so sure it will . . ."; "since my mother's illness my obsession has become my own failing memory" [76, 133]), and at one point even imagines her future senile self having a conversation in which she will ironically have no recollection of having written this book about her mother's loss of memory: "I wrote a book about my mother, you say? I don't remember" (227).[19]

She is also forced constantly to reinvent herself to adapt to the sudden shifts in her mother's personality, so that what may appear to outsiders as the natural intimacy of a mother and daughter with years of shared experience is "actually a relationship I have constructed to deal with this brand-new individual who has vestiges of her old personality. And I have to make up a personality for myself as well" (268). This process of (self)-renegotiation is complicated by the fact that her mother's "old personality" was itself neither stable nor transparent. Reproducing a photograph of her mother as a young girl dressed as a gypsy, Grant comments dryly: "Already she was taking on disguises" (23).[20] Later she refers to the "lifetime's habits of secretiveness that to us were part of her unreliable personality" (25) and describes her trying out a varied repertoire of masks: "In front of her three-way mirror, my mother practised showing her different faces to the world" (100). Here the literal fragmenting of her mother's image into three different reflections also functions as a metaphor for her slipperiness and duplicity. In this sense the disintegration of her identity brought on by her dementia seems, ironically, to be the culmination of a career of self-improvisation: "a lifetime of keeping up appearances had only prepared her for her greatest role, dementia, in which she did everything she could to pretend to the world that she was right as rain . . . she went on presenting a bold façade, artifice instead of authenticity" (130–31).

On the one hand, Grant presents her mother's preference for "artifice" as just that—a life choice, an expression (and paradoxically also an evasion) of her own particular personality. On the other hand, she is at pains to locate it in a cultural context. Grant tells us that she "grew up amidst a conspiracy of liars, show-offs and storytellers" (50), in "a family where the past was shifting and untrustworthy"; truth was so elusive that as a child she "thought all forms of lying were normal" (95). This, Grant emphasises, is the result not of a congenital predisposition to insincerity or a pathological delight in deceit for its own sake, but rather a pragmatic response to centuries of persecution: "My family had by necessity reconstructed itself and its past for the life it would live in a new land. . . . All the lies and evasions and tall stories are what you must have when you are bent on self-invention. Now my mother has a similar task, that of continuously inventing for *herself* . . . a coherent identity and daily history" (156; italics in original).

According to Grant's account, there is a direct relationship between the historical circumstances of her family and their tenuous relationship with their own history. It is hardly surprising, she implies, if, having "for the first time in centuries . . . felt the stranglehold of antisemitism lifted from round their necks" (35), her family decides to jettison its past, and to repress its memories of the Holocaust: "Buried in the hearts of the parents of all my generation are untold traumas of destruction and loss" (66). Her mother's was a generation of "damaged people" (66); the war "cast the longest shadow" over their children; "history breathed down [their] necks" (66, 33). If the loss of memory is traumatic for anyone, it is doubly so for Jews, Grant argues, because "while all cultures are to do with memory, none more so than the Jewish community in which everything is about what was" (269).[21] Moreover, in Rose Grant's brain "resided the very last links with her generation," so that what is at stake in this case is not simply the dignity and sanity of an old woman but a whole family's history.

The sense that Rose Grant's predicament (and that of her daughter) is exacerbated by her Jewishness—that her dementia constitutes an attenuation of collective Jewish memory, as well as a deprivation for the Grant family—is pervasive in Grant's book, from the epigraph at the head of this essay; to the passage in which she points out that Yom Kippur, the Day of Atonement (the holiest day in the Jewish calendar), is "also a day of remembrance" and refers to the "public memory of the nameless dead of the Holocaust" (17);

to her insistence that her mother conformed precisely to a "Jewish stereo-type" (44) in terms of her ambitions for her daughters; to her apothegm that "[m]emory . . . [is] rootless, the Wandering Jew of our physical selves" (289). This is also clearly the case for Figes's mother, though in her case the amnesia is willed rather than the product of a neurological condition.

As a child growing up in a secular German Jewish household in the 1930s, Figes was insulated from the increasingly ugly atmosphere of antisemitism through her ignorance of her own ethnicity and through the concerted efforts of those around her to preserve that ignorance. Even the debris left by the events of *Kristallnacht* is explained away by those around her as part of a rebuilding project. Reflecting on her anomalous position, Figes observes that "[c]hildren whose parents had not abandoned Judaism might have some inkling, not only of what was happening, but why. I was six years old, still waiting for Father Christmas. I had no notion why he failed to arrive during the winter of 1938" (*Tales*, 162).

Although the older Figes of *Journey* displays a profound ambivalence toward her Jewish identity (at one point stating that "until recently, I made a point of calling myself Jewish" [*Journey*, 82]), in this passage the use of the phrase "abandoned Judaism" contains an implicit reproach for her parents' decision to sever their connections to their Jewish past, and for their conse-quent failure to inform her of the reality of the situation in Germany in 1938. This note of reproach is explicit in *Tales*, when Figes writes of her mother's continuing determination to evade the truth of the wartime atrocities in which her family had suffered: "As I was growing up, long after I had grown up, my mother turned 'not knowing' into an art form . . . when I had the temerity to ask, she told me that her father had been deported to Warsaw and met his death in an air raid. I knew this to be an impossibility, that no trans-ports from Berlin had ever left for the Polish capital" (*Tales*, 87).

In a sense, both *Tales* and *Journey* can be seen as attempts to recuperate this lost history, to articulate what, in *Little Eden*, she calls the "dark hor-ror at the heart of the family which could not be spoken about" (*Little Eden*, 129). The catalysts for this process of retrieval are her grandchild in *Tales*, who "ask[s] questions [that] . . . we have avoided facing up to for so long" (*Tales*, 140), and Edith, her mother's housemaid from prewar Germany, in *Journey to Nowhere*. When Edith unexpectedly turns up at the Figes family home in Lon-don after the war and resumes her old position, Figes comments that "Edith was family, and I knew instinctively that this was her reason for seeking us out after such a long time, and from so far away. So it was with a growing sense of unease that I began to realize that my mother did not know this or, if she did, thought it of no consequence" (*Journey*, 59).

Figes's mother's rejection of Edith's emotional needs constitutes another, albeit in this case metaphorical, failure of maternal care, and it is Figes herself who undertakes this role in relation to Edith, in spite of being much younger than the maid. "Because my mother had failed her, Edith had developed a dependency on me . . . I thought about talking to my mother about it, but knew it was worse than hopeless. She would take umbrage, get annoyed with me . . . or, worse still, take her annoyance out on Edith, who was too vulnerable to speak for herself" (*Journey*, 106). By first offering protection to Edith and then telling her story—giving a voice to a woman who is "too vulnerable to speak for herself"—Figes might be said, in psychoanalytical terms, to be compensating not only for her mother's failure to mother Edith but for her failure to mother Figes herself. In other words, Edith functions in the text both as a surrogate child of Figes and a symbolic reflection of herself. In this context, it is significant that the most catastrophic failure of maternal care that Figes suffers—an incident so traumatic that she revisits it in each of the three books that I have been discussing—concerns the eventual revelation of the Nazi genocide that Edith narrowly evades, living in hiding in Germany, but which claims many members of Figes's family.

In *Little Eden*, Figes describes how, "one bright afternoon in early spring my mother gave me ninepence and sent me to the local cinema with the words 'Go and see for yourself'" (*Little Eden*, 131). The film that she sends Figes to see is a newsreel of the liberation of Belsen. Watching the "mounds of corpses, dazed survivors with huge haunted eyes staring out of skulls which had become too heavy for the frail, emaciated bodies," Figes has an epiphany: "At last I knew what it meant to be a Jew, the shameful secret which had been hinted at but kept from me for so many years, the mark on my head which I did not recognise but which Isolde had known about four years before . . . when I was a small child, innocent as Eve in the Garden of Eden, and as ignorant" (*Little Eden*, 131). In this first version of the episode, watching the newsreel becomes a second fall; the knowledge of good and evil gained, and the innocence lost, by Adam and Eve when they taste the forbidden fruit is used as an analogy for the (hitherto forbidden) knowledge of the evil committed in the Nazi camps that Figes acquires; her experience in the cinema is a metaphorical expulsion from the Eden of childhood innocence (and ignorance) that the title of the book evokes.

When she retells this story in *Tales,* however, the emphasis shifts. Whereas in the earlier account Figes registers neither surprise nor indignation at the fact that her mother sends her to the cinema unaccompanied, in *Tales* she points out that "this story shocked those who heard it" and goes on to pose the question: "Would it have changed anything if she had sat beside me, a loving parent, and held my hand in the dark? I might not have felt, as I did, that I was being punished . . . simply for being myself" (*Tales,* 126). Finally, in the version in *Journey,* the trauma of what she witnesses on screen is exacerbated, arguably even eclipsed, by the cruelty that Figes feels her mother displays in sending her to the cinema alone:

> She sent me on my own to watch the newsreel of horrors . . . I was so used to her treatment of me by that time that this struck me as perfectly normal until years later, when other people expressed their horror. "Go and see what they have done," she said that afternoon . . . in a tone of fury which felt as though it was directed at me personally. When I got back neither of us spoke for the rest of the day, reduced to a silence destined to last for years. (*Journey,* 47)

The neutral "Go and see for yourself" of the first account has become a personal attack, "Go and see what they have done," that results not in an allegorical fall but in a bitter, enduring breach between mother and daughter. Deliberately withholding information about the family's connection to the events of the Holocaust, Figes's mother paradoxically seems to hold her responsible for her ignorance, and to punish her for it, by subjecting her to the ordeal of watching the footage of the camps without companionship, consolation, or explanation. In this way, Figes's Jewishness seems to her like the mark of Cain, a shameful stigma that is literally and metaphorically unspeakable.

Jewishness plays a more peripheral role in Diski's nonfiction, but it permeates her narratives in subtle ways that are, again, connected to her relationship with her mother. Alluding in general to the modishness of ethnic autobiographies, and perhaps in particular to the spate of works during the 1980s and 1990s by Jewish women excavating their family histories,[22] Diski observes in *Skating to Antarctica* that "[t]he search for roots is a legitimate excuse for travel these days, but I'm a middle-aged Jewish Londoner, and there was not much chance of finding the source of these aspects of myself in the South Polar regions" (127). With characteristic self-irony, Diski distances herself from the idea that her voyage to Antarctica is in any sense one of self-discovery by drawing attention to the incongruity between her identity and her destination. Yet the title of the previous section of the book— "Whatever Happened to Jennifer?"—explicitly articulates a desire to (re)discover a lost self. Moreover, the terms in which Diski describes herself—"a middle-aged *Jewish* Londoner" (as opposed to "a middle-aged English woman," for example)—suggest that she is more concerned with the question of roots than might at first appear to be the case.

In this context, there is a remarkable episode in *Skating* when Diski befriends an elderly couple: "Emily and Manny Roth were not just the connected older couple I liked to imagine, but lively and verbal, and Jewish too" (73). It's not clear here whether "too" means "to boot" (i.e., in addition to being lively and verbal) or whether Diski is making a connection between their Jewishness and her own (i.e., *they* were Jewish as well), but at any rate it seems to be a factor in drawing Diski to them.[23] After engaging them in discussion, however, her enthusiasm swiftly evaporates, as she realizes that their political views are the polar opposite of her own. She reflects then that "[a]s far as they [the Roths] were concerned, I was a lost Jew, and that must have seemed as ugly to them as they appeared to me," but at the same time recognizes that "despite my dismay at their views, I none the less wanted their approval" (77). Diski acknowledges that she has a tendency to project upon older couples whom she meets a "fantasy" of the "good" parents she never had, but this fantasy seems to operate with particular intensity around the figure of the Jewish mother. So it is that Diski finds herself puzzling over the fact that "I still found Emily attractive, in spite of loathing her opinions" (76).

Later in the narrative, Diski finds herself similarly surprised by the affection she feels for Mrs. Rosen, an old next-door neighbor and friend of her mother's, whom she finds is still living in the block of flats where the young Diski grew up. When Diski first contacts Mrs. Rosen by telephone, Diski comments, "I liked the sound of her voice. London Jewish" (96), and after an initial interview with her and a number of other Jewish women[24] who remembered her parents, she agrees "not to use their real names in my book. . . . They are regular people, regular Jewish people at that, for whom scandal meant a good deal" (192). In both of these quotations, the word "Jewish" seems to be invested with a positive meaning: it imbues Mrs. Rosen's voice with charm, and it functions as a (moral) intensifier to the word "regular," implying that Jews are more easily scandalized than others because of the value they place on social order and harmony. In her final meeting with her, Mrs. Rosen recalls that even at the age of four Diski had been a feisty, intellectually precocious girl ("You could talk! You could argue!" [214]); Diski is grateful for this "unexpected moment of good mothering," which, she says, provided "a real, atavistic, mother-and-child moment of satisfaction for me" (216).

One of the most memorable moments of *Stranger on a Train* is also precipitated by Diski's encounter with a maternal figure—this time a "bad" rather than a "good" mother—on a ship. Diski decides to travel by sea rather than air for part of her American odyssey as an "[e]xercise in sensory deprivation" that recalls her trip to Antarctica in search of "a white oblivion."[25] In spite of her hope of enjoying "all that silence and lack of interference," however, she soon finds herself being drawn into the orbit of a German couple, Stan and Dora, who "talked without stopping, without thinking, it came to seem" (26, 27). At first merely irritated by their insensitivity ("They buzzed like flies across all the careful boundaries" [27]), Diski becomes profoundly disturbed when Dora asks her how old she is, announces "in a blue-eyed monotone" that she "could be your mother," and then "plant[s] a brisk kiss on my . . . cheek" (29). Diski's response to Dora's suggestion that she might be her mother is visceral—"I had to fight the gasp that rose in my throat," and when Dora kisses her, she "froze through the maternal moment" (29). The next day Dora sees her ironing a shirt in the wash room and informs her that "you must open the buttons to iron correctly" (29), at which point Diski loses her cool:

> "NO." I actually bellowed at the harmless old woman as you might shout at a child to prevent yourself from lashing out. "Leave it alone. Don't touch it. Do. Not. Touch. It."

> My face must have matched my warning tone. Dora started and then backed away. She was alarmed and quite baffled by my excessive reaction to her helpfulness. I didn't care to discuss with her how much she couldn't have been my mother. (29–30)

Diski recognizes that the vehemence of her reaction to Dora's unsolicited advice is disproportionate ("I actually bellowed at the harmless old woman"), but offers no explanation for it. Those readers of *Stranger on a Train* who have also read *Skating to Antarctica* may, however, be able to identify the obscure objective correlative for Diski's rage. For in the earlier book Diski describes how, "with the arrival of a sense of sexual privacy" at the age of fourteen, she begins for the first time to deny her mother access to her body:

> She slipped a hand around my pelvis and down between my legs . . .

"Don't do that," I snapped.

"It's all right . . . There's nothing wrong with your mummy touching her little baby."

"Stop it," I shouted . . . and pulled away from her. (*Skating,* 116)

It seems to me that, in spite of Diski's insistence that Dora "couldn't have been my mother," it is her resemblance to her—the way in which Dora claims an inappropriate intimacy on the basis of spurious maternal feeling, echoing her mother's attempts to justify her abuse as a legitimate expression of motherly affection—that accounts for the unaccustomed violence Diski struggles to suppress. In another sense, however, Diski's emphatic rejection of any connection between Dora and her mother is not necessarily a case of protesting too much but rather a reflection of a fundamental difference between the two women that suggests an alternative—or additional—source of Diski's distaste for Dora. Earlier in the book, Dora declares, as part of a series of apparent non sequiturs: "Ah, you cannot change the past. My mother always said that Hitler would be bad for us" (28). Diski does not respond to these observations, or comment on them, but when Dora first claims that she "could be your mother," Diski admits that it was "chronologically possible" but "historically and geographically inaccurate" (29). Diski's synesthetic description of Dora's voice ("a blue-eyed monotone"), and her euphemistic reference to history and geography, together with the self-pardoning, self-pitying tone of Dora's remarks about Hitler, all suggest that if, at one level, Diski identifies Dora with her mother, on another she identifies her with the Nazi regime, or at least with those Germans whose passivity in the face of the Nazis contributed to the Holocaust.

Whereas Grant and Figes refer explicitly to the Holocaust and its legacy for Jews of their generation on many occasions, Diski never names it, but it is present implicitly nonetheless. Witness, for example, her account, in *Skating to Antarctica,* of her discovery that she "was a tough child, right from the start, with a strong sense of herself":

A survivor. . . . Since then, I may have split my selves into manageable parts, but back then, and all along, there may have been some continuing consciousness that knew exactly who and what it was, and remained solid in that knowledge. Sometimes I am ashamed of this survivor, . . . But the fact was, there was this survivor to put against the flaky genes and the training in hopelessness. I suppose . . . I had gone to Mrs Rosen to . . . check that there had once been and always was that survivor. (216)

Is it possible that a writer as self-aware as Diski is not alive to the historical resonance—particularly in the memoir of a self-styled "middle-aged Jewish" woman—of the word "survivor," which recurs four times in this passage? (Figes also uses the term to describe herself in *Little Eden,* asserting that "I knew myself to be a survivor" [138–39].) Or of the associations of experiencing shame at having survived? Certainly her "sense of herself," and of her mother's self, is inflected not just by her biological inheritance (the "flaky genes"), but by the legacy of Jewish history, and its transmission through what I have been calling Jewish memory.

Nicola King, in *Memory, Narrative, Identity: Remembering the Self,* points out that "[t]he late twentieth century has . . . seen an increased focus on questions of memory as the generations which experienced the atrocities of two world wars die out . . . a renewed desire to secure a sense of self in the wake of postmodern theories of the decentred human subject."[26] In this sense, the nonfiction of Figes, Grant, and Diski can be seen in part as products of, or at least responses to, a particular historical moment. Rather than attempt to reconstruct a unified Cartesian subject, however, these writers participate in its deconstruction, acknowledging that, as Figes puts it, "the journey of memory is not a regular trajectory from now to then" but a meandering path that "turn[s] back on itself, so yesterday and last year are wreathed in an indeterminate fog" (*Tales,* 43). In fact, all three authors meditate self-reflexively on the provisionality, mutability, and unreliability of memory.

I find myself drawn to . . . [n]ot only personal memories, but memory as myth, the idyll of the story book, the invention of childhood itself, girls with long hair, boys in sailor suits, rolling hoops in the park, looking for fairies in the bottom of the garden, finding elves in the attic. (*Tales,* 31)

Memory is continually created, a story told and retold, using jigsaw pieces of experience. It's utterly unreliable in some ways, because who can say whether the feeling or emotion that seems to belong to the recollection actually belongs to it rather than being available from the general store of likely emotions we have learned? (*Skating*, 154)

The self isn't a little person inside the brain, it's a work-in-progress. . . . Memory . . . is a fabrication, a re-interpretation, a new reconstruction of the original. Yet out of these unstable foundations we still construct an identity. It's a miracle. (*Remind Me*, 295)

For Diski, Figes, and Grant, memory is intrinsically, inescapably imaginative, something that is not retrieved or recovered but rather (re)created, (re) invented, and (re)constructed; and therefore identity itself is neither stable nor fixed but is constantly being revised. That all three writers should deploy metaphors drawn from art ("myth," "idyll," "story book," "invention," "a story told and retold," "work-in-progress," "fabrication," "original") to describe this process is hardly surprising, given their careers as novelists. Yet the fact that they do so in the context of works of nonfiction has generic and philosophical implications, which form part of the subject matter of these works.

In *Tales* Figes points out that "[i]n every story there is a story which is not told" (58), implying not only that she is producing a counter-narrative to the one that her mother has passed on (or failed to pass on) to her but also that her own account is contingent, partial, incomplete. In *Skating* Diski signals even before her main narrative begins that her version of events is just that—a subjective, and therefore unreliable, version of events—by using as an epigraph a quotation from Samuel Beckett's novel *Malone Dies*: "I wonder if I am not talking yet again about myself. Shall I be incapable, to the end, of lying on any other subject?" In *Remind Me*, Grant repeatedly draws attention to the unreliability of her narrative, and by implication to the fictional nature of all autobiographical narratives: "Can I confirm that everything I have told you is true? I can't. I only know what lives and sings in the oral tradition that is the history of every family. For all I know it could be a pack of falsehoods, fairy tales to send the children and grandchildren to sleep at nights. So we all lie, staring into the darkness, trying to conjure up the dead" (*Remind Me*, 52). She admits both to sharing the family predilection for self-invention ("like them I had edited and re-created my own history" [101]) and to omitting certain material "for fear of offending the living or the memories of the dead" (260), but she does not see any of this as compromising or undermining her project in any way. On the contrary, she believes that the strategies of fiction are entirely appropriate for a work of nonfiction, since "our lives are essentially stories" (293).

In her introduction to *The Mother Mirror,* Laurie Corbin warns of the dangers of reducing women simply to their function as mothers: in reading autobiographical accounts of mother-daughter relationships written by the daughters, she warns, it would be only too easy "to see the mother only in relation to the daughter" and thus "to continue a repression of the mother that has been part of the oppression of women." Instead of accepting the daughter's representations of their mothers uncritically, we should strive "to read through the daughter's language to try to catch sight of that other, the mother."[27] In the nonfiction of Diski, Figes, and Grant, their Jewish mothers emerge as oppressed and oppressing, damaged and damaging, both victims and perpetrators of traumas that originate in Jewish history and their ambivalent attitudes toward it. They also function as muses for their daughters, not in the celebratory way that we find in many African-American memoirs,[28] for example, but in the sense that their failure to transmit family history, whether through wilful obstruction, the onset of dementia, or flight, inspires their daughters to reconstruct the lost narratives, to reclaim the Jewish memory that, in their Jewish mothers, has been occluded, displaced, or repressed. Yet the mothers never simply become caricatures or scapegoats. In their books about their mothers and themselves, Grant, Figes, and Diski spare neither their mothers nor themselves: rather than producing accounts that claim authority, authenticity, or objectivity, they have written self-questioning works that disrupt the conventional self/other, mother/daughter binaries in favor of a more interrogative, skeptical inquiry into the relationship among identity, memory, motherhood, and ethnicity.

Notes

1. Linda Grant, *Remind Me Who I Am, Again* (London: Granta Books, 1998), 28. Further references to this edition will be cited in the text.

2. Eva Figes, *Journey to Nowhere: One Woman Looks for the Promised Land* (London: Granta, 2009), 10. Further references to this edition will be cited in the text.

3. Jenny Diski, *Skating to Antarctica* (London: Granta Books, 1997), 229. Further references to this edition will be cited in the text.

4. None of them has received much critical attention. In an essay on the fiction of Eva Figes, published in 2001, Anna Maria Stuby noted that "[d]espite the fact that she has won some prestigious literary awards . . . Eva Figes is not a widely known writer," an observation that still applies. See "Eva Figes's Novels," in *Engendering Realism and Postmodernism: Contemporary Women Writers in Britain,* ed. Beate Neumeier (Amsterdam: Rodopi, 2001), 105–16 (105). In the entry on Diski in *Contemporary British Novelists* (London: Routledge, 2005), Nick Rennison observes that her "fiction has never attracted the kind of attention . . . that its wit and inventiveness deserve" (54), and

this remains the case, although there is an excellent essay on *Skating to Antarctica* and *Stranger on a Train* in Heidi MacPherson, *Transatlantic Women's Literature* (Edinburgh: Edinburgh University Press, 2008). The only published essay on Grant's fiction to date is my own "Bellow at Your Elbow, Roth Breathing Down Your Neck: Gender and Ethnicity in Linda Grant and Bernice Rubens," in *"In the Open": Jewish Women Writers and British Culture,* ed. Claire Tylee (Newark: University of Delaware Press, 2006), 96–109, in which I discuss her third novel, *Still Here* (2000), as an intertext of contemporary male Jewish American fictions.

5. Eva Figes, *Little Eden: A Child at War* (New York: Persea Books, 1978), 12.

6. Figes, *Little Eden*, 54, 19, 73; Figes, *Tales of Innocence and Experience: An Exploration* (2003; repr. London: Bloomsbury, 2004), 128. Further page references to *Little Eden* and *Tales of Innocence and Experience* will be cited in the text.

7. For influential examples of this tendency, see Nancy Friday's *My Mother, My Self: The Daughter's Search for Identity* (1977); Nancy Chodorow's *The Reproduction of Mothering: Psychoanalysis and the Sociology of Gender* (1978); Jean Baker Miller's *Towards a New Psychology of Women* (1978); and Carol Gilligan's *Meeting at the Crossroads: Women's Psychology and Girls' Development* (1992). In part this should be seen as a project of rehabilitation—a response to the demonization of the mother in popular autobiographies such as Christina (daughter of Joan) Crawford's *Mommie Dearest* (1978). Adalgisa Giorgio, in her introduction to *Writing Mothers and Daughters: Renegotiating the Mother in Western European Narratives by Women* (New York: Berghahn Books, 2002), describes this backlash as "the shift from 'matrophobia'—hatred of the mother and fear of becoming her/like her . . . to 'mother-quest'—the daughter's search for her Self through a recuperation of her maternal heritage" (5).

8. MacPherson, *Transatlantic Women's Literature*, 109.

9. The fifth section of Diski's memoir, for example, is entitled "The Best Pram in Town," alluding to the fact that, according to one of her mother's neighbors, Mrs. Rosen, whom Diski interviews as part of her research for the book, "*Your* pram was the most expensive one. You had the best" (*Skating to Antarctica*, 186). In *Like Mother*, there is an elaborate description of the ornately decorated pram, with its "glassy black-lacquered coachwork with its sleek swirls of silver chrome decoration . . . [and] silver chassis," in which Ivy displays Frances (Jenny Diski, *Like Mother* [1988; repr. London: Vintage, 1990], 41). This theme recurs in *Stranger on a Train*, when Diski describes meeting an old childhood friend, identified only as "S," who "had read the account of my childhood in *Skating to Antarctica* with amazement at the tale it told," believing at the time that Diski "had everything" because of the lavish attention bestowed by her mother on Diski's appearance (Jenny Diski, *Stranger on a Train: Daydreaming and Smoking Around America with Interruptions* [London: Virago, 2002], 78). Further references to this edition of *Stranger on a Train* will appear in the text.

10. Diski, *Stranger on a Train*, 3.

11. Like all the titles of the different sections of the book, it appears only as a running head on the right-hand page throughout the section, but not as a heading at the start of the section.

12. Diski is alluding here to the conventional wisdom about mother-daughter relationships popularized by books such as Nancy Friday's *My Mother My Self: The Daughter's Search for Identity* (New York: Delacorte Press, 1977). She may even be parodying the opening

words of Friday's introduction to her book: "Understanding what we have with our mothers is the beginning of understanding ourselves. . . . We know this" (15).

13. Again, there is an echo here of Diski's novel *Like Mother,* in which, when Frances learns of her mother's sudden death, she "couldn't think of a single reason" to grieve (57).

14. A good example of this is Teresa Brennan's theory that the bond between mothers and daughters is characterized by a "fleshly memory" of "inter-uterine communication," quoted in Nicola King, *Memory, Narrative, Identity: Remembering the Self* (Edinburgh: Edinburgh University Press, 2000), 28. Diski's use of the clinical term "gestation site" is part of her attempt to demystify the mother-daughter relationship; where Brennan sees a primal bonding ritual, Diski sees a biological process.

15. Paola Splendore, "Bad Daughters and Unmotherly Mothers: The New Family Plot in the Contemporary English Novel," in *Writing Mothers and Daughters: Renegotiating the Mother in Western European Narratives by Women,* ed. Adalgisa Giorgio (New York: Berghahn Books, 2002), 185–214 (195, 196).

16. Ibid., 199.

17. Giorgio, *Writing Mothers and Daughters,* 7.

18. Janet Handler Burstein, *Writing Mothers, Writing Daughters: Tracing the Maternal in Stories by American-Jewish Women* (Urbana: University of Illinois Press, 1996), 11, 13.

19. In her article "Remembering Their Lives: Leila Berg, Linda Grant, Anne Karpf, and Louise Kehoe," in *Jewish Women's Writing of the 1990s and Beyond in Great Britain and the United States,* ed. Ulrike Behlau and Bernhard Reitz (Mainz: Wissenschaftlicher Verlag Trier), 107–22, Ulrike Behlau reads this episode literally, apparently not realizing that Grant is actually projecting her fears into a fictional future scenario. Behlau writes that "Grant increasingly identifies with her mother and her illness, which may be an effect of her unearthing more and more details of her mother's past, and of trying to take her point of view. This identification reaches, however, a disturbing degree when Grant claims towards the end of the book that she, too, has been 'diagnosed with a memory loss'" (115). In fact, Grant is imagining herself, sometime in the future, suffering the same fate as her mother.

20. Grant makes extensive use of family photographs in her narrative, inserting them without any formal identification, commenting explicitly on some, but not on others. The front of the Granta paperback edition of *Skating* reproduces what Diski claims in the book to be her only photograph of her mother: "She is smiling directly into the camera, a posterity smile, a mother who is content to be with her daughter. . . . Her shadow and mine blur together into a unified shape, as umbilical as . . . Shackleton's roped-together men trying to pull the *Endurance* through the ice floe" (156).

In an essay on the use of photographs in the original edition of Mary Antin's *The Promised Land,* Betty Bergland points out that there is a long tradition of deploying photographs alongside text in autobiographical writing by women from ethnic minorities and argues that we should "consider the photograph within ethnic autobiography as an integral part of the meaning of the narrative and the subjectivities posited." See Betty Bergland, "Photographs and Narratives in Ethnic Autobiography: Memory and Subjectivity in Mary Antin's *The Promised Land,*" in *Memory, Narrative, and Identity: New Essays in American Ethnic Literatures,* ed. Amritjit Singh, Joseph T. Skerrett, Jr., and Robert E. Hogan (Boston: Northeastern University Press, 1994), 44–88 (53).

21. Grant is quoting here from John Bridgewater, the head of residential care for the elderly in Jewish Care (a charity that provides support for vulnerable people in the Jewish community in the UK) at the time when Grant was trying to find a home for her mother. Grant herself reinforces the idea that memory has a particularly central role in Jewish culture, though she is ambivalent about the virtues of this Jewish preoccupation with memory: "I don't know if it is a tragedy or a blessing when Jews, who insist on forgiving and forgetting nothing, should end their lives remembering nothing" (15). The comments of two North American Jewish literary critics, writing about North American Jewish novelists, are pertinent here. Norman Ravvin identifies "a familiar post-war pathos that distinguishes much Jewish writing since the Holocaust: the promise of recovery among ruins, an acceptance of changes wrought by passing generations alongside a steadfast need to reincorporate . . . a world that has vanished." See Norman Ravvin, *A House of Words: Jewish Writing, Identity and Memory* (Montreal: McGill-Queen's University Press, 1997), 5. Victoria Aarons argues that the protagonists of Jewish American fiction are "haunted by a past they never really knew, one that existed only in the memory of parents and grandparents before them." See Victoria Aarons, "Telling History: Inventing Identity in Jewish American Fiction," in *Memory and Cultural Politics: New Approaches to American Ethnic Literatures,* ed. Amritjit Singh and Joseph T. Skerrett, Jr. (Boston: Northeastern University Press, 1996), 60–86 (62).

22. For a discussion of some of these texts, see chapter 4 of David Brauner, *Post-War Jewish Fiction: Ambivalence, Self-Explanation and Transatlantic Connections* (Basingstoke: Palgrave, 2001), and Behlau, "Remembering Their Lives."

23. The fact that she actively courts the attention of the couple is particularly striking, given that, throughout *Skating to Antarctica*, Diski characterizes herself—at times caricatures herself—as a loner, accommodating the socializing impulses of those around her reluctantly, but happiest in solitude. As she puts it in *Stranger on a Train:* "I am never lonely on my own, but I often feel estranged when in company" (69–70).

24. Diski is informed by her guide, Nathan, that "[n]inety per cent of these flats were Jewish" (103), Mrs. Rosen explaining that "[t]he flats had a shelter under the basement. The Jews knew how to take care of themselves" (104).

25. Jenny Diski, *Stranger on a Train,* 26; *Skating to Antarctica,* 2.

26. King, *Memory, Narrative, Identity,* 11.

27. Laurie Corbin, *The Mother Mirror: Self-Representation and the Mother-Daughter Relation in Colette, Simone de Beauvoir, and Marguerite Duras* (New York: Peter Lang, 1996), 5.

28. See Audre Lorde's *Zami: A New Spelling of My Name* (1982); Alice Walker's *In Search of Our Mothers' Gardens* (1983); bell hooks's *Bone Black* (1996).

11

OPENING SPACES

Sue Hubbard's Poetry of Place

LUCY WRIGHT

David Harvey has contended that "it is important to challenge the idea of a single and objective sense of time and space, against which we can measure the diversity of human conceptions and perceptions."[1] While this statement relates to the condition of postmodern society in general, it is especially pertinent in relation to a postmodern *Jewish* identity. Jews have historically existed in a complicated spatial relation with notions of place, such as "belonging" and "longing," "exile," "diaspora," and "home." This uneasy positioning of Jewish identity between a status of location and one of dislocation has meant that Jewish identity, more than any other modern identity, exists as a spatial and temporal construct. As a result, dialectics of time and space have always been central to an understanding of Jewish history and culture, for not only do they underlie the narrative of the Hebrew Bible but they form the basis on which Jewish culture—religious and secular—is built.[2] At the same time, contemporary cultural theory is placing new emphasis on the ways in which we think about the connection between place and identity. Concepts such as nation—until recently the most prominent paradigm for thinking about the link between territory and identity—are being interrogated by new conceptual questions that concern the relationship between the local and the global, collective and individual, migratory groups and host cultures, and the complex relationship between the professed homeland and transnational or diasporic communities. In other words, "space" has come to the foreground as a category of cultural analysis in its own right.

In this essay, I look at the work of Sue Hubbard, a British Jewish poet who has published a number of anthologies of written work. She is also a public art poet who creates site-specific poems that collaborate with visual arts. Her work evokes memory, loss, myth, place, and identity and is interested in disrupting the conventional contexts in which poetry is usually found. For Hubbard, an ambiguous relationship with her Jewishness has provided the dynamic platform from which to explore notions of subjectivity. She says of her Jewish identity: "I know that in my daily life I don't feel particularly Jewish, but know that having been born in 1948, but for a few years and a strip of water, Hitler would have defined me as such. There is an identity in knowing that. [. . .] But for me personally my writing about Jewishness has been a metaphor for self-realisation and a quest for individual as opposed to cultural identity."[3] Here, I explore the ways in which Hubbard's work recurrently employs a poetics of place that seeks to reclaim material sites of spatial belonging, such as landscapes, cities, rooms, and cultural artefacts, in order to engage with a politics of belonging of a more metaphorical kind. In doing so I argue that she consistently blurs the boundaries between public and private, minority and mainstream, and British and Jewish.

The question of what constitutes a Jewish identity is a persistent issue of critical contention due to the fact that, as Jonathan and Daniel Boyarin rightly contend, "Jewishness disrupts the very categories of identity because it is not national, not genealogical, not religious, but all these in dialectical tension with one another."[4] Furthermore, Berel Lang has argued that "in the world of nationalist and democratic modernity in which the worldwide Jewish community finds itself, Jewish identity has become intrinsically 'hyphenetic.'"[5] The nature of a hyphenated Jewish identity was the subject of a heated debate in the *Jewish Quarterly* in 2007–8: does it mean, as Adam Thirlwell argues, that "Jewish is always half-Jewish," or that Jewish must always be wholly embodied through being firmly situated on one side of the divide, as Cynthia Ozick suggests in her claim that "the hallmark of Jewishness lies precisely in its distinction-making," and that "the purpose of seeing distinctions is to make choices"?[6] Yet what remains clear is that for a British Jewish identity, the multifaceted and variable nature of what it means to be Jewish has often existed in a disjointed relation to a British and, in particular, to an English identity that "is based on a fixed and homogenous sense of self that is rooted in the past."[7] Consequently, in light of the recent social-spatial understanding of the self, British Jewish identity, with its diverse cultural, social, and linguistic influences, most fully encompasses the recognition that "no political, social, or cultural space exists in isolation from others or can be considered in isolation from others."[8]

Helpful also in theorizing postmodern British Jewish identity is the emergent tension between feminism, with its promotion of a stable notion of subjectivity for the purpose of forging a public voice of female solidarity, and postmodernism, which disrupts such models by threatening to undermine the very identification of "women," or any other category such as British or Jewish, as a collective subject. This concern has ultimately led to what Judith Butler articulates as "a fear that, by no longer being able to take for granted the subject, [. . .] feminism will founder."[9] My own application of these terms is not an attempt to define them in stable relation to postmodern identity but is a necessary prerequisite for my engaged critique of them. I aim to expound the discursive possibilities and potentials for what these categories authorize and what they exclude or foreclose when understood as what Judith Butler terms "contingent foundations."[10]

It is against this theoretical positioning of a situational politics of location and a contingent politics of identity that I wish to contextualize my reading of Hubbard's writing. By examining her aesthetic choices and thematic contexts, I aim to demonstrate that she employs a "politics of poetic form,"[11] which is sensitive to and engages with the ways in which we situate ourselves in space and time, as well as the way constructs of place and time such as landscape, history, and memory can also map various "selves." I analyze Hubbard's textual poetry alongside her site-specific public art installations and comment on how the relationship between visual art and poetry—in their overlaps, intersections, and contradictions—can shed new meaning on the materiality of the text and the subjective space among place, language, and identity. I examine how her work articulates a sense of self that has to negotiate the potentially contradictory social, political, and cultural positioning of being both British and Jewish, woman and poet. In this way, hers is not simply a politics of location that makes connections between identity and place, but the exploration of how these situated selves can be multiple and changing. As Caren Kaplan argues, "[A]ny exclusive recourse to space, place, or position becomes utterly abstract and universalizing without historical specificity. [. . .] We need critical practices that mediate the most obvious oppositions, interrogating the terms that mythologize our differences and similarities."[12]

Accordingly, I aim to establish the processes by which Hubbard works with and against the various traditions inherent in each of the constitutive elements of her identity by considering a multifaceted postmodern British Jewish female identity as a site of intersection between multiple dichotomous temporal and spatial constructs, for example, minority-majority, marginal-mainstream, private-public, inside-outside, history-memory, past-present, and tradition-modernity. Hubbard's poetry deconstructs the markers of space and time, those borders and boundaries of belonging and social networks, to create a politics of identity that goes beyond simply location to one of "relation."[13]

In this essay I also seek to build on recent critical work in the field of contemporary poetics, with a particular concentration on the ways in which form, voice, and performance claim certain subjectivities and create relationships to the public sphere. As Peter Middleton asserts, "It is not the cultural identity of the author alone which is significant but also the politics of subjectivity encoded in the poetry."[14] Recent debates concerning the public and private voice of poetry, in response to postmodernism's skepticism of the subject and the language that mediates it, have resulted in voice becoming the site for a new sort of struggle in poetry. As a result, as Alison Mark and Deryn Rees-Jones highlight, "[a] division which many critics—and the poets—seek to interrogate is that between the expressive and the discursive constructions of the poetic subject, articulating the fictionality of the poetic 'I,' even at its most biographical, while closely examining contextual material which attests to the historical, social and political specificity of that 'I.'"[15]

This becomes particularly pertinent to the representation of a female British Jewish identity that incorporates three different voices of marginalization—woman, poet, and Jew. While these voices of gender, ethnicity, and selfhood can never be fully separated, as Helen Cixous suggests through her coining of the compound concept "juifemme,"[16] and offer many points of intersection for study, as Marla Brettschneider has shown,[17] they also speak from diverse and multiple relations of belonging. For example, as a Jew living in Britain, a subject's communal identity may relate to the specific location in which she grew up, but as a poet she may relate to a wider tradition of diasporic writing. Even within the shared experience of being Jewish, women can identify differently. For example, Bluma Goldstein has pointed out that the positions of diaspora and exile often attributed to Jewish identity "[presuppose] an identity very different from the other: the former would construe distinctiveness through connection and coexistence; the latter would stress the necessity of uniqueness, separatism, and sovereignty."[18]

Form plays an integral part in shaping the historical, social, and political specificity of voice in poetry. The "lyric" has historically been home to the expressive and confessional "I"—"the supposed haven of the 'private' self"[19]—yet this relationship has been complicated by poetry's more recent engagement with other genres, media, and disciplines such as narrative, public art, and performance. As Charles Bernstein has suggested:

> [T]he performative dimension of poetry has significant relation to the text-based visual and conceptual art, as well as visual poetry, which extend the performative (and material) dimension of the literary text into visual space. [. . .] Such elements as the visual appearance of the text or the sound of the work in performance may be extralexical but they are not extrasemantic. When textual elements that are conventionally framed out as nonsemantic are acknowledged as significant, the result is a proliferation of possible frames of interpretation.[20]

Here, I explore the ways in which the performative aspects of contemporary British Jewish poetics invite a transgressive disruption of the conventional boundaries of poetry and in turn complicate the relationship between subjectivity and voice by claiming new types of public. I will be drawing on Michael Warner's theory of "publics" and "counterpublics" to argue that contemporary poetry's collaboration with other disciplines broadens its parameters of reception, thus blurring poetry's traditional designation as a private and, in popular culture, often a marginal expressive form.[21] Consequently, the normative relationship among reader, text, and author is disrupted, creating space for new communities and subjectivities.

"Opening Spaces" is taken from Sue Hubbard's essay "Opening Spaces: Poetry as Public Art," written in 2000 to consolidate her involvement with the Arts Council England's "Poetry Places" scheme, which sought to bring poetry to new audiences by installing it in public space. It is an expression that suitably articulates the transforming potential of poetry to reclaim and reconceptualize the location within which it is situated, and points to the broadening of poetry's own parameters from an essentially private act to a wider public force. It is also a phrase that encapsulates the thematic and aesthetic engagement with space that Hubbard's own poetic practice undertakes. As a public art poet, novelist, and visual arts critic, Hubbard has maintained a continuous engagement with the visual and spatial dimensions of writing, both on and off the page, exploring the relationships between image and text, surface and depth, and the material and the metaphorical that occur via the intersecting of these discourses. Her public art creates site-specific pieces, which "grow out of and engage with the space in which [they are] situated" in order to reframe the relationship between space and both individual and communal identity.[22] Hubbard's published poetry also recurrently figures constructs of space, whether in the form of landscapes, cities, countries, rooms, cultural objects, or historical artefacts, which provide openings for her extended explorations of the cognitive mapping of social space attached to them, such as exile, diaspora, nation, home, region, location, dislocation, and displacement. In doing so, Hubbard's work speaks to and interrogates the political positions and boundaries that are performed by these frameworks of belonging, such as public and private, personal and social, inside and outside, and history and memory, and in turn the subjectivities they produce.

While Hubbard does not class herself as a Jewish writer, and her work is readily positioned under universal themes such as love, loss, or memory, there is also an implicit "Jewishness" present in her creative preoccupation with concepts of place and the narratives of displaced spatial belonging they so often evoke. As Maeera Shreiber has pointed out, "Exile and displacement have long been figured as the requisite or ineluctable conditions of Jewish aesthetic production."[23] Growing up in the Home Counties without any real religious background, Hubbard saw her relationship with her Jewish identity as a precarious one that was for her always something ineffable and marginal against what Cheyette has identified as the "overbearing Englishness" and homogeneity of British culture.[24] As Hubbard explains, "Jewishness became a metaphor for much that I could not explain in my life. It was like my private secret."[25] Therefore, the exilic subjectivity and uneasy relationship with place expressed in Hubbard's poetry can be read in direct correlation with the "innate sense of being an outsider" underlying her Jewishness.[26]

The few poems in which Hubbard explicitly addresses her personal Jewish identity speak from this ambivalent position of belonging. "Assimilation," for example, articulates a childhood identity caught in the schisms between a secular and religious, historical and modern, and British and Jewish consciousness, embodied in the choice of "whether to say Amen."[27] The vivid corporeality through which Hubbard describes the struggle to perform this enunciation, and the resulting spiritual belonging it would represent, "dumb-lipped trapped by / the trinity of longing, fear, propriety, / the word still-born in my throat" (13), signifies an identity that is perpetually deferred from "being" as a consequence of a Jewish past constituted through a series of cultural absences: "I did not know where I'd come from," "I've never tasted the sweet wine of Kiddush," and the absence symbolized through the disclosure that "in my father's study / a tarnished silver samovar lay in waiting for tall glasses, lemon and a scoop of Russian tea" (13). Similarly, in her poem "Inheritance" Hubbard sets up an opposition between the rural customs of a middle-class, English upbringing with the forgotten ancestry of a working-class, immigrant London: "unlocking clouded memories, three generations' climb from East End tenement to this wooded Surrey Hill."[28]

Each of these poems evokes a fairly typical Jewish narrative of diasporic longing and displacement, supported by a traditional framework of an ethnically and religiously specific exile. However, on the whole Hubbard's writing has resisted such obvious representations of a Jewish identity at odds with English culture, and has instead chosen to explore a more fluid and plural subjectivity through various topographical "belongings." "Topography," as Amir Eshel has noted, "in its primary use, combines the Greek topos, 'place,' and graphein, 'to write.'"[29] Through employing a variety of spatial metaphors, evoking allegories of place, and positioning poetry as "site-specific interventions,"[30] Hubbard's work inscribes identity onto place and vice versa in order to offer new frameworks for figuring and understanding the existential self as a product and process of the spatial relations it inhabits. As a result Hubbard has been able to interrogate the presumed fixity of a Jewish poetics of exile,[31] as well as writing against the totalizing notion of Jewish identity as "an ethnic allegory for postmodern indeterminacy" that dehistoricizes the Other "out of space and time."[32] Instead, Hubbard's poetry of place demonstrates how identity in the postmodern world is never stable or connected to one exclusive ethnic, religious, or transcendent position but is rather perpetually constituted via a multiplicity of common historical experiences and shared cultural codes, which come about through being in a continuous and changing relationship with space.

Spatial Temporalities

The spatial construction of the past is an idea that has been rhetorically figured by many writers who have invoked history and memory in metaphorical terms. As Jonathan Boyarin contends, "the metaphorical structures of our language display a tendency to borrow terms connoting spatial relations in our references to change over time. [. . .] [W]e discuss temporal sequence in terms of spatial distancing and vice versa: we speak of distant times, and [. . .] we think of long-ago places, if not in so many words."[33] In *Ghost Station* (2004),

Hubbard probes the spatial and temporal dialectics of postmodern identity by conceiving of authentic cultural locations, household objects, and historical artefacts as sites of alternative, unwritten or forgotten narratives of the past. Hubbard's poem "Stereoptica," for example, explores the continuation of the past in the present through the spatializing and materializing of both history and memory in the photographic image. The stereoptica, a Victorian device into which photographs were placed so that they appeared three-dimensional, provides the frame for the poem through which the speaker considers the lives of the subjects that have become "frozen as history."[34] Because of its ability to synthesize time (the memory of the past) and space (through the material image being viewed in the present), the photograph provides an apt metaphor for considering the "time-space compression" of postmodern culture.[35]

The interconnectedness between space and time is perpetuated by "this lensed *masque*" (10; emphasis in original), which enables the speaker to "like Lazarus, make them rise / from their matt solitude" (10), but also through the dialogue between text and image in the speaker's narrative reconstruction of this process. For example, the specific and identifiable places through which the speaker locates these photographic fragments of the past, such as "Tower Bridge" and "Trafalgar Square" (10), imbue them with a sense of historical longevity sustained both through the image itself and by the continued existence of the architectural sites they depict. Such interaction with the photographs conflates surface and depth, past and present, space and time, and constructs a subject out of this inert object. Thus Hubbard's textual engagement with these photographs creates a pertinent dialogue between history and identity. The poem therefore writes against the "depthlessness" of postmodernity, identified by Frederic Jameson as that "which finds its prolongation [. . .] in a whole new culture of the image or the simulacrum" that results in a "weakening of historicity, both in relationship to public History [sic] and in the new forms of our private temporality,"[36] and instead asserts new narratives, meanings, and subjectivities in relation to the past.

Whereas "Stereoptica" portrays history as a subject whose "moment's true currency" is "now" rather than "then" (10), "Rooms" reflects on a present structured by past time in the form of an *absence* of history and memory and the displaced sense of self it creates. A detached third-person narration guides the reader in a continuous, slow movement through the recognizable domestic space of a house, positioning him or her as a distanced voyeur whose gaze is always being directed "out beyond" the forgotten objects of the room

(12). The spatial presence of the past evoked in this poem suggests, as Gaston Bachelard has argued, that our knowledge of ourselves in time "is a sequence of fixations in the spaces of the being's stability—a being who does not want to melt away, and who, even in the past, when he sets out in search of things past, wants time to 'suspend' its flight."[37] In the poem, memory is suspended through the material objects that in this case can act only as markers of loss. Through situating "an impossible longing" in the symbolized space of the home, Hubbard demonstrates that "'Home' itself is a shifting construction, contingent upon temporal, spatial, and affective investments in place and relations."[38] Consequently, "Rooms" evokes a haunting "spectrality,"[39] which disturbs the binaries of past-present, and absence-presence, subverting the domestic landscape of the home to represent a site altogether "unheimlich."[40]

While the Holocaust may well provide the subtext for the trope of over-whelming absence in this poem, as "only / something felt, something / inau-dible" (12), the resulting sense of dislocation is a direct effect of the poem's omission of any indication of the history underlying these abandoned objects. The absence of any such narrative leaves them stranded in space and time and the reader with the difficulty of reconstructing a notion of the past. The poem creates a situation by which the only possible identification the reader can make with these objects is through a narrative of loss that leaves them with the same "impossible longing" that is addressed in the poem. Both "Stereop-tica" and "Rooms," therefore, illustrate Stuart Hall's idea that "[f]ar from being grounded in a mere 'recovery' of the past, which is to be found, and which, when found, will secure our sense of ourselves into eternity, identities are the names we give to the different ways in which we are positioned by, and posi-tion ourselves within, the narratives of the past."[41]

Exiles, Modernity, and Artistic Landscapes

Alongside its examination of the spatial dynamics of identity constructs such as history and memory, *Ghost Station* also deals with more corporeal notions of spatial belonging through its representation of rural landscapes as a way to chart the relationship between these places and the marginal voices, experiences, his-tories, and identities associated with them. In keeping with her affinity for the visual arts, Hubbard chooses to focus on artistic representations of literal and symbolic terrains to explore the notion that "the construction of a landscape and the construction of identity are inseparable parts of one process."[42]

For example, in "The Sower" Hubbard performs a poetic reconstruction of Jean François Millet's nostalgic depiction of rural poverty in his painting by the same title. The poem gives a detailed account of the 1850s painting in keeping with its realist style, depicting the sower's "puddled armpits / rancid in the freezing wind" (20). In her poetic dialogue with the painting, Hubbard also makes connections between the destitute terrain and the stark agricultural hardship of the man who lives on and survives off it. For example, her representation of the sower is engendered through the characteristics of the land, such as "Big beetroot hands" (20), thus playing on the idea of an identity literally "rooted" in the landscape. Through keeping the anonymity of Millet's "Sower" in her use of the third-person pronoun "he," Hubbard's representation becomes a synecdoche for the cultural history and identity of a whole people. Furthermore, this representation of a man, whose "[m]emory of famine runs / atavistic through his veins" (20), evokes in particular the historic displacement of the Irish and the oppression they suffered as a consequence of the deprivation of their geographical positioning. Hubbard has spoken of how she "feel[s] a connection with the displacement of the Irish," seeing "in their exodus and statelessness parallels with Jewish experience."[43] Thus while Hubbard gives voice to a very real and lived displacement and cultural alienation, she simultaneously evokes a sense of *belonging* to a certain history and people by setting up a trajectory of loss and longing in relation to place, which speaks to other exilic and outsider communities, including Jewish and postcolonial identities.

In keeping with Hubbard's intertextual referencing with the visual arts, "Crows over the Wheatfields" takes as its inspiration the well-known painting by Vincent van Gogh, this time exploring the representation of a landscape as a symbol for the alienation and personal anomie of the artist who depicts it. Reconstructing an imagined situation through which the finished work emerged, Hubbard creates a textual representation of Van Gogh's "Wheatfields" perceived through the psychological state of inner turmoil and extreme isolation of the painter himself. In the poem Hubbard correlates the "leaden skies" that portray the deep, dark hues of the painting with the somber and depressive state of the speaker, who has literally and figuratively "done with the sun" (22). An atmosphere of foreboding is created through the image— "Across the wheat field crows / wheel in a ragged requiem towards me" (22)— heightened in its reference to the imminent death of the painter shortly after he produced this piece.[44] Once again Hubbard draws the analogy between psychological and physical exile by highlighting the ties between Van Gogh's ostracized mental condition and the landscape he perceives, as is symbolically rendered in the three diverging paths featured in the painting, which the speaker describes as "leading somewhere / going nowhere" (22).

Hubbard's choice to create narratives of exile via a dialogue between poetry and these two paradigmatic works of "the great modernist thematic of alienation, anomie, solitude, social fragmentation, and isolation"[45] can be seen as a deliberate attempt on Hubbard's part to reinstate a sense of self in the postmodern world. As she has argued, "Both painting and poetry are essentially private, expressionist maps, diagrams of 'becoming.' In these dog days of the late twentieth century, there seems an unnamed hunger—for art in the broadest sense—to give expression to this longing, to name what cannot be named, to fill the void of postmodernity."[46] Yet Hubbard's is not the quest for a unified, coherent subject in the face of this absence but rather, as is shown in her mixing of various art forms, a search for a plurality of modes and expressions of identity in relation to place. In particular, Hubbard's own response to these artistic representations of landscapes probes the relationship among identity, place, and belonging by contrasting the notion of place, as it is invoked as a creative and imaginative territory, and the reality of "what has been for so many: brute, choiceless fact."[47]

Urban Alienation: The City and Metaphorical Belonging(s)

If the rural landscape symbolized for artists a space of belonging against the impersonality of modernism, the city offers a decidedly postmodern location for identity. Jameson has highlighted the particular relationship between the alienated postmodern subject and the city as "above all a space in which people are unable to map (in their minds) either their own positions or the urban totality in which they find themselves."[48] Hubbard's poem "Across the City" pursues this idea by figuring London as a site of a specifically female loss and longing brought on through women's personal, social, and political exclusion from a male-dominated sphere. Situated on the inside looking out "[b]eyond the wicker blinds," the speaker is located in a position of obscurity that alienates her from the outside world so that she "do[es] not recognise this place where dreams have shrunk / to pinheads and longing has become / as dry, etiolated, as the bathroom / geranium we all forget to water."[49] The speaker depicts a daily life of solitude, "Again I wake alone" (41), left in the absence of a male-defined relationship, as she describes how "Loss forms the bass-note [. . .] and somewhere, out there, / you go on living" (41). However, while the city sets the location for this isolated existence, it also provides a site for the speaker to map a cognitive cartography of feminine belonging conveyed by her admission that "all across the city / I hear the urgent wail of women" (41). The description evokes a scene similar to the wailing of women after the loss of men at war, thus creating a sense of connectedness through time and space between this historical longing and the modern condition of women whose men are absent through choice: "My friend telephones to say / her man is too busy to see her" (41). The speaker seeks to fill the subsequent void for women like her who have previously been interpellated only via their traditional hegemonic roles such as wives and mothers. Hubbard therefore addresses the need for a resistive interrogation of these definitions of belonging, ending the poem with a hopeful but unresolved question of, "What other possibilities unfurl, as we wait in the quiet of vacant / rooms for our futures to define us?" (42).

Whatever the final answer, Jameson has suggested that, "[d]isalienation in the traditional city, [. . .] involves the practical reconquest of a sense of place and the construction of an articulated ensemble which can be retained in memory and which the individual subject can map and remap along the moments of mobile alternative trajectories."[50] By constructing a relationship between the empirical position of the alienated female subject and an abstract conception of feminine solidarity *through* this shared sense of estrangement, Hubbard creates a potential, although not yet fully realized, space where women can "find a common web / of words" (41) and thus "interrogate the conditions and effects of inclusion within various sites of belonging."[51]

Poetry and Public Art

While Hubbard's text-based poetry retains a multidimensional engagement with space and time through its discursive relationship with visual media, none of her work explores the dynamic potential for poetry to proffer new social-spatial understandings of individual and communal identity to the extent of her public art poetry. Hubbard has created a number of site-specific installations that have specifically functioned as ways for people to interact with their surrounding environment in new and innovative ways. These works seek to reveal the complexities underlying our understanding of spatial boundaries such as public and private, mainstream and marginal, inside and outside, and even British and Jewish. Through placing the previously private subjectivity of the poem into a public arena, Hubbard shows, as Middleton has argued, that "different poetries represent different relations between subjectivity and the public sphere," creating new positions of belonging for reader, text, and author.[52]

Hidden Histories in the Jewellery Quarter of Birmingham

"All that Glisters" (2000) was one such project, in which Hubbard created a series of poems situated in, and relating to, Birmingham's Jewellery Quarter.[53]

In order to actively engage with the social and historical specificities of this geographical location in a formal and thematic way, Hubbard wrote and placed these poems as "site-specific interventions" that "grew out from the mores of this particular culture."[54] For example, "The Assayist" was a poem that adopted the material presence of the cultural production of jewelry-making specific to the area, through being printed on gold-leaf paper and placed in ring boxes, which were hidden in various locations across the city. By assuming the characteristics of a precious jewel to be "discovered" within the city itself, Hubbard played on the idea of poetry as an equally valuable aesthetic production. In this way she connects two disparate forms of artistic craft and the traditions through which they have been established.

Another of Hubbard's pieces, "Metallic Pen-makers to the Queen," enacted this same archaeological process to different effect by appropriating the exact language and typography of an archaic advertisement for the pen factory in Victoria Street to create, quite literally, a "found poem." In the act of producing a personalized poetic expression out of the public language of an advertisement, Hubbard subverts and extends the conventional boundaries of these two styles of writing, again traversing the literary, cultural, and class boundaries belonging to these two artistic crafts.

The connection among language, place, and identity is also evoked in Hubbard's poem "The Jeweller's Mistress," which was inscribed onto the glass window of a currently trading jewelry shop. Simulating the commercial lettering common to such establishments, the poem reveals itself as such only on closer inspection. Its obscure identity again plays on the idea of a hidden history waiting to be discovered in Birmingham's locality. Not only does the text's form employ the traditions associated with the jewelry trade, but the poem itself is inspired by the specialized jargon of jewelry-making. Paying precise detail to this terminology, Hubbard uses it to embellish the voice of the jeweler's mistress in order to convey her emotional and psychological state: "she dreams of piercing / his electroplated heart." By articulating an aspect of social history through the technical idiom of jewelry-making, Hubbard augments Birmingham's past with a sense of local identity and regional specificity, thus disrupting the conventional relationship between place and language that assumes a national scale.

"The Gold Cutter's Daughter" once again gives a female voice to the history of the area, this time to pay tribute to the influx of the large Jewish population that settled in Birmingham from the eighteenth century and consequently formed a significant part of the city's minority cultural identity.

Spoken from the perspective of the daughter, the poem narrates her experience as a marginalized immigrant who identifies as "a stranger." Again linking in with the industrialism of the area, Hubbard overwrites this tradition with the language of Jewish history and culture, as the daughter pays tribute to her father: "That which you weave, / like Judea's first goldsmith, / Bezalel, into vineleaves of gold." The analogy with Bezalel, the chief architect of the tabernacle in the Hebrew Bible, performs its own act of interweaving, linking these two strands of history and tradition and thus evoking a sense of sacred space in relation to the secular practice of gold-cutting. Gold itself becomes a symbol for Jewish identity, whose "otherness" is marked in "a little Gold Star / so they may know me for what I am." In this way the manufacturing of jewelry becomes an act imbued with political, cultural, and spiritual significance.

In terms of the poem's physical relationship with the city, Hubbard describes how her collaboration with the artist Pat Kaufman "resulted in an evocative installation whereby she placed the text of one of my poems in a sealed room of an empty Victorian shop. With her subtle ethereal lighting, and re-arrangement of the old artefacts, the piece could be seen through the window and experienced from the street by the passer-by almost as a stage set."[55] The poem's covert positioning plays on the demarcations of secrecy, defined by D. A. Miller as "the subjective practice in which the oppositions of private/public, inside/outside, subject/object are established, and the sanctity of their first term kept inviolate."[56] The physical distancing of the poem from the main street also emphasizes the historicity of the poem's subject, enacting a museum-like preservation that relegates the poem to the realms of past space, superficially removed from contact with the present. Since the reader is unable to interact directly with the poem, his/her position is transformed into one of spectator. The poem's visibility was also reduced through being lit from behind only periodically, and therefore being accessible to the public only during these times. Through the text's physical placement, Hubbard subtly explores the relationship between mainstream British culture and hidden histories of its minority identities which often remain erased from view. By giving voice and space to this private and largely forgotten aspect of Birmingham's Jewish identity, Hubbard gives a moment existing outside the mainstream narratives of its history a real and tangible place in her poetry.

The Birmingham Jewellery Quarter series thus attributes a unique tradition and rich multicultural heritage to this historic region. Yet Hubbard also exposes how its working-class and ethnic minority heritage has been largely obscured. She therefore highlights the extent to which the understanding of identity and culture depends on a continual negotiation between public and private, individual and communal forms of history and memory and the material spaces they are given to exist in the present. By giving voice to unwritten histories and unacknowledged spaces of the city, and allowing them to become (albeit temporary) features of the landscape in which they are set, these poems become part of the local community's received history of the place. Finally, by taking an aspect of Jewish social history and placing it in a contemporary public space, Hubbard deconstructs Lyotard's notion of the Jew as the postmodern emblem for "non lieu" and re-inscribes Jewish identity in a space and time.[57]

Mapping Myth and Migrants in "Eurydice," London, Waterloo

Hubbard's public art poem "Eurydice" (1990) is a piece that epitomizes the process of positioning ourselves by and within the various familial, cultural, and historical narratives that we encounter. Situated as a now permanent feature of the underpass from Victoria Arch at Waterloo Station to the IMAX cinema, this poem was originally commissioned to perform the social function of encouraging the use of this walkway. Taking as her reference point the ancient Greek myth of Eurydice, whose soul was banished to the underworld, Hubbard exploits the similitude of "underworld" and "underpass" to reconfigure this myth as a trope for contemporary public travel. In doing so Hubbard transcribes past onto present, antiquity onto modernity and brings an element of classical pre-Christian culture into daily British life.

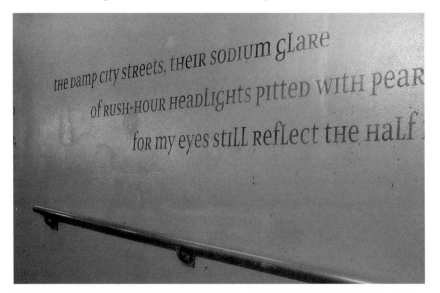

Photo by Orlando Valman

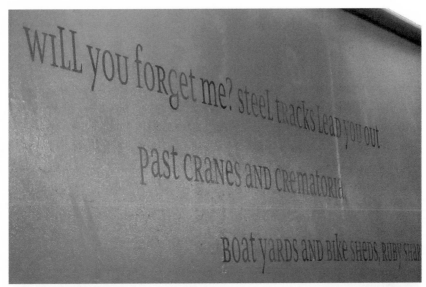

Photos by Orlando Valman

Once again the poem performs a dynamic encounter with its local surroundings. For example, Eurydice's journey into the underworld is evoked both literally and figuratively in the lines "I am not afraid as I descend / step by step."[58] These appear with the rest of the poem in a sequence of stepped three-lined stanzas that reflect Eurydice's descent to the underworld as well as enacting the movement of the reader/walker, forward and downward into the underpass. Ancient and modern time are also conflated through the mapping of this myth in real time, signified in the poem's reference to "rush-hour head-lights" and its setting against contemporary features of London's cityscape such as "the station clock" (significantly, also a modern marker of temporal-ity). Conversely, the antiquity of the city itself is evoked in the poem's allusion to London's own ancient history; for example, "roman glass and wolf-bone mummified in mud." In both ways Hubbard indicates that "[t]he viewer/read-er's relationship with a poem is not primarily spatial but temporal."[59] Another dimension of temporality in the poem is the aging of the physical work itself. Whereas the initial objective had been to create the effect of weathering by using a typography that appeared eroded and as if a natural part of the estab-lished landscape, since its original installation the poem underwent its own partial effacement through time (it was restored in 2011). The poem's ephem-eral nature thus demonstrates how the poem itself is altered by the place it inhabits as much as this space is transformed by the poem's presence.

The specific location of "Eurydice" by London Waterloo Station also pro-vides a significant site for the exploration of points of intersection between multiple dichotomous border constructs of belonging and the subjectivities attached to them. For instance, the display of this poem next to one of the largest stations in one of the busiest cities in the world means that the poem is able to reach an immense number and variety of people every single day, and is read by many of the same people each day. However, its audience is also unique and exclusive by way of the fact that the poem is available only to those people who use the underpass. Thus the poem's collective readership is characteristic of a "counterpublic," as a group defined by its tension with a larger public.[60] Furthermore, the spatial dynamics of the underpass itself offer a particularly apt site for a counterpublic arena; it is a liminal space of the city that provides a tension between notions of open and closed, above and below, and inside and outside. Finally, the metaphor of a journey that underlies the central theme of the poem, and which is enacted by each of its readers who travel past it, corresponds directly with a sense of belonging based on a politics of *relation* rather than location.[61] The transitory state of the commuter aptly renders a position that angles "the concept of 'subjectivity' away from 'individuality' and in the direction of the inclination toward the other, so that 'being' is constituted not first through the 'Self,' but through its own longings to be with."[62] By functioning as a counterpoint among strang-ers, "Eurydice" creates a sense of connection among disparate peoples away from their various homes. It is thus a space that empathizes with a position of marginality that is true of so much of Hubbard's work, since it makes us all, if only temporarily, migrant bodies.

Performing what Althusser has called "the representation of the subject's *Imaginary* relationship to his or her *Real* conditions of existence,"[63] "Eurydice" creates an exilic condition of belonging that each person can relate to via his or her own journey away from or toward home. This site of travel is thus the perfect space for depicting how all cultural identity is not fixed or stable but constructed through the spatial and temporal negotiation between positions of homecoming and exile, longing and belonging, continuity and discontinuity, and the communal and the individual.

Conclusion

The opening up of various types of space performed by Hubbard's poetry enables an extended exploration of the social-spatial self at different points in time. Her thematic study of the varying notions of place explores concepts of belonging, such as exile, home, nation, diaspora, region, and locality. Likewise, the critical engagement with the materiality of the text that Hubbard's public art poetry demands creates new types of subjectivities through displacing the normative relationship among reader, text, and author. Inasmuch as Hubbard's poetry of place has to do with mapping the self in space and time, it is also concerned with charting the *ways* in which we map multiple selves through our spatial positioning. Although her work examines the positions of alterity these identifications can create, it does not advocate a politics of difference but ultimately looks to examine the connections and alliances across and within the existential longing and isolation that is so characteristic of the postmodern world at large, as well as sharing resonance with Jewish identity. Hubbard thus advocates an aesthetic that "refuses the binary of the local and the global, and proposes instead the usefulness of thinking in terms of interested universalisms."[64] Finally, Hubbard incorporates into her inquiry a form of writing that draws on and collaborates with different visual arts, such as painting, photography, and installation, to show how different genres assume distinct relationships with the subjects they speak to and hence create different opportunities for belonging.

Thus, while Hubbard's poetry is not centered around uncovering any specifically Jewish identity, her creative preoccupation with concepts of place and her empathy with outsider positions largely at odds with mainstream society offer new ways of thinking about Jewish identity in contemporary

Britain. By viewing universal models of alterity across site-specific localities, Hubbard makes way for the production of complex figures of displacement that work against a notion of Jewish identity as the essentialist figure of exile. Her public art poetry in particular approaches this through providing a local intervention against the normative positioning of identity that we perform and take for granted on a daily basis. Hubbard therefore shows that all identity and the various belongings it forecloses are contingent upon spatial, temporal, and relational investments in place.

Notes

1. David Harvey, *The Condition of Postmodernity* (Oxford: Blackwell, 1989), 203.
2. For example, Amir Eshel discusses how space is central to Judaic worship, reflected in the ancient concept of *makom,* which literally means "place" but also evokes "God" in *Ha-makom.* Amir Eshel, "Cosmopolitanism and Searching for the Sacred Space in Jewish Literature," *Jewish Social Studies* 9.3 (2003), 121–38.
3. Sue Hubbard, cited from email interview correspondence, July 24, 2008.
4. Jonathan Boyarin and Daniel Boyarin, "Diaspora: Generation and the Ground of Jewish Identity," *Critical Inquiry* 19.4 (Summer 1993), 721.
5. Berel Lang, "Hyphenated-Jews and the Anxiety of Identity," *Jewish Social Studies: History Culture, Society* 12.1 (2005), 9.
6. Adam Thirlwell, "On Writing Half-Jewishly," in *Jewish Quarterly* 208 (Winter 2007), 4; and Cynthia Ozick, "Responsa," in *Jewish Quarterly* 209 (Spring 2008), 5.
7. Bryan Cheyette, *Contemporary Jewish Writing in Britain and Ireland: An Anthology* (London: Peter Halban, 1998), xiii.
8. Charlotte E. Fonrobert and Vered Shemtov, "Introduction: Jewish Conceptions and Practices of Space," *Jewish Social Studies,* n.s. 11.3 (Spring–Summer 2005), 2.
9. Judith Butler, "Contingent Foundations: Feminism and the Question of 'Postmodernism,'" in *Feminists Theorize the Political,* ed. Judith Butler and Joan W. Scott (New York: Routledge, 1992), 19.
10. Butler offers a poststructuralist perspective in answer to the problem of identity categories that seek to normalize foundations of human experience by suggesting that we should not do away with such categories as Jewish or female altogether but instead recognize them as always contingent and thus necessarily political and implicated in power (Butler, "Contingent Foundations," 3–21).
11. See Charles Bernstein, *The Politics of Poetic Form* (New York: Roof Books, 1990).
12. Caren Kaplan, "The Politics of Location as Transnational Feminist Critical Practice," in *Scattered Hegemonies: Postmodernity and Transnational Feminist Practices,* ed. Caren Kaplan and Inderpal Grewal (Minneapolis: University of Minnesota, 1994), 138.
13. See Aimee Marie Carrillo Rowe, "Be Longing: Toward a Feminist Politics of Relation," *NWSA Journal* 17.2 (2005), 15–46.
14. Peter Middleton, "Who Am I to Speak? The Politics of Subjectivity in Recent British Poetry," in *New Poetries: The Scope of the Possible,* ed. Rupert Hampson and Peter Barry (Manchester: Manchester University Press, 1995), 108.

15. Alison Mark and Deryn Rees-Jones, eds., *Contemporary Women's Poetry: Reading / Writing / Practice* (Basingstoke: Macmillan Press Ltd, 2000), xxiii.

16. Thomas Nolden draws on this idea in Thomas Nolden and Frances Malino, eds., *Voices of the Diaspora: Jewish Women Writing in Contemporary Europe* (Evanston, IL: Northwestern University Press, 2005), xxvii.

17. Marla Brettschneider, "To Race, to Class, to Queer: Jewish Contributions to Feminist Theory," in *Jewish Locations: Traversing Racialized Landscapes*, ed. Lisa Tessman and Bat-Ami Bar On (Lanham, MD: Rowman & Littlefield, 2001), 213–34.

18. Bluma Goldstein, "A Politics and Poetics of Diaspora," in *Diasporas and Exiles: Varieties of Jewish Identity* (Berkeley: University of California Press, 2002), 75.

19. James Acheson and Romana Huk, eds., *Contemporary British Poetry: Essays in Theory and Criticism* (Albany: State University of New York Press, 1996), 4.

20. Charles Bernstein, *Close Listening: Poetry and the Performed Word* (New York: Oxford University Press, 1998), 5.

21. Michael Warner, *Publics and Counterpublics* (New York: Zone Books, 2005).

22. Sue Hubbard, *Opening Spaces: Poetry as Public Art* (London: Poetry Society, 2000), 9.

23. Maeera Y. Shreiber, "The End of Exile: Jewish Identity and Its Diasporic Poetics," *PMLA* 113.2 (1998), 273.

24. Cheyette, *Contemporary Jewish Writing in Britain and Ireland*, xxxv.

25. Hubbard, email correspondence, July 24, 2008.

26. Ibid.

27. Hubbard, *Everything Begins with the Skin* (London: Enitharmon Press, 1994), 13. All future references to this poem will be from this edition and given in parentheses, as will all subsequent references to individual poems after the initial endnote.

28. Ibid., 21.

29. Eshel, "Cosmopolitanism and Searching for the Sacred Space," 124.

30. Hubbard, *Opening Spaces*, 9.

31. Therefore rejecting what Eshel has identified as "the essentialist trap of viewing Jews as the mere carriers of mythological, biblical 'genes' that condition their beliefs and literature in regard to the place." Eshel, "Cosmopolitanism and Searching for the Sacred Space," 124.

32. Bryan Cheyette, "'Ineffable and Usable': Towards a Diasporic British-Jewish Writing," *Textual Practice* 10.2 (1996), 298.

33. Jonathan Boyarin, "Space, Time, and the Politics of Memory," in *Remapping Memory: The Politics of Time Space*, ed. Boyarin (Minneapolis: University of Minnesota Press, 1994), 7.

34. Hubbard, *Ghost Station* (Cambridge: Salt Publishing, 2004), 10.

35. "Time-space compression" has been referred to as a condition of postmodernity, as suggested by David Harvey: "[W]e have been experiencing, these last two decades, an intense phase of time-space compression that has had a disorienting and disruptive impact upon political-economic practices, the balance of class power, as well as upon cultural and social life." Harvey, *Condition of Postmodernity*, 284.

36. Frederic Jameson, "The Cultural Logic of Late Capitalism," in *Postmodernism, Or, the Cultural Logic of Late Capitalism* (London: Verso, 1991), 6.

37. Gaston Bachelard, *The Poetics of Space* (1958; this translation, 1964, repr. Boston: Beacon Press, 1994), 8.

38. Rowe, "Be Longing," 40.

39. Jacques Derrida used the term "spectrality" to discuss "the *spacing* of public space" as something that is "neither living or dead, present nor absent: it spectralizes. It does not belong to ontology, to the discourse of Being or beings or to the essence of life or death. It requires, then, what we call, to save time and space rather than just make up a word, *hauntology*." Jacques Derrida, *Specters of Marx: The State of Debt, the Work of Mourning, and the New International*, trans. Peggy Kamuf (New York: Routledge, 1994), 51; emphasis in original.

40. I am using the German word for uncanny to show the correlation between the literal translation of "unhomely" and the later Freudian use of the term "uncanny."

41. Stuart Hall, *Cultural Identity and Diaspora: Identity, Community, Culture, Difference*, ed. Jonathan Rutherford (New York: New York University Press, 1990), 225.

42. Slawomir Kapralski, "Battlefields of Memory: Landscape and Identity in Polish–Jewish Relations," *History and Memory* 13.2 (2001), 35.

43. Hubbard, email interview, July 24, 2008.

44. Van Gogh suffered a fatal wound after shooting himself in similar fields to the ones he depicts.

45. Jameson, "Cultural Logic," 11.

46. Hubbard, "Preliminary Notes," *Poetry Society,* www.poetrysociety.org.uk/content/archives/publicart/hubbard/prelim (accessed August 2008) (para. 3 of 4).

47. Eavan Boland, *Object Lessons: The Life of the Woman and the Poet in Our Time* (Manchester: Carcanet Press Ltd, 1995), 163.

48. Jameson, "Cultural Logic," 51.

49. Hubbard, *Everything Begins with the Skin,* 41. All further references will be from this publication and given in parentheses.

50. Jameson, "Cultural Logic," 51.

51. Rowe, "Be Longing," 28.

52. Middleton, "Who Am I to Speak?" 108.

53. I am indebted to Hubbard's own lucid and detailed reflections on these works in *Opening Spaces*. www.suehubbard.com/sitemap.shtml#poet.

54. Hubbard, *Opening Spaces*, 19.

55. Hubbard, *Opening Spaces*, 12.

56. D. A. Miller, cited in Eve Kosofsky Sedgwick, "Epistemology of the Closet," in *Queer Theory and the Jewish Question,* ed. Daniel Boyarin, Daniel Itzkovitz, and Ann Pellegrini (New York: Columbia University Press, 2003), 41–63 (41).

57. Cheyette highlights how a translation of Lyotard's *Heidegger and the Jews* can be rendered as: "'The Jews' are the object of a *non-lieu*," translating literally as "non-place" or "noplace" (Cheyette, "Ineffable and Usable," 298).

58. The text of the poem appears at www.suehubbard.com/poet/eurydice_campaign/eurydice_release.shtml

59. Hubbard, *Opening Spaces*, 12–13.

60. See Warner, *Publics and Counterpublics*, 56.

61. As Rowe has highlighted, "The move [. . .] from location to relation, entails centering belonging as a starting point for naming and imagining location, as opposed to an effect of location" (Rowe, "Be Longing," 19).

62. Rowe, "Be Longing," 17.

63. Louis Althusser, cited in Jameson, "Cultural Logic," 51; emphasis in original.
64. Sneja Gunew and Anna Yeatman, eds., *Feminism and the Politics of Difference* (New South Wales: Allen & Unwin Pty Ltd, 1993), xiv.

CONTRIBUTORS

NADIA VALMAN, volume editor, is senior lecturer in English at Queen Mary, University of London. She is the author of *The Jewess in Nineteenth-Century British Literary Culture* (2007); has edited five books on representations of Jews in British and European culture; and recently co-edited an anthology of nineteenth-century Jewish literature from England, Germany, and France (2013) and *The Routledge Handbook to Contemporary Jewish Cultures* (2014).

DAVID BRAUNER is professor of contemporary literature at the University of Reading. He is the author of *Post-War Jewish Fiction: Ambivalence, Self-Explanation and Transatlantic Connections* (2001), and books on contemporary American fiction and the work of Philip Roth.

PHYLLIS LASSNER, professor at Northwestern University, has published *British Women Writers of World War II* (1998) and *Colonial Strangers: Women Writing the End of the British Empire* (2004), as well as books and articles on Elizabeth Bowen. Her most recent book is *Anglo-Jewish Women Writing the Holocaust* (2008). In addition to co-editing collections on antisemitism and philosemitism and on Rumer Godden, she is editor of the Northwestern University Press series "Cultural Expressions of World War II." She holds the International Diamond Jubilee Fellowship at Southampton University, UK.

PETER LAWSON has taught with the Open University in London since 2003. His research concerns post-1900 British and American literature, with an emphasis on Jewish writing in English. He is the author of *Anglo-Jewish Poetry from Isaac Rosenberg to Elaine Feinstein* (2006) and editor of an award-winning anthology, *Passionate Renewal: Jewish Poetry in Britain Since 1945* (2001). He has published many articles on twentieth-century poetry and Holocaust literature. Lawson is also the author of a volume of poems, *Senseless Hours* (2009).

RACHEL POTTER is a professor of modern literature at the University of East Anglia. She is the author of *Modernism and Democracy: Literary Culture,*

1900–1930 (2006), *The Edinburgh Guide to Modernist Literature* (2012), and *Obscene Modernism: Literary Censorship and Experiment, 1900–1940* (2013). She has also co-edited *The Salt Companion to Mina Loy* (2010) and *Prudes on the Prowl: Fiction and Obscenity in England, 1850–Present Day* (2013). She is currently starting a project on International P.E.N., writers, and rights.

SARAH SCEATS was formerly head of English at Kingston University, London. She specializes in twentieth-century fiction, particularly women's writing. She has published widely on food and eating, and on women writers including Angela Carter, Doris Lessing, Rose Tremain, Margaret Atwood, Elizabeth Bowen, and Betty Miller. She is author of *Food, Consumption and the Body in Contemporary Women's Fiction* (2000). She is currently working on life writing and a novel.

CYNTHIA SCHEINBERG is professor of English at Mills College and the author of *Women's Poetry and Religion in Victorian England: Jewish Identity and Christian Culture* (2002). Her articles and essays have appeared in *ELH, Victorian Studies, Victorian Poetry*, and *The Cambridge Companion to Victorian Poetry*. She has been awarded grants and scholarship from the National Endowment for the Humanities, The Carnegie Foundation for the Advancement of Teaching and the Harvard Divinity School.

LOUISE SYLVESTER is reader in English language at the University of Westminster. Her expertise is in historical semantics, lexicology, and language and gender.

CHERYL VERDON is an academic whose research centers on Jewish literature after the Holocaust. Published under the name Cheryl Alexander Malcolm, her works include *Unshtetling Narratives: Depictions of Jewish Identities in British and American Literature and Film* (2006), *Understanding Anita Brookner* (2002), three co-edited collections, and essays. For many years she actively promoted the study of Jewish literature in post-communist Poland and was, until recently, associate professor of English at the University of Gdansk. Now in London, she is writing a novel.

SUE VICE is professor of English literature at the University of Sheffield. She is the author of *Holocaust Fiction* (2000); *Children Writing the Holocaust* (2004); books on psychoanalysis, film, and television; and *Textual Deceptions: False Memoirs and Literary Hoaxes in the Contemporary Era* (2014).

LUCY WRIGHT holds an MA in Jewish history and culture from the University of Southampton.

INDEX